Books by Margaret Millar

THE BIRDS AND THE
BEASTS WERE THERE

Margaret Miller

The Birds
and the
Beasts Were
There

MARGARET MILLAR

Capra Press
SANTA BARBARA

Cover design by Victor Bickmore.
Interior design by Cyndia Burt.
Printed by McNaughton & Gunn, Saline, Michigan.

LIBRARY OF CONGRESS CATALOGING-IN-PUBLICATION DATA

Millar, Margaret.
 The birds and the beasts were there / Margaret Millar.
   p. cm.
 Includes index.
 ISBN 088496-324-1 : $10.95
 1. Birds—California—Santa Barbara Region—Anecdotes.
 2. Birds—California—Santa Barbara Region—Behavior.
 3. Millar, Margaret.
 I. Title.
QL676.M63 1991
598.251'09794'91—dc20
                                                    90-21649
                                                         CIP

CAPRA PRESS
Post Office Box 2068 / Santa Barbara, California 93120

To those of my fellow
bird watchers who have
completed their life lists:

Adelaide Garvin
Pat Haworth Higginson
Edouard Jacot
Egmont Rett

CONTENTS

FOREWORD

THE HOUSE in which this book was written barely survived the disasterous Coyote Fire of 1964 described in the final chapters of this book. But in 1977 it was completely destroyed in the Sycamore Fire and all that remains of it is this book.

Bird populations change and so do bird watcher populations. The dramatic increase in the latter accounts for the increase, or apparent increase, in the number of bird species observed since the beginning of my bird journal.

As this foreword is being written, October 1990, our city is in its fourth year of severe drought and wildfires. The mobility of birds helps them survive such disasters. In the nineties our canyons will still echo with the shrill calls of the red-shouldered hawk, "Here, here, come here!", the beguiling invitation of the quail to "Sit right down, sit right down," and on hot dry dusty days the very sensible request of the olive-sided flycatcher, "Quick, three beers! Quick, three beers!"

Who says birds have no brains?

— M. M.

Houdunit

It was the beginning of summer and I was approaching a corner in my life. I did not know that it was waiting for me, let alone that it would be of great significance; and when I turned it, there was no artillery salute, no bands played, no thunder rolled. The only sound was a quick, light tapping that seemed to be coming from the enclosed lanai on the lower floor. I was upstairs in the living room reading a book in an attempt to relax. My husband had left that morning on a trip to Mexico and I was already regretting my decision not to accompany him.

There was no one else in the house, yet the tapping continued. The dogs were lying beside my chair, not to indicate their devotion so much as to make sure I didn't go any place without them. Normally they barked at the drop of a decibel half a mile away, but they didn't stir until I reminded them sharply that they were supposed to be watchdogs. Then, responding to my tone, they started tearing up and down the room in a loud and disorganized demonstration of watchdoggedness. By the time they stopped, so had the tapping.

A few minutes later it began again, louder and more purposeful, as if the interruption had served merely to increase the performer's determination. That a performer existed I had no doubt: the noise didn't sound mechanical, like air in the plumbing or a defect in the water heater, and the wind wasn't strong enough to budge a butterfly.

I went downstairs, the dogs at my heels. The rooms—lanai and storage room, piano alcove, my husband's study and bath—were empty, as expected, and outside there was nothing unusual—no curious child from one of the houses across the canyon, no lost dog or straying cat. As I started back upstairs I heard the tapping again. This time it was closer and I could tell exactly where it was coming from—the window of the bath between my bedroom and my office. The new development wasn't exactly reassuring since that particular window was fifteen feet from the ground and no nearby tree provided access to it. The added fact that the dogs weren't making a fuss forced me to conclude that the originator of the noise was not of this world.

Twilight in the empty house did not provide the best occasion for speculating about the spirit world and who, among its occupants, might be trying to get in touch with me. I thought of various relatives and friends, and even my childhood hero, Houdini, who had promised his faithful followers that if he could possibly communicate from the spirit world he would do so on the anniversary of his death. I had to check several reference books before learning that he had died in Detroit, Michigan, the end of October, 1926. This was Santa Barbara, California, the end of June. It seemed unlikely that Houdini could have made such a gross mistake, so I crossed him off the list.

The ghostly noise stopped when darkness fell and I heard nothing more until the following morning, shortly after dawn. Once more I searched the house, upstairs and down, inside and out, and found nothing out of the ordinary. But I had no sooner gone out to the kitchen to make breakfast when the tapping started again from one of the east windows of the lanai; it was followed by a series of sounds as if someone was trampling around in the leaf litter underneath the ceanothus shrubs. The eeriest part of the whole thing was that the dogs didn't react to the sound, though their ears are twenty times keener than mine and they must certainly have heard it. Perhaps the performer was so well known to them that they considered him unworthy of their attention. If this was the case, why hadn't I seen him? Was my failure due to a deficiency of vision or of perception?

I was finishing breakfast when Bertha Blomstrand, who'd recently built a house across the road, telephoned to ask if I was wide awake enough to come over and see something peculiar. She advised me to make as little noise as possible, which, translated bluntly, meant to leave the dogs at home.

Bertha was waiting for me at the front door. She motioned me to be silent, then led me through the house to a window which looked out on the driveway, where her car was parked. It was a small foreign model, so common it could be seen on any street at any time. The only unusual thing about it was the left rear hubcap, which was being vigorously attacked by a brown bird. The bird would fling himself at the hubcap, beat it with his wings and peck it with such force that we could hear the sound clearly through the closed window. This was not love, like a parakeet seeing himself in a mirror. This was war. The chrome of the hubcap showed the bird a mortal enemy.

Thus the source of the tapping on my windows was discovered, and it was not Houdini whodunit. It was a little brown bird who acquired a name before he even had an identity—Houdunit.

I went back home, relieved that the culprit was nothing more formidable, yet curiously unsatisfied. What species did he belong to? Had he engaged in previous fights with his enemy in the left rear hubcap of Bertha's car and in the window of the lanai and of the upstairs bathroom? And why only this one hubcap out of four, these two windows out of many?

I had come to the corner and only one step was necessary to take me around it. The step seemed a very small one: later in the morning, when I went to the supermarket for groceries, I bought a thirty-nine-cent box of parakeet seed.

Some kinds of addiction are considered incurable. A heroin addict can be kept off his drug in a prison cell for years but the result is not a cure. A bird watcher can be confined to a room with the blinds drawn and the windows closed tight. But when one of the windows is opened and a snatch of bird song drifts in, when a blind is raised and a small creature wings by, or certain leaves in a tree stir without wind, the addiction is more powerful than ever. It carries with it, however, a lifetime guarantee. Wherever you go in this world—the rain forests of the Amazon, the Arctic tundra, the Mojave Desert, the Swiss Alps, the Taj Mahal, the top of the

Empire State Building or the middle of Main Street, Peoria, Illinois—no matter where you find yourself, there'll be birds to watch and you'll never again be bored.

I sprinkled half the parakeet seed on the ledge outside the living room. This ledge, which was to become the setting for hundreds of itinerant players to act their comedies and tragedies, was four feet wide and covered with roofing material which provided safe footing. It ran the length of two rooms, some fifteen yards, and had been intended mainly as an overhang for the lanai and patio on the lower level.

Nature had provided the ledge with a varied and colorful backdrop. At one end was a gnarled Australian tea tree, with a grove of ceanothus behind it. Entwined throughout the branches of the ceanothus were the strong, swift runners of a rampaging trumpet vine which had been in bloom since January. At the other end of the ledge we'd built a porch, which quickly became overgrown with cotoneaster and bougainvillaea. In the background an elderberry bush had grown to tree size, and beyond it stood a row of huge Monterey pines. Looking straight out across the ledge from the chair where I generally sat, I could see first a long privet hedge, unclipped and as tall as a man, a lemon tree and some young loquats, a pittosporum forty feet high and almost as wide, a number of old live oak trees and some enormous blue gum eucalyptus.

Our property slanted down about thirty feet to a flat area that had been an access road at one time. Though a previous owner had stuck a few concrete flagstones around it, it wasn't enough of anything to have a name. We called it the lower terrace only for purposes of identification. From here the ground sloped down into a canyon with a creek at the bottom. This creek, unlike most of the ones in southern California in the summer, had water in it. Its banks were strewn with boulders, and wildly overgrown with mugwort, native blackberry, deadly nightshade and poison oak. This last we made no attempt to get rid of, having learned that a fairsized patch of poison oak is as good a way to discourage trespassers as a fence and a Keep Out sign. The final backdrop was the Santa Ynez range of mountains, a changing mass of greens and grays and violets depending on the light.

This, then, was our ledge, a stage whose most dramatic moments up to that point were when Ken and I washed the picture windows.

The first customer for the parakeet seed was Houdunit—or his brother, sister, cousin, aunt—followed a few minutes later by a small, energetic brownish bird with striped underparts. It was promptly joined by another bird of the same size, shape and behavior but with a red breast and face. In spite of the difference in coloration they were obviously a pair. From their quick discovery of the food and their unhesitating descent on it, it also seemed obvious that they were a part of the neighborhood, a bright, lively, tuneful part. Yet I had never seen or heard them before. They might as well have been silent creatures of the darkest night. How could I have missed them?

This theme is a recurrent one among new bird watchers. To the uneducated eye, as to the incurious mind, much of the world is in darkness, and a thousand songs are lost on the unlistening ear.

That afternoon, for the first time in years, I went to the Santa Barbara Museum of Natural History. It is a charming place, a cluster of tile-roofed buildings with inner courts and stone archways and long open-air corridors rambling in all directions. A sycamore-lined creek runs through the area, which is shaded by massive old live oaks and dotted with huge boulders brought down by the creek during winter floods.

When our daughter, Linda, was in grade school, we used to take her and her friends to the museum on afternoons too hot to hike and too cold to swim in the sea. The children especially liked Bird Hall. They'd stand staring up at the condor and the white pelican suspended from the ceiling, or into the display cases which held the smaller birds, captives long past caring. The children's comments made it clear that they considered the stuffed specimens to be more like toys than real birds who had once walked on lawns or touched treetops or skimmed the surface of the sea. For them then, as for me now, the robin in Bird Hall has little connection with the fat, spectacled comic who appoints himself boss of the berry patch. The scrap of gray in the glass cage bears only a token resemblance to the bustling little busybody we call the bushtit, and the sight of the acorn woodpecker wired to a plaster post sets up no echo in my ears of the marvellously raucous and kinetic dialogue he conducts with his friends.

Movement is the very essence of a bird. The museum of the future should, and probably will, occupy itself less with collecting specimens and more with obtaining good color films and sound tracks of creatures alive, moving and meaningful.

In Bird Hall I found drab replicas of the birds I'd seen on the ledge—a brown towhee, and a male and female house finch. As I left, I paused to read the information sheet in the display case near the door. It stated that all of the birds inside were from Santa Barbara County and there were nearly 400 of them.

I had 398 to go.

How Sweet the Honey

On the way home I stopped downtown and blew the rest of the month's expense money on a pair of binoculars, a copy of Roger Tory Peterson's *Field Guide to Western Birds,* and a *Handbook of California Birds* by Brown and Weston. Thus equipped, I confidently expected to spend the balance of the day beside the window identifying all the birds that passed my way or stopped to eat.

My confidence was ill timed and misplaced. There were a lot of birds, certainly, but they were extremely uncooperative and so were the binoculars. When I was lucky enough to spot a bird quietly perched on a branch, I had to get the binoculars focused on it and adjusted to my eyes, then I had to go through all the illustrations in the *Field Guide* and the *Handbook* until I came to a picture that resembled what I'd seen. At this point I invariably discovered that my initial study of the bird hadn't been thorough enough and that I needed another look at it. By the time the binoculars and I were prepared for another look, the bird was halfway to Los Angeles and I was left gnashing my teeth and suffering from dizziness and a severe headache. (These symptoms are all common among new bird watchers; only the gnashing is permanent.)

About the middle of the afternoon a brash blue-and-gray bird joined the house finches feeding on the ledge and stayed long enough for me to identify it as a scrub jay. This was my first identification on my own, and though it was a small thing it went to my head like the smell of a cork to an old toper. I began to envisage my ledge and its surrounding greenery as a place to which birds of all kinds would irresistibly be drawn. I knew nothing whatever about attracting birds, but I'd had quite a lot of experience in attracting people and perhaps the same method could be used—food and drink. Obviously parakeet seed wasn't going to do the trick alone; I needed to put out several kinds of food.

I had a vague memory of watching my father, when I was a child in Canada, go through all sorts of shenanigans to keep the birds out of the cherry trees. Nothing had worked, so I reasoned that some birds must be inordinately fond of cherries. I didn't have any cherries on hand but I found a bunch of grapes, which might possibly be mistaken for cherries by a bird who was a little near-sighted. I also found some bread and four stale doughnuts. The grapes I fastened with a pipe cleaner to a branch of the tea tree at one end of the ledge. The bread I crumbled and scattered with the rest of the parakeet seed. One doughnut I slipped over a twig of the lemon tree, another in the cotoneaster, and the remaining two in the tea tree with the grapes.

If the arrangements looked as peculiar to the birds as they did to me, they would undoubtedly stay away in droves. To avoid disappointment, I decided not to sit around and wait but to go back downtown and purchase a few more bird-luring devices. It was on this trip that I met Harry.

Harry was the proprietor of a pet shop. Wearing his starched white coat and his sedate yet sympathetic smile, he looked more like a doctor about to diagnose my symptoms and treat the underlying disease. I didn't know it at the time but I was the kind of customer, or patient, Harry had been waiting for all his life. I had the disease for which he had the cure.

His first recommendation was a bird bath. Or rather, two bird baths. Some birds liked the ordinary pedestal-type bath, he said, while others preferred a container placed right on the ground. I didn't want to be accused of discrimination so I bought a four-dollar clay saucer in addition to the ten-dollar pedestal bath. ("Hang the expense," Harry said cheerfully.)

He also sold me a hopper-type seed dispenser and a humming-bird feeder which I was instructed to fill with a half-honey, half-water mixture boiled for ten minutes to kill the bacteria that would hasten fermentation. The bottle also had to be cleaned and the mixture renewed every second or third day to prevent the stuff turning into liquor and intoxicating the hummingbirds. Drunkenness, he hinted, was commoner among birds than most temperance-oriented bird lovers cared to admit.

Since that first talk with Harry I've seen a number of examples of intemperance—a flock of robins who'd gorged themselves on overripe pyracantha berries and were reeling around on a lawn like tumbleweed, and house finches tame as tulips after a feast of rotting peaches. Every winter I've watched a sapsucker imbibing fermented sap he'd tapped himself from a willow tree and trying to protect his source of supply from a thirsty and determined oriole. On a recent occasion I was nearly run down by a boozy bunch of waxwings who had arrived later than usual when the toyon berries were past their prime. But I have yet to see any drunken humming-birds. Perhaps they are indistinguishable from sober ones.

It was eight thirty and nearly dark by the time I finished arranging everything according to Harry's instructions. The pedestal bird bath was placed in the middle of the lower terrace at a safe distance from shrubbery that would lend cover to lurking cats. With the aid of a notched stick and some wire, I suspended a length of hose over the bath and left the water turned on just enough to provide a slight drip.

It didn't look very attractive, but I have long since discovered that birds and people frequently have opposite views about what is attractive. The tidy gardener will abhor the patch of weeds that is irresistible to the goldfinch. He will hasten to haul away the pile of brush where the wren finds its spider, the thrush its worm, the towhee its shelter. He will arrange to burn the stump where the bluebird nests and the woodpecker hunts for caterpillar larvae. He will use quantities of insecticide to get rid of mosquitoes while he simultaneously drives away their arch enemy, the cliff swallow, by knocking down its mud nest under the eaves in order to preserve the neatness of his house. He will not stand the sight of a tree skeleton, yet it is at just such a skeleton, the bare bones of an old blue gum eucalyptus standing at the west end of our property, where Ken and I have seen more species of birds than any other one place. Almost all the birds use it: for a lookout, as a place to rest, to meet, to court, to preen, to study the surrounding country, to watch for hawks, to converse, to sleep in the sun. The gardener who prides himself on his neatness pays heavily, and usually unwittingly, for his pride. Birds will be uncomfortable in his yard just as a human being is uncomfortable in the house of a perfectionist.

The hummingbird feeder I hung on the porch, with a couple of fuchsia blossoms taped near the tube to attract their interest. This feeder was discovered and taken over by a hummingbird the following morning. Such quick success is the exception rather than the rule and I attribute it not to the fuchsia blossom but to the fact that a neighbor up the street, Adelaide Garvin, had been feeding hummers for years. She kept eight containers of honey and water on her patio all year, so it seems likely that every hummer for miles around was well accustomed to them.

Mrs. Garvin had started out, one winter several years before, with a single feeder which was in due course discovered by a male Anna's hummingbird, the only species which is a permanent resident in our area. For a brief time things went smoothly, with Mrs. Garvin enjoying her guest and the hummer enjoying her hospitality. Then a second male Anna appeared on the scene. There was plenty of room in the garden for both of them, plenty of flowers to provide them with insects, and they could have lived harmoniously side by side, taking turns at the feeder. But if there's one thing a hummingbird can't stand it's the sight of another hummingbird eating. To him a feeder is merely another flower and he knows by instinct that a flower fades and there is an end of honey. To share it would be like a farmer sharing a well he knows is going dry—bad business as well as against nature.

Mr. Anna One welcomed the stranger with a vigorous and noisy frontal attack. The stranger, Mr. Anna Two, reciprocated in kind. And so it went, day after day. From the first feeble light of morning these tiny iridescent patches of rose-red plunged and dove and zoomed and dipped and hovered, and the air was filled with their excited sounds of combat, *tick tick tick—tick tick—tick tick tick tick tick.* . . . It was like listening to a battle between a pair of deranged flying clocks.

While no blood was shed, no clear-cut victory was won either, and the battle simply went on. Neither of the gladiators was ever allowed more than a few seconds at the feeder and Mrs. Garvin began to be afraid that they were going to starve to death and she would be responsible. She was at the point of taking down the feeder and forgetting the whole thing when she read in a magazine about a situation similar to hers. The solution, it seemed, was to place a second feeder, at some distance from and out of sight of the other, on the assumption that if each bird had its own feeder, peace would prevail. Mrs. Garvin, delighted at the prospect of such an easy solution, hastened to buy another feeder and put it up at the opposite end of the patio, hidden from the first by a giant yucca.

Mr. Anna One spotted the new feeder immediately. Before Mrs. Garvin even had a chance to fill it he was over, investigating, touching it with his beak and tasting it with his tongue, which was as long and quick and delicate as a snake's. This maneuver left the first feeder unoccupied and Mr. A II lost no time using his opportunity. It was probably his first—and positively his last—uninterrupted session at any feeder. Dining alone had certain obvious advantages, but A II evidently felt that they were outweighed by the excitements of combat because within a couple of minutes he went off in search of A I. They met at the new feeder just as Mrs. Garvin was in the act of filling it.

The ensuing fight lasted for the balance of the afternoon. A I would take a sip of honey water, then fly back to his perch on a twig about six feet away, moving his head constantly from side to side so as not to miss the approach of any trespassers on his new property. At this point A II would zoom out of ambush and take a hasty swig before being driven off. Then he would swoop back across the patio to the original feeder. Suspecting just such skulduggery, A I would immediately follow him, ticking so fast and furiously he seemed ready to explode like a time bomb. Back and forth between the feeders the two birds went, until dusk forced them to seek cover for the night.

In her quest for peace Mrs. Garvin had merely intensified the war and enlarged the battlefield. She was, naturally, disappointed but she was also beginning to get curious: what would happen if she put up a third feeder? Was it possible that the birds actually enjoyed fighting and were merely using the feeders as an excuse?

In order to prevent A I and A II from spying on her activites, she waited until the following night to place a third feeder in the arbutus tree at the other side of the house where it was almost completely concealed by the dense leaves. She had even left the formula uncolored and merely painted the end of the feeding tube with red nail polish. Though I have found that this works perfectly well, I still go on using the colored stuff. It looks prettier.

Both male Annas were much too occupied to go exploring. A neglected girl friend, however, often has plenty of time to kill, and one of these was browsing in the arbutus, sticking her beak into the tiny, white bell-shaped flowers, when she discovered the feeding tube. If she had had any sense she would have kept her find to herself and enjoyed a little security. But she couldn't resist the urge to brag to the male and lord it over him. She had no reason to spare his feelings; the previous spring, after a spectacular kiss-and-run affair, he had left her to face the consequences, a pair of twins, and raise them all by herself.

It was the beginning of February when Miss Anna discovered her feeder. At the same time, unfortunately, a male Allen's hummingbird arrived in the arbutus tree after a winter vacation in Mexico. He was tired and hungry after his long journey and even under the best of circumstances he is not noted for his placid disposition. Buzzing his wings, fanning his brown-red tail and squeaking vigorously at Miss Anna, he ordered her to get lost. Miss Anna retaliated with a thrust of her bill and a series of enraged *tick tick tick's,* which attracted the attention not only of A I and A II but of Mrs. Garvin as well.

She witnessed the ensuing four-way fight but it was such a bedlam of noise and color and speed in and out of the arbutus tree and around and around the house, that it was impossible to declare a winner. It was, however, quite obvious which bird had been defeated: the lower half of A I's bill was now at a 90° angle to the upper half. He appeared so pitifully wounded that Mrs. Garvin was in an agony of remorse for having started the whole thing.

Among most wild creatures the custom is for the defeated to shrink away and lick his wounds in hiding. A I evidently didn't think much of this custom. Instead of stealing quietly away, he became even more pugnacious, and while his broken bill may have looked pitiful to Mrs. Garvin, to the other hummingbirds it appeared more formidable with its double thrust. In fact, his injury wasn't actually very serious. It did not, for instance, interfere with his eating since he did that with his tongue, which was protected quite satisfactorily by the upper bill. In time, his lower bill atrophied and fell off and he grew a new one in much the same way as we grow a new fingernail.

A I may have lost the battle but he won the war. He became, at least temporarily, the undisputed owner of the original feeder.

Hummingbirds mate as they live, with great speed and intensity. In our part of California courtship begins as early as December for the Annas, February for the Allens.

I kept a daily record of a pair of Allen hummers who arrived at the beginning of February, 1965: the male on the 3rd, the female two days later. Courtship began immediately. On February 8, I watched the female gathering material for her nest from one of the wicker cornucopias I had filled with cotton balls and hung in a tree. She was a dainty little freckle-faced creature, most meticulous about what went into her nest. If she pulled out a piece of cotton which she considered too large, she promptly spit it out. If it wasn't large enough she added to it until it was exactly right.

On March 10, thirty days after I first observed Mrs. Allen gathering cotton, I learned by chance that she had completed her mission. Looking out at a dead ceanothus tree, I observed what I thought were two female Allen's hummingbirds sitting on adjoining twigs, each peacefully minding her own business. This was such an unlikely situation that I went running to get my binoculars.

They told the story: in the center of each white throat a small red spot was revealed. As the weeks passed, these spots would enlarge until they became the flaming orange-red throats of the male Allen's hummingbird. The two peace-loving "ladies" on adjoining twigs were Mrs. Allen's fine young twin sons, who hadn't yet been introduced to the joys of combat.

Of the 319 known species of hummingbird, in only one is the male believed to help with the incubation and raising of his family. Some hummingbird admirer had tried to explain this male absenteeism with the theory that if the male hung around the nest his brilliant beauty would draw too much attention to it and so endanger the young. I find it difficult to subscribe to this. Few birds are more conspicuously beautiful than the males of the hooded oriole and the black-headed grosbeak, both of whom are devoted fathers. Perhaps the real answer lies in the nature of the female hummer. She needs no help from anyone in looking after her family. I've watched her rout sparrow hawks, harass crows and drive off turkey vultures. The only opponent really worthy of her is another female hummingbird.

The third week of March also brought the first wave of migrating rufous hummingbirds on their way to the breeding grounds further north. The rufous shares with Allen the scientific name *Selasphorus,* flame-bearer, but it is even more applicable to him. During the five or six weeks the members of his family frequented our yard, we used to see them shooting through the trees and bushes like tiny balls of fire, so bright they hurt the eyes. Although they used our feeders and fought over them, they never took possession of one the way the Anna, Allen and black-chinned hummers did. Perhaps they knew they were just transients and could not afford to linger, no matter how sweet the honey.

Before the rufous hummers had finished migrating through our area, the black-chins began arriving to spend the spring and summer, nearly always within sight of a sycamore tree. The down on the underside of sycamore leaves was their favorite nest-building material; I've never seen a black-chin use the cotton which I provided and which seemed to please the other breeding hummers.

The courtship of these tiny creatures with the white-and-violet bibs involves the technique, used by other members of the family, of lightning-fast ascents and descents before the watching female. The black-chin has added something of its own to the mating ritual. While the female waits in a shrub or small tree, the male begins swinging rapidly and noisily back and forth in front of her like a pendulum, a performance intended to bedazzle his lady. It is not intended to bedizzy the human observer, but that's the effect it has.

The hummingbird characteristic which I find irresistible is its fearlessness. When I went out into their territory they not only showed no fear of me, they ignored my presence altogether except as an object that was in their way. I might have been a short tree or a tall stump. They shot past my nose, skimmed my ear lobes, wheeled round and round my head like animated corkscrews while I dodged and ducked. If I had on red nail polish they touched it with their bills to make sure it wasn't a rare flower or a new type of feeder. One of their favorite targets was a sweater of mine which had strawberries embroidered around the collar. It was, at first, an unnerving experience to be prodded on the back of the neck by a hummingbird.

The hopper-type feeder Harry had sold me I nailed to the main trunk of a young blue gum eucalyptus. This location was convenient to the drip bath I'd arranged on the lower terrace. But it had a serious disadvantage not apparent at the beginning—blue gums grow at a great clip. The feeder is halfway to heaven by this time and utilized only as a perch for sleepy doves to sun on. We're still asked some rather naïve questions about why we put a feeder up so high and how we put seed in it, and so on. The full explanation we used to offer has been minimized with the passing of the years: "Trees grow."

And so began my initial week of bird watching. While my husband was in Mexico, I entered an even more foreign and more fascinating world. No day began soon enough or lasted long enough. The field guides were never closed, the binoculars never returned to their case. Letters from Ken arrived and I would just be sitting down to answer them when some bird would fly past the window and I'd be off, perhaps only as far as the porch or the driveway, perhaps completely around the block.

The dogs always followed me on these excursions. They were well aware of my preoccupation, and they resented it and took a stand against it in the only way they knew how. Whenever our little caravan paused long enough, they staged a fight to attract my attention.

But all three of our dogs eventually became bird watchers. The davenport in front of the picture window facing the front yard was their favorite lookout. This window always bore evidence of their new hobby. At the bottom were the noseprints of Johnny, the Scottish terrier; a few inches above, the prints of Rolls Royce, the cocker spaniel; and a foot or so above these, Brandy, the German shepherd, left his unmistakable traces. The birds very quickly took stock of the dogs and judged them harmless. Right outside our back door, in a cotoneaster tree, I hung a plastic sunflower-seed feeder. When I opened this door to let the dogs out, the birds simply went on eating, but if they caught sight of me they flew away.

Occasionally I am asked what difference bird watching has made in my life. I can only repeat, the days don't begin quickly enough, and never last long enough, and the years go by too soon.

Wzschthub

Ten days after Houdunit and I met beside the hubcap, my husband returned from Mexico. His plane, delayed by fog, didn't land until nearly midnight, so that it was too late for me to explain the considerable changes which had taken place in our household during his absence. One of the most important of these was my enrollment at the University of California at Santa Barbara for a two-week field course in bird identification. Registration and orientation had taken place the previous day at the Museum of Natural History, whose ornithologist, Egmont Rett, was our instructor. The first class was to meet at seven thirty the next morning at Goleta Slough, an area of tidal mud flats and shallow ponds and inlets.

I got up at five o'clock with the idea of doing some observing before the others arrived. I hadn't yet tried to identify any shore birds. I only knew, from reading the Peterson guide, that they weren't going to be easy.

I fed the dogs, and then, over a cup of hot tea, I wrote a note to leave for my husband:

> *Dear Ken:*
> *Gone to class, will be back sometime this afternoon. Don't eat the grapes in refrigerator or the doughnuts in bread box.*
> *Leave living room drapes closed at front and open be-*

side my chair. Go very slowly past this window or else crawl past so you won't disturb them.

Love,
MM

Birds had so quickly and easily become an integral part of my life that it simply didn't occur to me that Ken might wonder what the class was about, why the grapes and doughnuts were out of bounds, and who "them" referred to. (He told me later he wondered a great deal when he read my message, not about grapes or doughnuts, but about marbles, whether some of mine had been lost.)

I was propping the note on his bedside table when he suddenly let out a loud groan and rolled over on his back.

"Don't wake up," I said. "I'm just going to school."

"It's the middle of the night."

"Not to me."

To me it was the beginning of a new day. As I backed the car out the driveway I felt curious and excited and a little nervous. It was like being eighteen again, on my way to my first class in Greek at the University of Toronto, but there was one big difference. This time I wasn't going because it was the thing to do, or in order to please someone else or even to educate myself to earn a living. This time I was going for the most important reason of all: I wanted to learn.

There is surely nothing more discouraging to the new bird watcher than the sight of a thousand gulls on a beach at low tide. This is especially true in an area that's frequented by a dozen different kinds of gull, nearly all of which change plumage every year for the first four years. Some also change bill and leg color every year, and still others show seasonal changes in plumage.

No matter how often I shifted position and readjusted my binoculars, the gulls on the beach that morning all looked exactly alike to me.

Fortunately for my morale, there were other birds in the slough more easily identifiable: a dozen great blue herons, some snowy and common egrets and a black-necked stilt. The herons and egrets ignored me but the stilt pegged me as an intruder and announced my presence with earsplitting cries while he flew over my head, his long black beak sticking straight out in front and his improbable long pink legs sticking straight out behind.

The new bird watcher often thinks that the birds he or she identifies at the beginning are those which are common in that particular region. The very first identification of a friend of mine was a wood duck at the local Bird Refuge. She assumed that this species was as common as some of the others that hung around the refuge—coots, ruddy ducks, mallards, cinnamon teal. Five years have passed and she's still searching for another wood duck. My experience with the black-necked stilt wasn't quite so extreme, but I didn't find a second one for almost a year.

A stilt, poised in a shallow pool on his incredible legs, looks so beautiful and so gentle that one isn't prepared for his loud, piercing shriek. Many shore birds have noisy calls—gulls and terns, godwits and willets come first to my mind—perhaps because they must make themselves heard above the constant sound of the sea and the wind. Ken and I spend much time on our beach and there are very few days in the year when the tide is low enough, the waves small enough and the wind soft enough for us to be able to converse in normal voices. At the beach, if you want to be heard, you scream. So does the stilt.

The stilt's manner of flying is also in contrast to his voice. It is rather slow and dignified. I was watching him in flight when a car drove up and parked beside the bridge where I was standing; and a small slender man stepped out. I recognized Mr. Rett, the instructor, but he didn't recognize me and I hardly expected him to —at least thirty people had signed up for the class the previous day, all but two of them women.

Mr. Rett, too, focused his binoculars on the stilt. Neither of us said anything. Watching the stilt together seemed the only form of communication necessary. When Mr. Rett finally spoke it was not to me in my language, but to the stilt in his: "Key up, key up, key up."

The startled bird paused above our heads and hovered for a moment with his legs dangling like strands of pink rope frayed at the end to form a foot and knotted in the middle to simulate a knee. (The Greek word *himas,* meaning thong, forms the basis for his scientific name, *Himantopus mexicanus*.) Then, with one final cry, the stilt took off over the bridge toward the other end of the slough. It was only after he had landed out of our sight that Mr. Rett turned to me.

"Are you in my class?"

"Yes." I told him my name.

"Margaret Millar," he repeated, watching me carefully as though making sure he would remember what species I belonged to. "You're early."

"I wanted to do some extra work on shore birds."

"Extra work?" Now he was really staring at me. "Where do you teach?"

"Why do you assume I teach anywhere?"

"Most of the class does. These field courses in natural history are set up for teachers to earn a couple of quick credits without interfering with the regular summer session. No exams are given. All you have to do to get a B in this course is to keep breathing."

"I'd like an exam," I said, "and the chance to work for an A."

"You mean you signed up because you're interested in *birds?*"

"Yes sir."

"Well, I'll be damned."

It was such a shock to his nervous system that he completely forgot my name and kept referring to me for the next two weeks as Mrs. Whatchamacallit-who's-interested-in-birds.

Few teachers have either the desire or the opportunity to live their subjects. The man who conducts classes in Shakespeare may frequently quote the bard but he doesn't talk in iambic pentameters and wear long hair and a pointed beard. But for Mr. Rett birds were not only a livelihood, they were a life. He had been in museum work since his early teens. He was now in his sixties, a very small, spare man who bore a certain physical resemblance to a bird. He was light on his feet and his movements were quick and precise. Sometimes on very early morning field trips when he was hunched inside his sheepskin jacket he looked like a sparrow who had fluffed out his feathers to insulate himself against the cold.

In the midst of a conversation with people about birds, he would suddenly switch and start talking about people to birds. When he called them, they would answer. Hot, dry stretches of mountainside that seemed too desolate to support any kind of existence would suddenly come alive with the exuberant ringing of wrentits or the fretful cluckings and mutterings of California quail, or the clear, haunting octaves of a cañon wren.

Of all western bird songs, the cañon wren's must surely be the one that everyone notices and remembers, even tone-deaf nature haters. The first time I heard it was when Mr. Rett took the class on a walk through the Botanic Garden, sixty acres in the foothills above the Old Mission, planted entirely with native California trees and shrubs and flowers.

It was the last week in July. A trickle of water was still running in Mission Creek and the garden was lush and green. Mr. Rett kept pointing out birds but I was still having trouble using the binoculars and the field guide, as well as the check list Mr. Rett had given to each of us. I spent most of my time trying to focus the binoculars, looking at the check list and the index of the field guide and shouting, "Where? What tree? What kind of bird? I don't see any—"

When I had finally located the bird and attempted to match him up with his picture in the book, Mr. Rett and I were a quarter of a mile apart. In the intervening space the rest of the group were strung out like mismatched beads.

Some of the types I was to meet on many future birding trips were represented in the class. There were the Eaters, and though they carried binoculars, field guides, notebooks and extra sweaters and sun hats, they always managed to hold a sandwich. There were also the Talkers, and though some of them looked quite young in years, their life histories already seemed inordinately long.

Then there were the Shutterbugs, a busy lot indeed. They took pictures of the Old Mission and the Old Mission dam, each other, members of the class getting into cars and getting out of cars, Mr. Rett pointing west, Mr. Rett pointing south, Mr. Rett pointing east by northeast. A person examining the entire collection of pictures taken during those two weeks would be lucky if he found a single clue that the class was about birds.

Such a group would have proved most disheartening to Mr. Rett as a teacher if he had taken it seriously, so he didn't. At least he didn't until that morning at the Botanic Garden when he stopped at the bridge over the creek. Three members of the class stopped with him—myself, out of breath from sprinting to catch up after the last pause, a shutterbug who used the bridge railing to park her gear while she changed film, and a little old lady I couldn't remember seeing the previous day. She had a soft, benevolent smile and pure white hair which was drawn back in a simple bun at the nape of her neck. She wore a khaki skirt, a long-sleeved plaid cotton shirt with matching hat and a pair of navy blue sneakers. It was the kind of versatile outfit an outdoor person needs to be comfortable in our area where there is a wide range of temperature in any twenty-four hour period—a cold, foggy dawn, a hot noon sun, a brisk sea wind in the afternoon.

She also wore, suspended on a strap from her right shoulder, a leather bag where she kept some obviously old, German-made binoculars and a field guide protected by a plastic wrapper. Across the top of the wrapper, in black marking pencil, was printed the word BEALS. The make and condition of her binoculars, if nothing else, should have tipped Mr. Rett off. Perhaps a succession of Eaters, Talkers and Shutterbugs had dulled his perceptions. Anyway, he was unprepared for BEALS.

"There used to be a cañon wren living around these boulders," Mr. Rett said. "Let's see if he's still here."

He whistled the wren's song and the sound of it was so piercingly beautiful that even some of the Talkers paused to listen. A few seconds later Mr. Rett's answer came from the creek.

The degree of success in translating a bird song into human syllables depends on the listening ear, certainly, but also on the song itself. That of the yellow warbler sounds to my ears like *see see see see, witty me*. But even in the case of a simple song like this one, there are differences in the ways it is translated by various people: R. T. Peterson hears it as *tsee-tsee-tsee-tsee-titi-wee*, George Gladden as *sweet, sweet, sweet, sweeter, sweeter*, Ralph Hoffman as *tsee, tsee, tsee, tsitsi wee see*.

In the case of a much more complicated song like the cañon wren's, the range of differences widens. Peterson calls it "a gushing cadence of clear curved notes tripping down the scale," with which

I agree; but then he interprets it as *te-you, te-you, te-you tew tew tew,* which is surely inadequate. Hoffman despaired of translation and used description instead: ". . . the cañon wren pours out a cascade of sweet liquid notes, like the spray of a waterfall in sunshine." Perhaps W. L. Dawson gives the best impression of the song, not in the syllables he chose, which seem more pharmaceutical than faithful, but in the way he wrote them:

cuick
　cuick
　　cuick
　　　para
　　　　para
　　　　　goric
　　　　　　goric
　　　　　　　goric poozt teetl

Mr. Rett kept imitating the cañon wren in an attempt to bring him out into the open where we could all see him. The trick didn't work that day, and the little singer remained hidden behind his boulder. (This same boulder is the site of a wrenery every spring, and if you're lucky, you can catch the young ones in the act of practicing their songs.)

Meanwhile another small brownish bird landed on a sycamore branch hanging out over the water. Merely the way it sat, motionless, erect, alert, would have indicated to a novice bird watcher that it was a flycatcher. But I wasn't even a novice yet, and all it meant to me was one more clumsy search through the field guide for one more small brownish bird.

Mr. Rett identified it, for anyone who was interested, as a Traill's flycatcher.

Immediately BEALS lowered her binoculars and raised her eyebrows. "It's an Empidonax, certainly. But Traill's?—how can you be sure?"

For a few seconds Mr. Rett looked too stunned to reply. Then he said, "I know a Traill's when I see one."

"Really? Some people, some quite knowledgeable people, in fact, are content to call the whole group Empidonax and let it go at that."

She turned away with an elaborate shrug. It was the kind of

gesture I'd seen performed in court when a lawyer was attempting to cast doubt in the minds of the jury about a witness's credibility.

The jury, in this case, wasn't paying much attention. Some were out to lunch, some were discussing more important topics such as themselves, and the two lone men in the group had found a sunny redwood bench to sprawl out on and were, to all intents and purposes, asleep. That left me, still plodding through the field guide in search of small brownish birds. I was beginning to suspect that the day was still far distant when I could pronounce and spell Empidonax let alone identify one. Obviously I needed a system, some way of knowing which of the sixty color plates in the book would most likely contain the bird I was searching for. (During the first year of bird watching, my field guide was reduced to a handful of loose, limp sheets of paper. The one I'm currently using is my third.)

My efforts, involving as they did considerable paper-rattling, groans of frustration and muttered maledictions, did not go unnoticed.

"What on earth are you doing?" Mrs. Beals said.

"Trying to find a picture of that bird."

"What bird?"

I couldn't point, since by this time the bird had moved. I couldn't remember the word Empidonax and it would have been rather tactless to call it a Traill's flycatcher, so I said, "The one Mr. Rett *believed* to be a Traill's flycatcher."

"Why shouldn't he believe it? It was."

"But you—"

"Even the experts must be kept on their toes. Unless they're challenged now and then, they tend to get sloppy or take things for granted."

It turned out that Marie Beals was something of an expert herself: at her place on Long Island she had banded more than 15,000 birds!

Mrs. Beals pointed out to me my basic mistake. For every minute I spent studying a bird, I was spending ten minutes looking at the book.

"Try reversing this. You'll have plenty of time later to study the book. It won't fly away. The bird will."

In fact, it already had. But a minute later I located it on the jutting branch of an elderberry.

"Now," Mrs. Beals said, "suppose you look at the bird not as an object that must be matched up with a picture in a book, but as a living creature intent on survival. What is he doing?"

"Well, he seems to be staring down at the water at his own reflection."

"Nonsense. Only human beings have time to waste admiring themselves. He is looking for food. Among the smaller birds, the search for food occupies most of their waking hours. The next time you hear the expression, 'to eat like a bird,' remember that a robin can eat sixteen feet of earthworms in a day. It would be much simpler for him," she added thoughtfully, "if he could eat one earthworm sixteen feet long, but perhaps that wouldn't be so pleasant for the rest of us. It would certainly cause a sharp decrease in the number of home gardeners."

The bird, meanwhile, had sallied forth, picked a small dragonfly off the surface of the water and returned to its perch. I watched him while Mrs. Beals explained that the first thing I should do when I encountered a new bird was to notice the shape and size of his bill because this indicated what type of food he was best equipped to eat. The thin bill of the little flycatcher wasn't intended to crush seeds like the short bill of the even littler Oregon junco who'd come down to the creek to bathe. In general, she said, insect eaters like flycatchers, warblers, thrushes and wrens had thin bills, while seed eaters like finches and grosbeaks and buntings had thick bills.

It was the kind of simple basic lesson I needed and wanted, but a long time was to elapse before I automatically looked first at the bill of a new bird.

By now, Mr. Rett was some hundred yards ahead of us. As Mrs. Beals and I hurried to catch up with him, I asked her why she had signed up for the course. She explained that she had just moved to Santa Barbara and wanted to find out about our best birding areas, and, since she didn't drive, ways of reaching them and people to go with. On this last score, she indicated, the class was a big disappointment—as far as the members were concerned, it could just as well have been a course in skin diving or diamond cutting; none of them paid the least attention. I clued her in, as gently as possible, to the fact that the class was for credits, not condors or cranes.

Mr. Rett hadn't missed our company. We found him sitting on a boulder, talking to a small yellowish bird that was moving impatiently through the narrow gray leaves of a low-growing shrub. Mrs. Beals identified the bird for me as a yellowthroat and the shrub as a variety of buckwheat.

It was a charming scene, the little man and the little bird engaged in earnest conversation.

"*Check.*"

"Double check."

"*Check, check, check, check, check.*"

What they were saying, I don't know. But I like to think that I was witnessing something more than just a man imitating a bird. (This scolding or protest note of the yellowthroat, which sounds like *check* to me, Dawson translates as *wzschthub.* Try saying this with your mouth full of peanut butter—it's the only way to do it.)

At the time of this writing, a pair of yellowthroats are the star boarders at our feeding station. Although these are birds of the marsh and tule, the salicornia and slough, they can also be birds of the porch and the ledge or any other place where they're able to cadge their favorite food, doughnuts. When the larger birds like the jays, thrashers and flickers, and the flocking ones like the cowbirds, house finches and white-crowned sparrows, have finished eating and deserted the premises for a while, the smaller and more solitary birds start to appear, normally singly, sometimes in pairs: the wrentit, the orange-crowned warbler, the Lincoln sparrow, the Bewick's wren, and of course, the yellowthroat. We usually see the male first. His black mask edged with white may serve as effective camouflage among the lights and shadows of a tule marsh, but on our ledge he is as conspicuous as a butterfly in a bathtub.

The female, having no black mask to hide behind, is more circumspect. We don't see her as frequently, and when we do she is seldom on the ledge. She prefers less open, less obvious places, like under the floorboards of the porch, or the shrubbery around certain bird baths, or the bottom parts of the privet hedge and the bougainvillaea vines.

Beginning birders, on catching sight of the female yellowthroat, are inclined to mistake her for other warblers of our area, especially the orange-crowned and the yellow. She is much more wren-like than either of these, both in profile—her head is flatter and her bill longer and somewhat downward curved—and in habitat, preferring the ground and low shrubbery rather than trees. The yellowthroat was, in fact, formerly known as the tule wren and the scientific name for the species, *Geothlypis trichas,* means a bird that's confined to the ground.

When disturbed, both the male and the female will utter the protest sound, *check,* or, if you prefer, *wzschthub.* But only the male has the ability to sing. *Bewitchedy, witchedy, witched, bewitchedy, witchedy witched.* Perhaps he is warning the bird world that he is indeed bewitched, but that at any moment the spell will end and he will take off his mask and reveal what he really is, at least an eagle.

During the mid-morning break I had a chance to ask Mr. Rett about Houdunit's strange relationship with the hubcap and the two windows. He said that most birds, and many mammals as well, will defend their territory vigorously against other members of the same species. This territorial fighting among birds is more or less ritualized and no real harm is done to the contestants, though some observers have seen blood drawn in boundary disputes between brown towhees.

The towhee in the hubcap, the second one in the lanai window and the third in the bathroom window were, to Houdunit, interlopers who had to be driven off, contenders for his title, his food supply and his nesting sites. The trio's persistence must have cast doubts in Houdunit's mind about his ability as a fighter, but he didn't give up. Instead, the sun gradually changed position in the sky and obliterated his enemies.

I also asked Mr. Rett to imitate the call note of a brown towhee. He replied what sounded to me exactly like *chink.*

Would you believe *wzschthub?*

You're a Stool Pigeon, Mother

At noon the class returned to the Museum of Natural History for lunch. The meal was planned, prepared and served by Junior Aides—a number of girls in their early teens who did volunteer work at the museum during the summer and after school hours. The girls also made up their own menus, which were printed on a blackboard and offered such delicacies as:

goop soup · sand witches
false furters · dam burgers
kookies

We ate outside at redwood picnic tables under a huge live oak tree. Unfortunately there was a heavy infestation of oak moths that year so the Junior Aides were able to add an unexpected item to their menu, oak moth larvae. The wiggly little creatures seemed to hang from every leaf, and the lightest brushing against an overhanging branch netted at least fifty of them on your clothes and in your hair, and naturally the odd one dropped into a sand witch or a dam burger. Some members of the class made fast and shrill departures.

Marie Beals was undismayed. "It's all good honest protein."

The oak moth larvae turned out to be the lesser of two evils associated with eating in the museum patio that summer. The other was Melanie.

The name was well chosen since it comes from the Greek word for black, and Melanie was black indeed. Black as coal, black as night, black as ebony or jet, black, in fact, as the raven she was; black of feather, of foot, of bill, of eye, and most definitely, of heart.

I was later told that Melanie had been found when she was about a month old, on Santa Cruz Island, some twenty-five miles offshore from Santa Barbara. Raised as a pet by a family who lived near the museum, Melanie spent her first year developing her wings and practicing the aerial acrobatics of her kind. She stayed close to home since she was fond of her adopted family and knew a good thing when she saw one. There was an additional reason: ravens are very scarce in our area. She was not tempted to join a pair of strong black wings tumbling and soaring and diving in the air, and no male voice, curiously softened and symphonized by love, called her away.

It is almost an axiom that the more intelligent a creature is, the more ways he discovers or invents to amuse himself. By this standard Melanie was a genius. At the beginning of her second spring she found out what sport there was to be had on the grounds of the museum—people to laugh at her, animals to snap at her, caged birds to denounce her. There were little girls to howl if she merely, by the purest accident, pulled out a few strands of hair in an attempt to make off with a barrette or bobby pin, and little boys to shriek if she stole their pocketknives or poked them in the stomach while trying to determine if silver belt buckles were detachable. In all fairness to the children, I would like to draw the reader's attention to the size of a raven. Melanie was two feet long, and with her wings spread, four feet wide, and her beak measured three inches in length and was one inch deep at the nostril. This is a lot of beak attached to a lot of bird.

A good deal of Melanie's attention was lavished on middle-aged matrons. She had no particular affection for them as such, but they happened to wear more jewelry than any other class of people. Earrings and necklaces, wrist watches, bracelets, jeweled pins and buttons—Melanie adored them all, not because she was female but because she was a raven. I have never heard a satisfactory explanation of why birds of this family find shiny objects irresistible. Perhaps there is no explanation that can be properly translated from ravenese into humanese.

Melanie's only legitimate jewelry consisted of a pink plastic name band on her right leg, which was meant to indicate to the general public that she was no ordinary bird. She occasionally chewed the band, not with any intention of getting it off—she could have accomplished this in short order with her powerful beak—but in a lazy, desultory way, like a bored teen-ager chewing gum in class.

Melanie also had a weakness for nipping ankle socks. Her friends claimed she didn't know that socks contained ankles or that the owners of same would object vociferously. A class of visiting schoolchildren was worth at least an hour of good clean noisy fun. Some of the noise Melanie supplied personally, since ravens are capable of making a wide variety of sounds. The cost of first aid equipment was running high and the number of excuses for Melanie's conduct was getting low. The result was inevitable—the museum officials decided to banish Melanie from the grounds. As a member of the staff succinctly put it: "One of these days she's bound to take a hunk out of somebody who doesn't want to give a hunk."

The cooperation of Melanie's adopted family was, of course, necessary. When Melanie's misdeeds were spelled out to them, they professed great astonishment: "You can't mean our Melanie. She's as gentle as a lamb. There must be another raven around."

This was possible, but the family finally conceded that it seemed rather unlikely there would be another raven wearing on her right leg a pink plastic ankle band with the name Melanie printed on it. At any rate, Melanie was banished.

Her departure caused many changes around the museum. Visiting classes of schoolchildren were oddly quiet and monotonous. A sudden shriek splitting the air conveyed none of the *now-what?* excitement of the Melanistic days. The explanation was usually quite dull: a lady had turned her ankle, a Junior Aide had tried to pet the porcupine, a little boy had fallen into the creek or out of a tree.

The mynah bird, who had taken to using Melanie as a confidante, lapsed into a depressed silence and could not be coaxed into repeating the sentiment he had picked up in some mysterious period of his past:

"You're a stool pigeon, Mother."

Meanwhile, Melanie's fame had spread and people from out of town arrived daily, demanding to see "that trained raven," and taking a dim view of the fact that they'd driven fifty or sixty miles for nothing more than a mynah bird that wouldn't talk and a porcupine that couldn't be petted.

Melanie became, *in absentia,* a kind of folk heroine whose presence had been unappreciated and motives misunderstood. The same people who'd complained most bitterly about Melanie's conduct now inquired after her health and hinted at her return. The children who'd screamed the loudest over her advances, now vehemently protested her banishment. Teachers who'd accused Melanie of disrupting their classes, ladies left with a single earring and Junior Aides with ankle scars—everyone wanted Melanie back. So back she came.

For the first couple of days after her return Melanie was a changed character. Showing the modesty becoming a folk heroine, she received the extravagant greetings and compliments of her admirers with quiet dignity, and accepted tidbits of food graciously, hardly even maiming a finger. Perched on the railing of the little bridge over the creek she watched with regal detachment the parade of brightly-colored bobbysocks, and ponytails held in place by jeweled clasps. Her performance was so convincing that one patron accused museum officials of feeding her tranquilizers, or of doing away with the real Melanie and trying to palm off on the public an inferior substitute.

It was Melanie herself who prevented this accusation from developing into a full-fledged rumor. Her new role, in spite of the fact that she was so good at it, bored her. She was too intelligent and curious for the docile life. She missed the excitement of children racing for cover, the slamming of doors and the honking of horns and the blowing of whistles.

On the third morning after her return, a group of young girls from an out-of-town boarding school arrived at the museum. The girls were in the charge of two nuns, both of whom wore prayer beads. For poor Melanie this was temptation enough, but there was a greater one, something quite new to her world: one of the girls had attached to the laces of her saddle shoes tiny silver bells that tinkled when she walked. The bells—their gloss, their movement, their enchanting sound—were too much for Melanie.

The girls were strangers to Melanie and she to them. Sensing this, she chose surprise tactics. Without a shadow or a whisper of warning, she swooped into the middle of the class, croaking, lunging with her beak and flapping her huge wings. No two witnesses tell the same story about what happened after that, but stories agree that the scene ended with children scattering in all directions and Melanie soaring over the oak trees, carrying a silver bell in her beak while the mynah bird screamed after her: "You're a stool pigeon, Mother! You're a stool pigeon, Mother!"

Darkness set in before the last of the children was finally located, so it was not surprising that two days later the museum received a sharp and rather uncharitable letter from the head of the boarding school. A meeting was held, at which three decisions were made:

1. Melanie was Melanie, and any thought of reforming her was ridiculous.

2. All schools should discourage girls from taking up nonsensical fads like wearing bells on their shoes.

3. Visitors to the museum should be asked, on entering the grounds, to remove all jewelry before it was removed for them.

The preceding events were, of course, unknown to me when I first met Melanie. She introduced herself by landing, apparently out of nowhere, on the redwood table where Marie Beals and I were having lunch.

Marie was delighted, I was somewhat less so. A raven in the air is one thing, a raven sharing a table with you is another. And to complicate matters, I didn't even know what kind of bird Melanie was. To me she was simply the biggest, boldest and blackest I'd ever seen. For a full minute she stood motionless, with her eyes on me, like a vampire bat locating in advance the most vulnerable portion of the jugular vein.

"It's obviously somebody's pet," Marie said. "I wonder if it's hungry."

Marie tossed a piece of bread on the ground. Melanie didn't even bother glancing at it. Instead, she walked sedately toward my plate, removed a frankfurter and began to eat it.

Marie watched placidly. "She needs plenty of protein."

"So do I. That's my lunch."

"Ravens, as you probably know, are scavengers. They eat carrion. So do we, if you come right down to it. A frankfurter is simply carrion that's been cooked."

Viewed in this light, the loss of my lunch didn't seem so bad.

Marie, who turned nearly every occasion into a bird lesson, was explaining to me what distinguished the raven from the crow—the heavier beak, the wedge-shaped tail, the shaggy throat feathers. If the two species are seen side by side, the most obvious difference is one of size. But birds are seldom that cooperative, and anyway, using size as a means of identification is chancy. The far raven looks no larger than the near crow. (As an example of this deceptiveness I cite the experience of a friend of mine who was out on a condor survey with a Forest Service official. My friend was taken aback when the official pointed out as a distant condor—wingspread, $8\frac{1}{2}$ to $9\frac{1}{2}$ feet—a not so distant turkey vulture—wingspread, 6 feet.)

The difference to look for, Marie said, is that of flight pattern: ravens soar like hawks, keeping their wings stiff and straight, while crows flap a great deal, and when they set their wings to glide, the wings are bent upward. Though the habitats of the two species may overlap, in California the crow generally prefers to roam in flocks through the more cultivated areas. The raven is more of a loner, and like many other loners he seeks a mountain fastness or the solitude of the desert.

Melanie was no doubt surprised to hear this but her only comment was a hoarse, low-pitched *Grub*. She had finished my frank-

furter, or cooked carrion, and was walking around the redwood
table with the expectant air of a small boy at a circus: will the lion
escape from his cage? Will the aerialist fall? Surely the bear will
attack his keeper? Will the sword-swallower choke, the fire-eater
burn, the elephants stampede?

For Melanie none of these things would have been nearly so
exciting as what actually happened. In an effort to put a more
comfortable distance between Melanie's beak and myself I stood
up too abruptly and my purse fell off my lap, strewing its contents
on the ground—wallet, comb, lipstick, checkbook, pillbox, and my
keys for the house, the car and the safe-deposit box. The lipstick
was in a gold case trimmed with a green glass emerald, the pillbox
was turquoise enamel on copper and the five keys were attached to
a silver dollar. It didn't require more than two seconds for Melanie
to decide which item she wanted. Before I even realized what was
happening, my key ring was airborne. Up, up, up, over the toyon
tree, over the oak, over the sycamore, and to all intents and purposes, out of my life forever.

"Note the speed of a raven," Marie said, "and its mastery of—"

"Those are my keys."

"—air currents."

"I can't get home without them."

"Ravens are what are known as static soarers, like the buteo
hawks . . . Your *car* keys?"

"Yes."

"Dear me, that *is* awkward. I was hoping you'd give me a lift as
far as the courthouse."

Melanie had disappeared for a moment, but now she emerged
from behind an enormous Monterey pine tree and took up a position on the very top of it. According to Marie, who was watching
through binoculars, Melanie still had the key ring in her beak.

"So far, so good," Marie said. "However, she may have a cache up
there—magpies and crows often have special hiding places for their
treasures; perhaps ravens do too. My climbing days, alas, are over."

"Mine haven't begun."

"Well then, there we are, aren't we?"

There we were, and there we seemed likely to remain.

By this time a small crowd had gathered, including a Junior

Aide who told us a little about Melanie's background, enough to convince me I'd better either call the garage or start walking. The idea of telephoning Ken occurred to me but was quickly cast aside. It is difficult for two professional writers living under the same roof to keep each other's writing hours inviolate. But it must be done, and Ken and I had long ago worked out a system: he handles emergencies in the morning when I am writing, I handle them in the afternoon when he is writing. It was afternoon.

At this point Melanie looked down, saw the size of her audience and decided to improve the show. With a flirt of her tail she sallied forth from the pine tree. Circling it once to make sure all eyes were on her, she dropped the key ring, did a complete somersault while it was falling, then swooped down and picked it out of the air. Catching a thermal updraft she repeated the performance half a dozen times, each time letting the key ring fall a little longer and a little further. I could almost feel my heart fall with it, but Marie took a more philosophical approach to the new turn of events: "At least it tends to dispel the theory that she has a secret cache in the tree, and that's all to the good."

"I still don't have my keys."

"Forget about them. Admire the bird's performance."

Although it's always somewhat difficult to admire a performance put on at your own expense, I did my best.

Since that day I've never seen any bird engage in such a complicated aerial game involving an object, though I've heard that golden eagles will play with stones in a similar fashion, and on a number of occasions I've watched them do barrel rolls while attempting to get rid of Swainson's and red-shouldered hawks. Many birds drop and retrieve in the air, but the objects involved are usually food. I've seen ospreys and kingfishers go after fish that have escaped them, white-tailed kites after mice, jays and flycatchers and mockingbirds after insects. But only Melanie have I seen playing with a silver dollar and five keys.

Melanie had the stamina to continue her dazzling display indefinitely. Her span of concentration, however, was short and it was only a matter of time before she got tired of the game. The question was, At what point would she quit, before she dropped the key ring, or after?

The question was soon answered. One moment my key ring was glinting in the sunlight, the next moment it disappeared somewhere in the middle of the chaparral-covered hillside, and Melanie was flying, empty-beaked, back to the top of the pine tree. A long groan went up from the onlookers and almost immediately they began to disperse as if the show had ended.

There was no use in attempting a search. The hillside was full of ticks and poison oak, and the chances of finding one small key ring in all that brush were minimal. A Junior Aide with the name Connie stitched on the pocket of her working smock claimed that Melanie had extremely sharp eyes and would certainly be able to find the keys if she wanted to. What would make Melanie want to was anybody's guess.

Meanwhile Melanie remained on her perch on top of the pine tree. Perhaps she was merely resting. More likely, she was wondering what had happened to her audience and how she could get it back again. There is no such thing as an ex-exhibitionist.

Connie, it turned out, was something of an authority on Melanie since she lived with her family in the immediate neighborhood of the museum.

"She used to come to all our barbecues," Connie said.

And why, I wanted to know, had Melanie stopped?

"She didn't, we did. We haven't had a barbecue since last Easter."

I didn't ask what had happened last Easter. I felt that under the circumstances I was better off not knowing.

At Connie's suggestion we decided to try a new tactic based on the fact that Melanie couldn't stand being ignored. Marie, Connie and I sat down again at the redwood table and pretended to be completely engrossed in the contents of Connie's social studies textbook. For reasons which will remain forever unknown, the mynah bird chose this moment to start showing off his rather limited vocabulary.

"You're a stool pigeon, Mother! You're a stool pigeon, Mother!"

Whether Melanie was galvanized into action by the mynah's voice or by our ignoring her, we will never be sure. But galvanized she was. She swooped down low over the hillside, and without an instant's hesitation, located the key ring in the underbush and picked it up.

The speed of her performance raises questions: did she remember where she'd dropped the key ring? Or could she actually see it in the middle of all that brush? I'm inclined to believe she used her memory rather than her eyes, partly because I know how dense the underbrush is in that area and partly because of similar experiences I've had with dogs, our German shepherd, Brandy, in particular. Frequently while playing on the beach he loses a ball or a stick, yet he has no trouble finding them when told to. He doesn't track the object down by smelling—this breed is not very keennosed anyway—and his eyesight isn't half as good as my own. I must conclude that he remembers, not in the human way—where-did-I-drop-that-blinking-ball?—but in his own and Melanie's way, which we still do not fully understand.

Keepers of parrots, cockatoos, budgerigars and the like usually have tales to tell about the prodigious memory feats of their pets. Usually, too, ornithologists put a grain of salt on these tales. Experiments conducted on wild birds indicate that some species have a remarkable capacity to remember. Joel Carl Welty cites one such experiment in his definitive work, *The Life of Birds:*

> *The Nutcracker,* Nucifraga caryocatactes, *in Sweden lives on hazel nuts and spends its full time for three months in the autumn gathering and storing the nuts. In a series of observations by Swanberg [1951] the birds were observed to fill their throat pouches at the hazel thickets and fly as far as six kilometers [about four miles] to bury them in their spruce-forest territories, in small heaps covered with moss or lichens. The Nutcrackers live on the nuts over winter and feed their young on them the next spring. Apparently the birds remember where they have stored the nuts, for of 351 excavations, some of them through snow 45 centimeters [about 1½ feet] deep, 86% were successful.*

Probably we will never know exactly how Melanie located my key ring with such speed and will have to be content with the fact that she did find it. She landed on the redwood table, wearing the key ring proudly in her beak. Both Marie and I made attempts to grab it away from her, but Melanie let out a reproachful croak and daintily stepped beyond our reach.

"You'll never get it from her that way," Connie said. "My dad tried that at Easter and Melanie still has his gold-plated monogrammed bottle opener. If you want her to give up something, you should offer her a substitute. Do you have any jewelry you wouldn't mind losing?"

Marie wore no jewelry, and all I had on was my wedding ring. I made it clear that I would prefer to walk the six miles home rather than add my wedding ring to Melanie's collection of trinkets.

We finally decided, after a brief caucus, that we would have to appeal to another aspect of Melanie's greed. She was always hungry, Connie said, and frankfurters were her particular weakness, especially if they were doused with ketchup or barbecue sauce, perhaps to give them a more authentic carrion appearance. Connie went to the kitchen and returned with two ketchup-covered frankfurters on a paper plate. She put the plate on the ground about ten feet away from Melanie, who had turned her head and was ignoring the whole business.

"She's not hungry," I said.

Connie disagreed. "She's just pretending. Keep watching and be ready to grab the keys when she drops them."

For the next few minutes Melanie gave an Academy Award performance as she-who-couldn't-care-less. She took a few dainty steps and gazed pensively up at the sky; she studied the oak trees and the sycamores; she lifted her right foot and examined her name band like a bored young woman consulting her wrist watch; she cocked her head to listen to the mynah bird who was still telling mother she was a stool pigeon.

Then, suddenly, Melanie plunged to the ground. I think she meant to pick up both frankfurters while still retaining the key ring, but even Melanie's formidable beak wasn't capable of managing such a load.

There are probably few times in life when a person is grateful for a ketchup-covered key ring. That was one of them.

Even now, Melanie's admirers point out that it was a hot summer that year, and if excuses are made for human misconduct during a heat wave, they should certainly be made for corvine delinquency. The fact is that ravens are as impervious to climate as they are to environment. They are at home in the treeless Arctic tundra and in thick forests of spruce or alder, in town and country, in the mountains, on the coast and in the desert. While driving through the Mojave Desert in a severe windstorm with the temperature well above 100° F., when it seemed no living creature could exist, I have seen ravens looking as sleek as if they'd just stepped out of a cold shower.

No, it was not the heat that was responsible for Melanie's repeated indiscretions that summer; it was the restlessness in her bones, the quickening of her blood. Melanie was growing up. While her misdeeds were not planned to call attention to the fact that the time had come when she needed the company of another raven to carry out her purpose in life, this was the effect of them. It was decided that Melanie should be returned to Santa Cruz, the island where she was born.

Her journey across the twenty-five miles of channel was taken in style on a boat borrowed for the occasion by her adopted family. Melanie rode in the galley, sitting part of the time on the refrigerator, the rest on the top bunk. She was very quiet and refused to eat. Perhaps she was seasick or tired. I can't, however, discount the possibility that she was quietly remembering her first sea voyage and all the things that had since happened to her—and to a lot of others!—and her fine collection of admirers and earrings and silver bells that had to be left behind. Any ornithologist will tell you ravens don't think, but any friend of Melanie's will insist they do.

Santa Cruz Island, twenty-three miles long, from two to six and a half miles wide and comprising 62,000 acres, is a ruggedly beautiful area, privately owned and almost completely uninhabited. Conservation organizations, led by the Sierra Club, have been working for some time toward the goal of making Santa Cruz part of our National Park System.

Most of the shoreline of the island, which was once part of the mainland, is composed of cliffs rising straight out of the water. Here and there tides have eaten into the cliffs and formed caves. One of these, Painted Cave, is seventy feet high and can be explored in a small boat when the tide is low and the sea calm—two distinctly different conditions which may or may not occur together. The cave's inner walls have been painted, not by intrepid Indians, but by the chemical action of salt water on the various rock formations.

Some parts of the island are shale, sandstone and volcanic rock, almost bare of vegetation. A few areas have enough water to support groves of Monterey pines and oaks, in addition to the various chaparral shrubs like ceanothus. These sections are inhabited by a bird that is found nowhere else in the world. The Santa Cruz Island jay, once considered a separate species, is currently listed as a subspecies of the scrub jay.

The differences between the two jays are many: size, color, voice, behavior, body-wing-tail ratio, dimensions of nests and of eggs, even the shape of the beak, which, in the island bird, is the same length but bulkier, almost half an inch deep at the nostril. This jay is heavier, has a longer tail and a sturdier body, but to me the most striking difference is in color. His plumage is a deeper and more vivid blue. Though some of his calls and actions resemble those of our mainland jay, his disposition is gentler, perhaps softened, as Dawson suggests, by the year-round food supply for which there is little competition, the equable climate, warmed in winter and cooled in summer by the sea, and by the lack of human interference with his affairs.

Because his wings are too weak to support his body in any sustained effort of flight, the Santa Cruz Island jay is fated to remain forever on his lonely island. There we see him every May and September when the Santa Barbara Audubon Society crosses the channel to check the migrations of pelagic birds like shearwaters, petrels and alcids. In order to land on the island, permission from the owners is required. This is often tedious, and for our purposes unnecessary, since the straight cliffs of the shoreline permit boats to cruise or anchor very close in. The flirt of a bright tail among the live oaks, a patch of cobalt blue gliding up through the Monterey pines as if it were attached to a sky hook—these mark the Santa Cruz Island jay, a bird unique.

Melanie was released from the galley fifty yards offshore. Rising on her toes like a ballerina, she lifted her great black wings and flew straight toward the land of her birth and of her destiny. She didn't look back.

Since that day I have visited Santa Cruz Island many times and have seen in the sky bald eagles, peregrine falcons, red-tailed hawks, and of course, ravens, many ravens. But none of them wore a pink plastic band on its right leg. The band is probably gone anyway: she would have long since chewed it off as the last vestige of her flighty youth.

Morgan

Addiction to bird watching may happen very suddenly as it did to me, or it may be a slower and quieter thing, as in my husband's case.

From the beginning he adjusted well to the necessary changes in our household. He ate our much simpler meals without complaint, he was careful to avoid getting too close to the picture windows, he looked and listened with patience while I pointed out the ordinary birds that were now coming daily to the ledge and the feeders, and the grapes and doughnuts in the trees: house finches, song sparrows, scrub jays, mourning doves, wrentits, mockingbirds and towhees. The brown towhee, Houdunit, was practically a member of the family by this time, but of the rufous-sided towhee we could catch only glimpses as he foraged, both feet at a time, in the underbrush or flew low across the canyon. We had to wait until the following spring to see him right out in the open, singing his wheezy waltz: *too-wheee—1, 2, 3—too-wheeee—1, 2, 3—too-wheee—1, 2, 3.*

On very rare and special occasions the rufous-sided towhee has come up into the tea tree for a furtive bite of doughnut, but to this day he has never appeared on the ledge or any of the feeders. Often, especially just before twilight, we hear his plaintive question: *Aaay? Aaay?* From bush to bush he goes, asking over and over again, *Aaay? What is life? Aaay? How did it start? Aaay? Where will it all end?* But nobody ever answers.

Perhaps the nearest thing to an answer appears in the month of May. We catch sight of it as it hurries through the underbrush of the canyon, looking like a large black sparrow. Only the choice of flyway and the white outer tail feathers identify it as a young rufous-sided towhee.

The critical point in my husband's conversion came one morning in early August. I was in my office working on a book. When I emerged for a tea break I found Ken at the dining-room table with the two field guides open in front of him and my binoculars hanging from his neck. "Have you ever seen a band-tailed pigeon?" he said casually. "There's one on the feeder in the eucalyptus tree."

The first band-tailed pigeon is an event, an experience. This is partly because of his size—he's larger than the domestic pigeon— and partly because he is wild, a bird of the woodlands, not of the city streets or the ledges of office buildings. He also differs from the domestic pigeon in having, at maturity, a white crescent around the nape of his neck and a light gray, sometimes almost white, band at the end of his tail, which is very broad and can be spread out into a fan—hence the common misnomer, fan-tailed pigeon. Unlike all other North American pigeons and doves, he has a yellow bill with a purplish-black tip, and feet that seem to have been painted to match, yellow with purplish-black toenails. He looks as though the moment of his creation had been a summer morning and the place a wild elderberry bush and one ripe dewy berry had clung to his beak and one to each toenail.

While these birds most frequently nest in oaks, and acorns are a main part of their diet, it is with eucalyptus trees that I associate them. We see them perched in these trees more often than any others. When the blue gum eucalyptus is very young, or when an older tree is putting out new leaves, the leaves are so different in color and shape from the older ones that they appear to belong to a separate family. These leaves are a soft velvety blue-gray, exactly like the plumage of the bandtails perched among them. No doubt this is just a happy accident, though it sometimes seems that the eucalyptus, like a good host trying to please his guest, grows new leaves to match the bandtails.

What is the difference between a pigeon and a dove?

People frequently ask this question and seem disappointed in the answer: there is no difference. The terms are interchangeable, and the birds eating milo and cracked corn on our ledge could just as well be called band-tailed doves and mourning pigeons. Although in general practice smaller birds are known as doves and larger ones as pigeons, this isn't a rule. The Supreme Court of bird watchers, the American Ornithological Union, lists the domestic pigeon under the name rock dove.

However the columbine grapevine works—perhaps in a kind of pidgin English—it is quick and efficient in spreading the word about a new feeding and watering area. By week's end our bandtail's immediate family was well established and every hour brought a new batch of obscure in-laws and fifty-second cousins and friends of friends of friends. They all took an immediate fancy to the bird bath with the continuous drip. They stood on it, they drank from it, immersing their beaks to the nostrils and drawing in the water; they showered, lifting first one wing, then the other, letting the drip trickle down onto their wing pits.

Band-tailed pigeons share with some other flocking birds a custom that serves the species well in the wild but is not expedient at a feeding station. A bandtail arriving at dawn for breakfast doesn't immediately go to the feeder and start eating. Instead, he perches in one of the eucalyptus trees, and even though he must be hungry he waits quietly for his friends, now and then thrusting his head forward and back to appraise his surroundings more accurately. When a certain number of birds have arrived, as when a critical mass is reached in nuclear physics, the action starts. Suddenly, like clumsy blue butterflies, the pigeons begin falling out of the trees onto the feeder and the lower terrace. At one of these eucalyptical gatherings of the clan I have counted ninety-eight bandtails.

There must be some kind of signal to start this mass movement. If it's a voice signal, I've never heard it; if it's kinetic, either I haven't seen it or don't recognize it. It seems likely that one of the bandtails is the accepted leader and sets an example for the rest to follow. When he decides to eat, everybody eats—providing the dining area is a two-acre field, not a seed hopper with a perch meant for half a dozen birds.

The lone bandtail is a quiet bird with little to say as he goes about his business. But when twenty or thirty of them attempt to land on a narrow perch the resulting noise sounds as if they were approaching the boozy climax of an avian cocktail party with every guest trying to communicate at once in grunts and clucks and squawks. From a certain distance this cacophony is very human-sounding and I sometimes think that if, instead of a party, they were holding a meeting with rules of procedure to give each of them a turn, I might be able to understand what they meant.

By the end of that first week in August, it was becoming obvious with the arrival of each new in-law and fifty-second cousin that we needed a much larger pigeon feeder, placed in an area apart from the other feeders so that the smaller birds wouldn't be frightened away. Not that the bandtails were aggressive—I've never seen a bandtail indicate rancor toward a bird of another species even in self-defense, and I've watched many of them being bullied and birdhandled by acorn woodpeckers, scrub jays, mockingbirds, even house sparrows. The size of the pigeons and their number, however, were discouraging some of the shyer species. The wrentit, the Oregon junco and the song sparrow seemed reluctant to share a table with the bandtails, without having any real cause to fear them.

The second pigeon feeder had a trough placed between two pine trees some distance from the house, and could accommodate twenty pigeons. Almost as soon as Ken had driven in the last nail, we began to learn of the existence of an ornithological principle new to us: people with a six-pigeon feeder have twenty pigeons, people with a twenty-pigeon feeder have fifty, and for people who have two feeders, a ledge and a charge account at the feed store, the sky's the limit—unless nature steps in and sets a limit of her own. And that is what happened next.

The conclusion of the bird course hadn't meant the end of my association with Mr. Rett and Marie Beals. Both had been to our house to see the bird-feeding setup, Marie and I went birding together whenever possible, and I frequently visited the Museum of Natural History for advice and information from Mr. Rett. On one of these occasions he asked me if Ken and I had been coming across any dead mourning doves or band-tailed pigeons in our area. Two doves had been brought to the museum, one dead and the other greatly emaciated and unable to eat. Autopsies had in each case revealed a large growth in the throat caused by a protozoan parasite, *trichomonas gallinae*. Birds so afflicted were unable to eat but they kept trying and regurgitating, thus passing the parasite on to others, especially at a feeding station. He advised me to be on the lookout for dead or emaciated birds, and if I found any, to suspend feeding operations immediately in order to prevent a serious outbreak of trichomoniasis.

I didn't like the idea of suspending feeding operations. It seemed to me that a well-nourished bird would be more resistant to disease and that a bird already infected would be even more dependent than usual on a steady food supply and lots of fresh clear water. Closing down the station would be a little like closing down a hospital because people were getting sick. Mr. Rett admitted that he'd never witnessed an actual epidemic (or rather, epizootic) outbreak of trichomoniasis, but he'd received government pamphlets warning of such a thing and advising people to beware. I assured him that we would beware.

As the week progressed there were manifest indications that we were losing some of our pigeons: cracked corn and milo left untouched on the lower terrace and in the trough between the pines, fewer and scantier gatherings of the clan in the eucalyptus trees, the sounds of partying more sober and subdued. We found no dead birds but this was not surprising since much of our area is a jungle of underbrush. Here a dead or dying bird could lie undetected or be eaten by a cat, a sharp-shinned or Cooper's hawk, or a turkey vulture. Whatever the cause, we were rapidly losing our pigeons.

The following Monday, when I went down to scrub out the drip bath, a bandtail was waiting for me on the terrace. He watched my approach without alarm, making no effort to move away or take cover. When a wild creature departs from its usual behavior pattern like this, you can be pretty sure it's sick; its survival instincts are not operating. The bird was not emaciated. Frequently on our winter beach walks Ken and I come across oil-soaked and grounded scoters, grebes, gulls and loons. Our friend and fellow birder, John Flavin, who has rescued, cleaned, fed and put back into circulation any number of these creatures, taught us how to predict with some accuracy a bird's chance of surviving the various steps of this difficult treatment. If the breastbone appears very sharp it means the bird hasn't eaten for a long time and is a poor risk.

Our bandtail's breastbone appeared to be well fleshed. I kept the bird under surveillance all morning. Mostly he dozed in the sun, sometimes he picked up a few grains of milo and ate them with no sign of difficulty in swallowing. By noon he was dead.

This was the first bird we lost at our feeding station and it was a blow to me. I had fallen into the habit of accepting the California sun as a fetish that would dissolve disease and hold death in abeyance.

I had to drop in at the veterinarian's that afternoon to pick up a case of the special diet my Scottie needed, so I decided to take the bandtail with me and find out what had caused its death. If an epidemic was about to start I wanted to be ready for action, preferably immediate and drastic.

The vet, a soft-spoken, pleasant man, was surprised when he opened the carton containing the pigeon—and not one hundred percent delighted. "What am I supposed to do with it?"

"Find out why it died, whether it had trichomoniasis or not."

"Good grief, what's that?"

I repeated what Mr. Rett had told me about trichomoniasis. The vet, while examining the pigeon briefly, said he didn't know very much about avian diseases, except those affecting domestic species like parrots, budgerigars and canaries, but that the bandtail appeared to be young, uninjured and well nourished. This ruled out old age or accident as the cause of death, as well as trichomoniasis.

I said, "Are you positive?"

"There's no sign of a swelling in the throat."

I had gone into the vet's office all set to fight an epidemic and I was not about to leave again without one to fight. "But it could be something equally serious that the other birds might catch?"

"Could be. Diseases caused by bacteria or viruses are usually communicable."

Bacteria and viruses were more along my line than protozoan parasites, and I warmed to the subject: "What would you do if, for instance, you had a flock of homing pigeons and wanted to prevent the spread of a disease?"

"Well, if there was any urgency about it, I'd give each of them an intramuscular shot of antibiotics."

The thought of trying to catch several dozen wild pigeons and administer an intramuscular shot of antibiotics to each of them was enough to dampen the enthusiasm of even the keenest epidemic fighter. "What if the urgency wasn't so great?"

"I'd dissolve the stuff in their drinking water."

"Suppose they didn't like the taste and refused to drink it?"

He said he didn't know if it had any taste but for the sake of science—and a three-dog client who paid her bills promptly—he would find out. He brought from his supply cupboard a plastic bag containing a pink powder. He mixed a little powder in some water, drank it and declared the stuff was delicious and he felt better already. He put the bandtail back in the carton and closed the lid.

"I'm leaving town for a couple of days so I won't be able to perform an autopsy right away. But I'll do it as soon as I return. My secretary will call you when there's something definite to report."

"The bandtails could all be dead by then."

"If you're worried, take along some of the powder. If they're sick, it'll help, if they're not, it won't hurt." He wrote the mixing instructions on a piece of paper and gave it to me.

I was halfway home before it occurred to me that getting wild pigeons to accept an antibiotic solution in place of water might be almost as difficult as giving them an intramuscular injection. Our bandtails, unlike the hypothetical homing pigeons I'd mentioned to the veterinarian, were free. They had choices: come or go, take it or leave it. With their swift, direct flight they could range many miles during a day, and if our bird baths contained a new mixture instead of water, they didn't have to drink it. There were lots of other bird baths, and a few creeks which were still flowing, however sluggishly.

We had some things working for us though. The first was food: the range of the birds was restricted by their desire to stick fairly close to their source of supply, especially of milo. This was their favorite food, more because of its size and shape than its taste. One of nature's economies was not to bother providing pigeons with much sense of taste because they bolt their food. It goes down the esophagus and into the crop with such speed that even the most sensitive taste bud wouldn't know what hit it.

The second factor in our favor was habit. Like people, birds develop habit patterns. The bandtails had taken a particular fancy to the drip bath on the lower terrace and to a very large ceramic saucer we kept on the ledge. We let the other bird baths go dry and substituted, for the smaller birds to use, tin pie plates which the pigeons would only tip over if they tried to stand on them. In the drip bath and the ceramic saucer Ken put the antibiotic solution. The arrangement worked very well. Evidently pigeons' discernment of color is no more highly developed than their sense of taste, for right from the beginning they treated the pink mixture with the foam on top as if it were the purest water.

For the balance of the week the bandtails drank, bathed in and waded through antibiotic. (So did a lot of the other birds, including Houdunit, the brown towhee, who spent a great deal of time breaking the bubbles with his beak.) Keeping the containers full was quite a job, but we had the satisfaction of seeing that the flock was no longer on the decrease. It had leveled off at about fifty bandtails—all of whom looked healthy, or at any rate not sick. Meanwhile we heard nothing from Miss Ames, the vet's secretary, who was supposed to call us. On Friday I decided to call her since our supply of the antibiotic wouldn't last through the weekend. I asked her if I could pick up some more of the stuff.

She hesitated for a moment. "Are you sure you need more? You probably don't realize how expensive it is. I've been making out the bills and just the amount you've already used is costing you eleven dollars."

Miss Ames's sudden concern for my bank account was unexpected, and when I thought of the whopping bills she'd cheerfully sent me in the past, downright ominous. "Something happened, Miss Ames?"

She admitted that something had happened which probably wouldn't have if it hadn't been Tuesday, and if the doctor hadn't been on the point of departure, and if I hadn't put the pigeon in a box. "The doctor was leaving just as the rubbish collectors were coming up the driveway for the Tuesday pickup. I was busy in the front office admitting a pair of Schnauzers to board. I thought I heard the doctor say something about refrigerating a pigeon, but by the time I got the Schnauzers settled, I couldn't find any pigeon. . . ."

Our bandtail had truly been collected.

We never found out what had killed the pigeon. We did learn, a year later, however, what had happened to many of his relatives and friends that autumn.

The following spring and summer brought a sharp increase in the number of bandtails at the feeding station. Some were adults, males and females identical; some were young, easily recognized by their tameness and the lack of a white crescent on the nape of the neck. Then, in early fall, we began to notice the same signs as we had the previous year. Corn and milo were left untouched in the feeders and on the ledge. There were fewer and quieter gatherings of the clan in the eucalyptus trees. Approximately half of our pigeons departed, but no viruses, bacteria or protozoan parasites were involved.

They migrated.

Many volumes have been written on the migration and homing ability of birds. An account of Morgan, the pig-headed pigeon, will add little to the scientific body of evidence, but as a study in determination Morgan's story deserves telling.

He appeared one late winter in the back yard of Mary and Tom Hyland, who lived on the north side of Santa Barbara. The neighborhood at that time was new, with the shrubbery only half grown and the trees just getting started. In order to compensate for this, the Hylands had gone to great lengths to attract birds.

For bird baths Tom had arranged a series of saucers, graduated in height and size, the one at the top overflowing into the one below, and so on. Every shrub, tree and flower had been planted to provide various kinds of birds with food, nesting sites or shelter. Even a weed, tree tobacco, was included because hummers and orioles loved its sweet yellow flowers. There were feeders everywhere, for sunflower seeds, for the smaller grains, for bread, for raisins and apples and oranges. Just beyond the yard was a barranca left in its wild state and filled with scrub oak, elderberry, toyon, ceanothus and sycamore trees growing right out of the creek bed. (A birder in our part of southern California can spot creeks a mile away by looking for stands of sycamores. In the dry season this is necessary since the presence or absence of water usually means the presence or absence of birds.)

On my first visit to the Hylands' back yard I came upon a scene of eerie stillness which, at a feeding station, always indicates the presence of danger. The baths and feeders were all empty, and not a twig moved or a leaf stirred.

I soon found out why. Sitting on a fence post waiting for a piece of action, or rather of the actors, was a sharp-shinned hawk. Its plumage marked it as immature, its size as a female. The only other bird in sight was the pigeon, Morgan, on the roofed perch Tom had built for him just outside the living-room door. Even without the hawk's juvenal plumage as a guide, I'd have estimated both birds to be very young. An adult pigeon would have had sense enough to remove himself, and an adult sharpshin, especially the much larger, stronger female of the species, would have almost surely attacked. There was other evidence, later on, that when Morgan arrived in the Hylands' back yard in February, he was very young.

He was certainly very hungry. He ate grain out of Tom's hand while Mary looked on with mixed feelings. The pleasure of seeing a hungry creature eat was marred by the knowledge that pigeons attract pigeons. There were already a great many in the neighborhood and she had been trying to keep them away from the feeders so they wouldn't drive away the smaller birds, especially the white-throated sparrow which had recently arrived. The white-throated sparrow is a rare winter visitor here, and unlike his common cousins, the whitecrowns and goldcrowns, he is almost never spotted except at a feeding station. Mary wanted him to stay so that her fellow birders would be able to see him.

Perhaps our world is more interesting because so many of our decisions are based on emotions rather than common sense. A friend of ours who breeds dogs tells us that when the time comes to sell a litter, she can bear it only if the pups haven't been named. I have found this true about birds too. The death of Old Crip, the departures of Li'l Varmint and Big Boy Blue are more poignant and memorable because these birds were not just a purple finch, a Tennessee warbler and a Steller's jay—they were our birds and they'd become ours because we'd named them. It may have been the immediate naming of Morgan that made his staying a sure thing.

"He reminds me of Bob Morgan," Tom said as the pigeon fed out of his hand.

So Morgan he became and as Morgan he remained.

He was no beauty—his plumage could be described as white mottled with black or black mottled with white—but he was faithful. Though I've seen geese used as watchdogs, Morgan is the first pigeon I've known to assume this role. There was very little traffic in the vicinity of the Hylands' house, since it was the next to last one on a dead-end street, and perhaps this was why Morgan assumed that that end of the street belonged to him. He would perch on top of the chimney or the telephone pole, moving his head back and forth as our bandtails do when they're curious. Any approaching car or pedestrian, any dog or cat ambling past on the way to the barranca, Morgan would challenge with a kind of warning grunt, "Who? Who?"

Mary and Tom always knew when someone was coming. The baying of hounds couldn't have sounded a more effective alarm than Morgan's rather soft, ominous question, "Who?"

He had other noises, among them a typical coo which he used to communicate with the other pigeons in the neighborhood. At first the Hylands translated this cooing as an invitation to the other birds to come for dinner or at least drop in for a friendly visit. As time went on, however, they were forced to amend the translation.

Human beings with no way of interpreting an animal sound have to judge its intent and meaning by its effect. For example, let's picture two men standing on a city street. One of them whistles and a cab stops in front of him; the other whistles and the pretty girl passing him blushes or smiles. Without any analysis of pitch or tone, the girl and the cab driver know perfectly well what each whistle means and so does everyone else. If you need proof of this, try using the wrong whistle next time you need a cab.

The Hylands eventually agreed on the translation of Morgan's pronouncements from the telephone pole: "Listen, you guys, I've got a good thing going here. You can come over and look, but don't louse it up by staying."

The other pigeons and doves did indeed come over to look, and some even attempted to use the bird bath and steal a few grains of food. When this happened Morgan flew into a terrible rage. He paced back and forth on his perch in a frenzy of activity, flapping his wings, puffing out his feathers, inflating and deflating his throat, from which emerged a weird wild mixture of grunts and clucks. It is no tribute to the brain power of the other pigeons that they got the message and took off.

We have all seen animals exhibit anger in ways that are quite nonhuman. The dog snarls and his hackles rise, the bull lowers his head and charges, the cat spits, the porcupine bristles. But I never expected to see an angry pigeon. Certainly I didn't imagine that an angry pigeon would look so ludicrously similar to an angry person —the pacing up and down and flailing of arms, the heavy breathing and the wild incoherent speech. To this day I never see a person in a fit of rage without thinking of Morgan.

That first year Morgan fitted smoothly into the Hylands' routine. He guarded the premises and kept other pigeons away, he followed Mary around as she worked in the garden and he superintended Tom washing the car. As summer progressed and the weather grew warmer, Morgan spent the hottest part of the day in the house, sleeping beside the heirloom clock on the ledge of the brick fireplace, or up on the cornice above the living-room drapes.

Everything went well until the following spring. The Hylands noticed no change in Morgan's vocal efforts. That such a change had taken place, however, was clearly indicated by the behavior of the other pigeons. Some of them began to come quite boldly into the yard to eat and drink, and a small dapple gray one even landed on Morgan's perch. Morgan was furious, naturally, since he happened to be on it at the time, but almost immediately his rage turned into display. Indeed, many of the same ploys that had been used to indicate anger now served to show what a fine, strong, handsome fellow he was—the pacing (now an obvious strutting), the inflated neck, the wing flapping.

The Hylands watched the budding romance with considerable misgiving. Their fondness for Morgan did not blind them to his faults. He was, for one thing, set in his ways like an old bachelor and resisted the slightest change in his routine. As for Dapplegray, his mate, she was not so much smitten by Morgan as she was by his perch, which she'd been eyeing covetously for months from a neighbor's roof.

As if to invalidate the Hylands' low opinion, Morgan and his bride started to set up housekeeping. Pigeons and doves are inept nest builders anyway and the efforts of Morgan and Dapplegray were pathetic. Dapplegray wanted to build right on the much-admired perch, but the sticks she brought simply fell down. Eventually a nest of sorts was put together, though it was precariously situated on a tiny ledge under the eaves.

Mary Hyland, who had strong nest-building instincts of her own, refused to tolerate such sloppy housekeeping and went to the pet-supply store and bought a substitute nest of the kind used by raisers of homing pigeons. But every attempt to persuade Morgan and Dapplegray to use it came to nothing. Morgan, in fact, attacked the substitute nest as if it were a rival and eventually Dapplegray laid two white eggs on the meagre pile of twigs under the eaves. One rolled out almost immediately. The other, incubated by both parents, hatched in about three weeks.

The fledgling appeared healthy and Morgan and Dapplegray were attentive to its needs. It was, nevertheless, doomed, its fate having been decided at the time Morgan refused to accept the substitute nest. Dapplegray's flimsy cluster of sticks had been fairly adequate as an incubator; as a nursery it wasn't. Fledglings develop at a very rapid rate. In order to carry this increasing weight their legs must grow correspondingly strong and they can't do this without proper support in the nest.

As soon as Morgan and Dapplegray became aware that their offspring was crippled they abandoned it. The Hylands made an attempt to feed the little creature themselves and when that failed they took it to the Museum of Natural History, where the trouble was explained to them. The fledgling was straddle-legged and would not survive.

Meanwhile Dapplegray had already started building another nest on the opposite side of the house. What was the seventh or eighth twig to Dapplegray was the last straw for the Hylands. They could visualize a whole series of inadequate nests and crippled babies left to starve. Morgan and Dapplegray were given one more chance to accept the nest from the pet shop. When they refused, Tom built a trap and baited it with Dapplegray's favorite food, Spanish peanuts. Dapplegray made no fuss as the trap door closed behind her. Either she was so crazy about the peanuts she didn't care what was happening, or else she was rather relieved to be getting out of a situation she couldn't handle. Tom drove her down to the wharf and released her in the middle of one of the flocks of pigeons that hang out along the waterfront.

It was the Hylands' hope that Morgan, deprived of his mate, would return to the innocence of his youth, the uncluttered days before Dapplegray. Morgan had other ideas. The day after Dapplegray's enforced farewell, her successor was ensconced on Morgan's perch and the whole sequence began again—the collection of sticks and twigs and the refusal of a substitute nest. After a long discussion it was decided that in fairness to all—the smaller birds which Morgan kept chasing away, the Hylands themselves and Morgan's future progeny—Morgan should be taken to the Bird Refuge, another pigeon hangout.

The trap was set, Morgan entered without hesitation and the trip down to the Bird Refuge began. It was a sad occasion, with Mary moist-eyed in the front seat and Morgan moping in the back. At least the Hylands assumed he was moping. My own feeling is that he must have been quietly memorizing the landscape, because when Mary and Tom arrived home, Morgan was already on his perch waiting for them.

"Who?" he asked when the car drove in. "Who? Who?"

"Who do you think," Tom said crossly.

Morgan's second trip, to Carpinteria twelve miles away, was more of a workout for him but still no real problem. It was becoming increasingly clear that more drastic distances would be necessary. The Hylands had, for a long time, been planning a visit to the Southern California Audubon Center at El Monte, about 110 miles south of their home. Morgan accompanied them, settling down to enjoy the trip as if he'd planned it himself.

The Hylands' return without Morgan seemed final. Mary removed his food dish from the patio and Tom took down his perch and stored it in the garage. For a few days Morgan's new mate hung around, but then she too departed and there was no reminder left of Morgan except a little pile of sticks on the ledge under the eaves.

It was the middle of May by this time, and with Morgan and his pals no longer hanging around, a number of the small migrant birds were coming in to eat and bathe. Some, like the black-headed grosbeaks, brought their fat, fuzzy balls of babies, while others, like the male hooded oriole, came alone to filch the honey water out of the hummingbird feeder. Though the Hylands bought a special oriole feeder for him and he learned to use it, he kept returning to the hummingbird feeder as if making sure their food was no sweeter than his.

This tendency of certain birds to drink or attempt to drink hummingbird mixture varies from neighborhood to neighborhood. Some people are forced to take down their hummingbird feeders because the house finches empty them as fast as they're filled. Others claim that the house finches don't go near their hummingbird feeders, and only on one occasion have I observed a house finch trying to drink from ours. In the summer the hooded and the Bullock's orioles use it by perching on the spout, in the winter the Audubon warblers use it by hovering, not very successfully, hummingbird style. Sometimes I see an orange-crowned warbler take a sip, and very infrequently, a plain titmouse, this latter species being one of the few which don't show a pronounced weakness for sweet things when they're available.

On the first Saturday in June, the Hylands returned from a shopping trip downtown to be greeted by a familiar sound from the top of the chimney: "Who? Who?"

Mary quickly rolled up the car windows, but it was too late. Tom had already heard. "Good Lord," he said, "it can't be Morgan."

But good Lord, it was. Nor had he come back alone. Somewhere in the course of his 110-mile, nineteen-day journey from El Monte he'd picked up a lady friend who was now sharing the chimney with him. She might have been one of the neighborhood belles like Dapplegray or she might have flown all the way from El Monte with him, led on by pigeon pleas and promises. In any case the twig gathering began again, again the nesting site was the tiny ledge under the eaves, and again the Hylands decided that Morgan must go and stay gone.

This time their preparations were more careful, based on greater awareness of Morgan's capabilities. Through a friend they contacted a pigeon fancier in Bakersfield, some 150 miles inland. He agreed to take Morgan and his new mate, and keep them penned with his other pigeons for two or three months before releasing them. After this long a period he was sure that Morgan's home ties with Santa Barbara would be cut and new ones formed with Bakersfield.

He was correct. Somewhere on the outskirts of Bakersfield right now one pig-headed pigeon is flying fancy free.

As this is being written it is March and many of our bandtails are getting ready to nest. Mates have been chosen and display is the order of the day. An important part of this display involves the male flying out from a eucalyptus branch, making a soft buzzing sound and wiggling his wings as he passes the female, a maneuver that should remind you, according to your age group, of human displays like the shimmy and the watusi. The male bandtail also uses inflation (to a lesser extent than the domestic pigeon) and a mating call that sounds like *ca——hoo,* the *ca* part being more like an inhalation of air than an intentional sound. Though it is not particularly loud it has a carrying quality, especially in a canyon area like ours. All day long the *ca-hoos* of the bandtails mingle with the incessant *oo-hoo-hoos* of the mourning doves. As the sun begins to set—sometimes even before—the great horned owls start in, *hoo-hoo-hoo-hoo-hoo,* and a little later the screech owls, with their tremulous *hoohoohoohoohoohoohoohoo,* until our canyon becomes a veritable hoos' hoo in America.

Companion to Owls

Masculinity in our society is usually associated with larger size, greater strength, more aggressive instincts and a deeper voice. Conditioned to these notions, Ken and I made all the wrong assumptions the evening we saw our first horned owls.

It had been a hot day and we were watching the beginning of the California twilight. (If you don't watch the beginning, you see very little of it—our twilights are brief, the least possible compromise between day and night.) I must have heard owls before, both here and in other parts of this country and Canada where we've lived, but those remembered sounds lacked reality, position in time and space, because I heard them before I was interested in birds and aware of what I was listening to. For the record, then, that warm clear evening in Santa Barbara was the occasion of my first owl.

Fortunately for me it was the great horned species, which makes a distinctly owl-like hoot, recognizable even to someone who has only read about it. Some of the other owls hoot infrequently, if at all, and make a variety of non-owlish noises: the saw-whetting sound that gives the little saw-whet owl his name, the sneeze of the barn owl, the sharp yipping of the desert elf owl, and the daytime stuttering of the burrowing owl which differs greatly from its own nighttime cooing. Tiny, the burrowing owl who's been a pet at our local Museum of Natural History for several years, has a sound I've never heard this species make in the wild. When I stroke the side of his neck and ask him for a kiss, he nudges my hand gently with his beak, if he happens to be in an affectionate mood. If he's not, he turns away with a peremptory "Zhut!" as Bronx a cheer as I've ever heard in California.

Ken and I went outside to see if we could locate the source of the sounds we'd heard. It wasn't difficult. There was plenty of light, since the sun had barely started to go down, and the two owls were calling and answering each other, one from our television antenna, the other from the top of a Monterey pine tree two hundred feet away. The birds were identical except in size and voice, the one on our antenna being smaller and having a voice considerably higher in pitch. This, we learned later, was the male. His inferiority to the female in size is shared with a number of species, mainly predators like hawks and eagles and other owls, but also unrelated birds like phalaropes and kingfishers.

As we watched, the female swooped down from the top of the pine tree and passed over us so low that though I heard nothing I felt the air being displaced by her great wings. The male followed, also in utter silence, also barely clearing our heads. Were the birds trying to frighten us away? Or were they aware, as wild creatures are so often aware in advance, that something unnatural was about to happen? Perhaps it had already happened and they had heard it. Owls have so acute and accurate a sense of hearing that they can pinpoint a mouse in utter darkness.

Our faulty and underdeveloped human senses told us nothing. Even when we saw the sky changing we thought at first it was caused by jet trails. But the trails kept enlarging and spreading, forming weird moving patterns splashed with color intensified by the light from the setting sun.

Most enthusiastic bird watchers are able to remember in detail their initial meeting with any given species. Ken and I are unlikely to forget our first great horned owls since we happened to see them at the very moment that an intercontinental ballistics missile, just launched from a nearby base, was discovered to be defective and ordered to blow itself up over the Pacific Ocean.

Ken suggests another explanation why the owls, on that one

occasion only, flew so audaciously low over our heads. We happened to have Johnny, our little black Scottie, with us at the time. Since the great horned owls eat many mammals like rabbits and skunks, it's quite possible that their behavior was due not to any ICBM being blown up, but to curiosity whether Johnny was a black bunny or a stripeless skunk.

The female superiority in size among certain birds leads to a number of questions, some of them along the line of which-came-first-the-chicken-or-the-egg? In the case of at least one species, the sparrow hawk, there is evidence that the female, who is responsible for preparing and distributing to the young the food brought to the nest by the male, feeds the female nestlings oftener than she feeds the males so that the latter are some twenty percent smaller and considerably more docile than their sisters. This system of preferential treatment can be called a matriarchy.

For a more extreme and better known example of it, however, we must go to the phalarope family. Among phalaropes the rôles of male and female are reversed. The females are bigger and more aggressive—if such a term can be used to describe these gentle little birds, of which all three species visit our shores. She assumes the gaudy breeding plumage and does the courting. Mundane affairs like nest building, incubating, feeding and caring for the young she leaves to the male, while she, freed from chicks and chains, rejoins the giddy friends of her girlhood. As a matter of curiosity I sometimes ask my fellow bird watchers the name of their favorite bird and the reason for their choice. I no longer have to ask the mothers of young children. Their choice, and the reason for it, is unanimous—the phalarope.

To the amateur student of psychology this business of asking people to name their favorite bird can be highly interesting. I have a long list of birds chosen, and the reasons for each choice. A kind of rough pattern emerges from it. Surprisingly, not too many of the birds listed were picked for their beauty and those that were—among them, the western tanager, mountain bluebird, hooded oriole, vermilion flycatcher, lazuli bunting, rufous-sided towhee—were nearly always selected by rather plain-looking people. This pattern of opposites keeps repeating. Among oldsters there is a strong tendency to choose birds connected with their early youth. People who live alone are most likely to choose companionable birds, song sparrows and whitecrowns, robins, mockingbirds, meadowlarks. Timid people tend to favor the aggressors like hawks and falcons, and sad people to favor the clowns like the roadrunner, the chat, and the acorn woodpecker.

Ask the man in the street how an owl looks and sounds and he will be able to tell you, although the chances are he's never seen or heard one. The field check list for our area mentions eight species of owl, yet the average birder is fortunate to find half this number in a year and our annual Christmas bird count for the last six years lists only some sixty owls.

Owls are not, like the doves and pigeons which very early found their way into recorded history, a very obvious or regular part of everyone's life. Yet they have captured the imagination and inspired the painter, the poet, the sculptor. They are found on Egyptian wall paintings, Chinese screens and Indian vases. An owl stands guard beside Michelangelo's statue of Night at the tomb of the Medici. Owls are mentioned in the works of Homer, the Bible and the Shakespearean plays, and there are to my knowledge five Greek and four Latin words for owl.

During the fifth century B.C., and later, the staple currency of the Aegean consisted of coins known as "owls." Manufactured in Athens, mainly of silver, each coin showed the head of Athena on the obverse side and the figure of an owl on the reverse. An argument might be made that both were intended to represent aggression and conquest since Athena was originally goddess of war and owls had the same habits then as now. But Athena later became the goddess of wisdom and it is generally accepted that this is what the coins symbolized. The choice of an owl to represent wisdom astounds people familiar with these birds. Adu and Peter Batten, who have lived as intimately with wild creatures as it is possible for human beings to do, give the owls second prize for stupidity, first prize going to the little puffbirds of the Amazon jungle. A number of observers, however, point out that great horned owls show great caution in the presence of gunfire. Our pair of horned owls gave us an example of this caution without a shot being fired.

One evening I was sitting in my lookout chair in the living room. It was 1965, the end of April and the end of a day and I was waiting for two species of birds; the great horned owl and the Vaux' swift, and hoping they wouldn't arrive simultaneously. The night before, they had missed each other by less than five minutes. Except for this habit of hunting at dusk, the two species had little in common, least of all size. The great horned owl is some two feet in length, the Vaux' swift is four inches. Seen for the first time against a darkening sky the latter can quite easily be mistaken for a large and capricious insect.

The initial appearance of the Vaux' swift at our place came at the beginning of May, 1964. It wasn't entirely unexpected. The birds are known to migrate through our area in the spring, though they aren't often seen when weather conditions are favorable to them. That spring, however, brought a series of heavy overcasts and the Vaux' swifts were caught in one and grounded. A flock of fifty or so stayed, appropriately enough, at the Bird Refuge for several days. Another, much larger flock was trapped on a fairly well-traveled road north of town. Unable to orient themselves, and blinded by traffic and streetlights, they flew wildly into the windshields of passing cars and died by the hundreds. An impressionable friend of mine unfortunately happened to be driving along this road after seeing Alfred Hitchcock's film *The Birds,* and the combined effect was almost disastrous. She is still careful to omit Mr. Hitchcock from her prayers.

Time passed, the fogs lifted and the swifts passed on their way northward to their breeding grounds. All except one—our bird was still appearing every evening with astonishing punctuality. In the middle of May he was joined by another swift, presumably female. Where she came from is anybody's guess—was she a late migrant? Was the meeting accidental? Or did he go looking for a mate, and persuade her to accompany him to our canyon? At any rate we were delighted because there was no official record of the Vaux' swift nesting in southern California and we had considerable hope of supplying one. It seemed easy enough. All we had to do was watch and see which hole in which dead tree the birds emerged from and returned to. Since these birds also nest in chimneys we would have to be chimney watchers too.

Every day, when the sun had set, I began my vigil, sometimes inside the house, sometimes outside, at the back, at the front, on the driveway. It hardly mattered, since the appearances and disappearances of these birds were like those of a magician's rabbits. Suddenly they were there and just as suddenly they weren't. Their speed, their unpredictable twists and turns and the number of hiding places available made constant observation impossible. I was lucky to get my binoculars on them for a fraction of a second.

On July 19 a third swift appeared with the other two, and while I didn't witness any feeding maneuvers, I was as certain as I could be under the circumstances that the pair had mated and this was their fledgling. During the following week a new ornithological rule emerged from my experience: it is just as easy to lose track of three Vaux' swifts as it is to lose track of two. Right under my nose (presumably) the birds had mated, built a nest and raised a family and I still hadn't the foggiest notion which dead tree or which chimney held the secret.

My twilight vigils, covering a period of eleven weeks, had come to nothing of a positive nature, so I gave them up. Out of habit, however, I still glanced at the sky when the sun had set. During August and September I saw the Vaux' swift on a dozen occasions, always just a single bird and probably the same one each time. On September 22 the Coyote fire started early in the afternoon and by sundown every schoolchild in Santa Barbara, Montecito and Goleta knew it was going to be a bad one. Many families living in the foothills were already packing their belongings in cars and trucks and borrowed trailers. Ken had the rainbirds going on our roof—these had been installed after the previous fire on the advice of the Montecito fire chief to all canyon dwellers—but the water pressure was dropping and the fire was racing toward us across the explosively dry mountains. I walked up the road to consult a neighbor about what we ought to do. As we stood watching the flames, the Vaux' swift suddenly darted over our heads.

"Did you see that?" my neighbor screamed above the roar of helicopters. "It must have been a bat."

It hardly seemed the time or place for a bird lesson, so I agreed that it must, indeed, have been a bat.

We didn't see the bird again that year. Vaux' swifts are said to winter in the tropics and I have a notion that he headed straight for some nice wet rain forest.

The following spring the migrating Vaux' swifts either missed us entirely, or, since the weather was unusually warm and clear, passed over us at a great height. We saw none of the birds at all until our friend of the previous year arrived back on April 25. He fell immediately into the same pattern, appearing out of nowhere to cross the darkening sky between the two largest Monterey pines, and becoming as regular a part of evening as the scent of star jasmine and the sound of May beetles striking the windows when I turned on the lights.

This swift, then, was the bird I was waiting for when I learned firsthand of the caution of the great horned owls in the presence of gunfire. The swift showed up on schedule, stayed within eye range for all of five seconds and disappeared.

I sat still, hoping for another glimpse of him and some inkling of where he was hiding out. My chances of finding a nest were considerably better than last year, since a great many of the dead trees in the area had been burned to the ground during the Coyote fire. Suddenly I heard what I thought was a shot. Then further up the canyon I saw a rocket-type firecracker rising in the air. Fortunately it was more crack than fire—it fizzled out at less than a hundred feet. Firecrackers are illegal in California and particularly dangerous in heavily wooded foothill areas, so I tried to determine the exact location of the explosion before reporting it to the fire department. Suddenly I saw the male great horned owl swoop past our house at chimney height. He didn't make a sound. About three minutes later the female followed him, also without a sound. Always before when we'd seen the owls they had alerted us to their presence by calling to each other. That night, and every night for the next two weeks, though there were no more "shots," the owls remembered the first one and passed through our canyon as mute as moths.

Year after year Santa Barbara's Christmas bird count would list one screech owl. Readers of Audubon Field Notes, where the Christmas-count results are published, couldn't be expected to know that it was always the same screech owl. The little bird's

name was Hermie, which stood not for Herman or Hermione but
for Hermit since no one was sure what sex he belonged to, though
he was referred to as "he."

And a hermit he was indeed. Some years ago he established
squatter's rights to a four-inch tunnel that ran horizontally under
the apex of the red tile roof of the Natural History Museum. This
setup was so ideal that no mere chemical urge could compel him to
share it with a partner. Or perhaps he'd already had a partner and
lost her, and since screech owls mate for life, he was destined to
spend the rest of his days alone. At any rate he made the best of
things.

Hermie's quarters, warm and dry in the winter, cool in
summer and secure from enemies, permitted him to have a rather
lively social life for an owl. When he felt like fraternizing he would
come to the entrance hole of his tunnel and sit in the sun and
watch the people going in and out of the front door of the museum. If they seemed particularly interesting he would watch with
both eyes; if not, he would close one eye. Often he went to sleep
entirely and at these times, without the glitter and movement of his
eyes to draw attention to him, he looked like part of the building
and even people who knew he lived there had trouble spotting him.
He didn't like too much attention. When a group of noisy schoolchildren pointed at him or bird watchers trained their binoculars on
him with too much interest he retreated with sour dignity into the
fastness of his tunnel.

The curiosity which can kill cats also kills many birds. This is
what started Hermie's trouble—though it was human ignorance
that caused his death, as it does for so many wild creatures. Flying
down to investigate some workmen who were putting in a new
parking lot for the museum, Hermie got trapped in the wet black-
top. One of the workmen, seeing Hermie's struggles, killed him
with a shovel "to put him out of his misery," a phrase that can
cover a lot of unnecessary killings. And Hermie's was unnecessary.
Waldo Abbott, now curator of ornithology at the museum, says
that if the little owl had been brought to his lab, no more than fifty
yards away, the blacktop could have been removed from his feathers quite easily and Hermie would still be occupying his penthouse.

In heartening contrast to the shovel-wielding workman are the people like Gloria Forsyth, a friend of mine, who found a very young baby cliff swallow which had fallen out of its nest under the eaves of the Forsyth's house. The experts whose advice Gloria asked about raising the tiny creature all told her the same thing: forget it, it's too difficult to keep a baby swallow adequately supplied with insects. Gloria was not easily discouraged and she had, moreover, a steady source of food because she kept riding horses. For the next two weeks she could be seen at any time of the day walking around the corral, swatting horse flies, picking them up carefully from the ground with eyebrow tweezers and placing them in a little gold pillbox. Neighbors and passers-by must have received a distinctly odd impression but the swallow thrived, and the last Gloria saw of it, it flew expertly off her forefinger toward the corral. *Sic transit Gloria's hirundo.*

There is something both absurd and awesome about the very tiny owls. The elf owl is the smallest and has the distinction of being the only member of the family in which the male is as large as the female—though at five inches it hardly seems to matter. The elf owl caught by a flashlight beam as he peers out of his hole in a sahuaro makes a captivating sight, but it is the pygmy owl which intrigues me most. The size of a sparrow, he has the courage and skill of an eagle. He has been known to kill birds as large as a meadowlark, mammals as large as squirrels and reptiles a foot long.

Pygmy is different from other owls in many respects. He does not share the gross eating habits of the larger ones who devour their victims, bone and feather, and fur and teeth, and regurgitate the indigestible parts in the form of pellets. Pygmy eats daintily (though not in quite the same manner as Tiny, the burrowing owl at the museum, who holds his food in one claw and lifts it to his mouth like a picnicker eating a chicken leg) and he leaves no pellets to betray his presence.

There are other differences. Pygmy is unperturbed by the approach and observation of people. He hunts by day and his flight is different from that of most owls, both in manner and sound. He makes a distinct noise as he swoops down on his prey because his wings lack the adaptation of nocturnal owls, the sound-deadening filaments on the feather tips. There has been some disagreement about whether this adaptation was intended to permit the night owl to sneak quietly up on his victims or to make it easier for him to use his sense of hearing to locate his victims in the dark. The latter seems more reasonable. It would surely be inconsistent on the part of nature to silence an owl's wings to conceal his presence and do nothing about moderating his voice, which gives him away to every mouse in a meadow miles away.

The pygmy owl is especially intriguing to me because, after years passed without one being reported in our area, Jewell Kriger and I found a pair nesting in Refugio Canyon. Refugio Canyon is perhaps best known to birders for its yellow-breasted chats, which can nearly always be found in May and June in the willow thickets along the stream. (The canyon is also known for its tarantula migration, an event not likely to appeal to many spectators.) Sometimes patience is necessary to see the chats. It certainly was on that day. We could hear them sounding off, first from one side of the road, then the other, but we couldn't manage to get one in the binoculars. This spring repertoire of raucous noises contrasts sharply with the absolute silence of the chat who visits us every fall for a month to feed on grapes and bananas.

Suddenly Jewell said in a rather surprised voice, "I didn't know sparrows would eat mice . . ."

Nor did I. I focused my binoculars on the limb of the dead oak tree she was looking at and the "sparrow" turned his head slowly and transfixed me with a pair of the brightest yellow eyes I've ever seen.

The little owl showed not the faintest sign of nervousness or alarm at our intrusion. He casually resumed his business, which was not eating the mouse but removing certain inedible portions of it. I began to suspect that he had a mate nearby and that the mouse must be intended for her. He was in no hurry to let me know for sure. He picked fastidiously at the mouse's carcass, turning every now and then to look at Jewell and me in a manner that reminded me of an earnest biology teacher giving a lesson in dissection and checking to see if his pupils were paying attention.

Meanwhile we weren't the only creatures to discover the presence of the pygmy owl. Suddenly the air around us was filled with wingbeats and the sounds of avian alarm and anger, buzzes and cluckings and rattles and squeaks and squawks. The swallows appeared first and were most abundant, tree swallows and violet-greens and cliffs. One would swoop down on the owl so low it almost touched him, then rise in the air to let the next one swoop down, until there was a steady strafing of outraged swallows. Other birds hastened to join the action—Bullock's orioles, Oregon juncos, ash-throated flycatchers, red-winged blackbirds, black-headed grosbeaks—until the place was a riot of sound and color and motion. Many of the birds were larger than the owl, but if he was disturbed he didn't show it. He calmly continued his task with only the occasional blink to indicate his thoughts: *Look at these idiots railing at me when I'm only doing my duty . . .*

After about ten minutes he flew to a hole fifteen or twenty feet up in the main trunk of a dead sycamore tree. He dropped the remains of the mouse over the edge of the hole so that its tail and hind legs hung down, then he let out a sound which was half-hoot, half-whistle, and flew down low, straight across the road, and out of sight. Except for a dozen or so swallows who followed him, the other birds dispersed and went about their business.

We kept our binoculars focused on the hole in the sycamore and as we watched, the mouse seemed suddenly to come to life and start crawling over the edge into the hole, wagging its tail back and forth. It was an eerie sight indeed, even though one was aware that Mrs. Pygmy was the principal behind it. We waited, hoping she would show herself, but she didn't. Many times on subsequent occasions I saw her yellow and black eyes peering out of the little round hole in the sycamore. She looked like a jack-o'-lantern set in the window of a tree house at Halloween. Her eyes, incidentally, appeared quite different from the male's. Since she spent most of her time in the darkness of the nesting cavity, her pupils were greatly dilated and the narrow yellow rim of iris seemed to have been added as an afterthought by someone with a dab of leftover paint.

Jewell and I decided to postpone finding the chats until another day so that we could hurry back to town and put the pygmy owl on the Rare Bird Alert.

The R.B.A. was started in Santa Barbara in 1963. It works

simply. People who sign up for it are given cards with a list of six or seven names and phone numbers. When they are contacted by the person whose name precedes theirs on the card they must contact the next person listed below. Thus, in as little as fifteen minutes, every eager bird watcher in town can be informed of the whereabouts of a rare bird. There is one essential rule—the birds so found must not be molested or disturbed in any way.

In certain other localities the R.B.A. has been sadly abused. Collectors for museums and universities have operated with such callous disregard for birds and birders alike that many expert birders no longer report their findings to the R.B.A. This will continue to be the case, I am assured, until collecting is outlawed in the United States as it was some time ago in England when the English became aware that a little collecting here and a little collecting there added up to an awful lot of dead birds. Collectors actually exterminated one species of hummingbird, Loddige's racket-tail, before naturalists had a chance to study the birds in life. Only about forty California condors survive in the world today, though there are 112 dead ones in public collections and nobody knows how many more in private collections. I think we can safely assume that very few of them died of heart attacks. But perhaps the prize for the most stupid act of collecting must go to the famous ornithologist who saw the last authenticated flock of Carolina parakeets in 1904 in Florida. There were thirteen birds in the flock and he shot four of them.

Biologists themselves are becoming alarmed at the way many of their colleagues waste our natural resources. At the upper levels there is much unnecessary, even foolish, duplication in research. At the lower levels, class experiments all too often involve senseless destruction of mammals, birds and marine life. I recently came across, in an ornithological journal, the report of a study of hybridization between Baltimore and Bullock orioles as evidenced by differences in the amount of black and orange pigmentation. The birds could easily have been mist-netted, examined, banded for future observation and released. Instead, 623 orioles were collected—and this was for only one study among many done on the same subject.

Biology, which means the study of life, has come more and more to mean thanatology, the study of death. Biologist Farley Mowat wrote of being "sorely puzzled by the paradox that many of my contemporaries tended to shy as far away from living things as they could get, and chose to restrict themselves instead to the aseptic atmosphere of laboratories where they used dead—often very dead—animal material as their subject matter."

To an increasing number of people, collecting is a dirty word. I would never have reported the pygmy owl on the Rare Bird Alert if I hadn't been sure it was safe from collectors. Jewell made a note of the time of day, the mileage on the odometer, the species and height of the tree containing the nesting hole, and so on, while I hunted around for a marker to place on the side of the road. I found a section of board that had been painted red. This was a piece of good luck. (Every year there is talk of our local Audubon branch designing simple markers and distributing them to members who spend considerable time in the field. Nothing ever comes of it, probably because most of us have learned that you find the rare birds only when you're not prepared for them.)

Some members go out on just a few of the bird alerts, but there are others who will instantly drop whatever they're doing and set out to wade through a marsh for a wood stork, climb a mountain for a white-headed woodpecker or go to sea in a dense fog looking for a Xantus' murrelet.

Perhaps the most difficult alerts to follow through are the warblers, since they are so tiny and so active. Easterners accustomed to seeing warblers in migration through leafless trees aren't happy about having to locate our California birds in the dense foliage of live oaks and sycamores and eucalyptus. Many warblers reported on the R.B.A. are never seen by anyone but the original finder. Quite a few, however, are. A rare palm warbler, put out on the R.B.A. as seen "in Gaviota State Park, near picnic table No. 9; look low and watch for tail wagging," stayed all fall, seldom venturing even as far as picnic table No. 10. A chestnut-sided warbler —a first record for Santa Barbara—spotted by the Hylands on a lemonade bush along the bridle trail in Hope Ranch, was found the following day and the day after by Nelson Metcalf and Ken and myself in the very same bush.

The pygmy owls, committed as they were to a fixed location which was well marked, proved the easiest of all the R.B.A. birds to locate. The tiny pair became our star attractions, all the more so after Nelson Metcalf discovered that if the male was off hunting when visitors arrived, he could be coaxed back by an imitation of his call notes. It didn't matter how poor the imitation was—I've never learned even to whistle properly, but by pursing my lips as if I were about to whistle, then saying "hoo-hoo" instead, I could always evoke a response from the little owl, who would answer from a considerable distance and come flying in with his obstreperous escort of swallows.

Refugio Canyon is too far away to permit anyone with a job to perform to keep the owls under close observation. But they must have raised their young in a manner satisfactory to them because they returned the following year to the same nesting hole accompanied by what surely appeared to be the same escort of swallows. Eventually a road construction crew bulldozed over the red marker I'd put out, but by that time every birder within a hundred miles knew exactly where to find a pair of pygmy owls.

Another member of the owl family, much rarer than the pygmy and probably the most difficult to find of all eighteen North American owls, couldn't be put on the Rare Bird Alert because private property was involved, and the owners, after losing a valuable colt to a trespassing hunter, had the area posted and patrolled.

It was a canyon near Santa Maria, with steep sides heavily wooded, the preferred habitat of this particular species of owl. The trees along the stream were mainly cottonwoods, willows and sycamores, and on the slopes, mature oaks, both deciduous and evergreen, with an abundant undergrowth of poison oak, more popular with owls than with owlers. Mary and Tom Hyland had received permission to watch birds on the property, and it was here on an April twilight in 1966 that they came upon a pair of spotted owls. With the enthusiastic help of Mickey and Ed Williams, the Hylands kept the birds under observation for four months.

Mary had called me from Santa Maria in late April when she and Tom found the owls, and again in May to urge me to drive up and see them. Once the owls were located early in the morning in a particular place, Mary said, they could almost certainly be depended on to stay in the same place for the balance of the day. The trick was to locate them. Many owls are seen more often by day than by night—the burrowing, the pygmy, the short-eared, the snowy, the hawk owl—but spotted owls are nocturnal. The best time to find them is at night when they call to each other as they hunt. The best time to observe them, however, is in the daytime while they doze in a tree.

Though I certainly wanted to see the owls I wasn't keen about driving seventy-five miles by freeway, then searching through a remote canyon on foot to try to find two silent, motionless birds endowed with almost perfect protective coloration. I decided to wait.

On June 7, Mary called to tell me that while none of the observers had been able to find a nest, the evidence that one existed had been photographed the previous day—two baby spotted owls perched on the limb of a valley oak some fifteen feet above the ground. How the babies, still in natal down without tail or wing feathers, had gotten out of the nest and onto the limb of the oak tree was a mystery. Presumably the parent birds moved them, because when I visited the canyon the next morning, only a single baby owl was in evidence, and according to Mary, he was in a different tree from the one he'd shared with his sibling the previous day.

It was 9:30 A.M., a time for all nocturnal creatures to be asleep. Baby Spot evidently hadn't been told this. He was awake, his large dark eyes wide open and as luminous as two smoked agates. He was about twelve inches long, a little more than half-size, and so fuzzy all over that he appeared to be wrapped in cotton candy which someone had colored light beige instead of pink. The presence of five observers—Mary, Mickey Williams, Jewell Kriger, Nelson Metcalf and me—didn't alarm him in the least. He dozed off while we watched him, his claws hooked securely around the limb of the oak tree, his head sunk into his shoulders, giving him a completely neckless appearance. With neck and eyes hidden he looked not so much like a bird as like a kind of large oval-shaped fungus growing out of the tree.

Thinking that Baby Spot was settled for some time, we decided to drive further up the canyon to a meadow where Mary had recently seen a blue grosbeak and a flock of the tiny, temperamental Laurence goldfinches. We missed the grosbeak, an uncommon summer visitor in our part of the state, but we found the goldfinches, the largest flock I've ever seen. Some two hundred of them were feeding on the seeds of low-growing plants none of us could identify.

Here, beside the meadow, we ate our lunch and watched the goldfinches eat theirs. Then after another long, futile search for the grosbeak we returned to the oak tree where we'd seen Baby Spot perched that morning. It was empty. The night baby who was supposed to sleep all day, who had no wings to fly and no tail to steer, had somehow managed to reach another oak tree, some seventy-five feet from the first one, and settle on a branch about twelve feet from the ground. Had his parents moved him? If so, why? And where were they now? And what had happened to the other owlet, Twin Spot?

Baby Spot was awake and he was hungry. He twitched and fidgeted on the branch, pecking fretfully at his toes like a little boy biting his nails. Every now and then he let out a long sigh which was no more an owl sound than the sound of any young animal wanting food and attention.

We waited for one or both of the parents to respond to Spot's needs but they failed to appear. The amount of information I'd been able to obtain about spotted owls from my bird books was meagre. By all accounts, though, the birds were tame, stupidly tame, in fact, so it seemed unlikely that the presence of observers was keeping the parents from attending to Baby Spot. To make sure, however, we moved a considerable distance away to watch the oak tree and its forlorn occupant through binoculars.

It was five o'clock. I had a most uneasy feeling that the three missing owls had met with disaster. There was no need to communicate these thoughts to my companions. Their expressions made it clear that they were thinking along the same lines: if Baby Spot was an orphan it would be up to one of us to take him home and look after him until he was grown and fully feathered and could hunt for his own food.

Before such a step was taken, however, we decided to do more investigating. Mary and Mickey were wearing heavy hiking boots so they volunteered to climb up the hill through the poison oak in search of clues. Baby Spot, still fidgeting back and forth on the oak limb and intermittently chewing at his toes, watched their approach with minimal interest.

Meanwhile Nelson had reached the tree where we'd seen the owl that morning, and it was he who found the first bunch of owl feathers. They were the feathers of a baby spotted owl and they were scattered all over the ground underneath the tree. Not just five or six of them, but whole handfuls. There were no hawks in the area likely to take on a spotted owl, and it seemed likely that the other predators, such as bobcats and coyotes, preferred game that was tastier, more plentiful and easier to catch. That left the most undisciplined and dangerous predator of all—man.

"A hunter or a collector," Mickey said quietly. "To a dead bird it hardly matters."

Mary suggested that since we weren't getting anywhere standing around worrying, Nelson and Jewell and I might as well drive back to Santa Barbara, and she and Mickey would go and make dinner for their respective families, then return to the canyon at dusk to see how Baby Spot was faring.

I reached home about the time they were setting out for the canyon again. After a quick meal I assembled all the available information concerning the spotted owl.

Most bird books gave it either no mention at all or merely a sentence indicating it was the Far Western counterpart of the Eastern barred owl. In *Birds of America,* edited by T. Gilbert Pearson, and *Birds of the Pacific Coast* by Ralph Hoffman, it rated a paragraph. I found only two accounts that were by any means adequate, in A. C. Bent's *Life Histories of North American Birds,* and W. L. Dawson's *Birds of California.* Both Bent and Dawson quoted the same sources, articles published in the ornithological journal *Condor,* one by Lawrence Peyton (1910), the other by Donald R. Dickey (1914).

Dawson also included two of Dickey's photographs of young spotted owls. The picture of a single owl, a dead ringer for Baby Spot, was captioned "A Feather-Bed Baby." The other picture showed the same young owl with his sibling perched on an oak stump some fifteen feet from the ground and a hundred yards from the nest. Underneath this picture was a quote from Dickey's article: "That the young could have reached the spot unaided seems incredible."

The alternative he suggested was that the parents, fearing for the safety of their offspring, had moved them. But he didn't seem too happy with this explanation. Faced with the identical situation fifty-two years later, I wasn't too happy with the explanation either. Baby Spot, while still technically a baby, would have been an awkward load to haul down from a perch twenty feet in an oak tree, across seventy-five feet of rough terrain and up twelve feet into another oak tree. And, even if spotted owls were as stupid as their detractors claimed, what would be the point of such a transfer? It wasn't enough of a move to foil any predator worthy of the name, and the second tree offered no better concealment than the first.

Later that night the fifty-two-year mystery was solved in a ten-minute phone call from Mary Hyland in Santa Maria.

She and Mickey had returned to the canyon shortly before dusk to find Baby Spot in the same tree as we'd left him. He was still alone and obviously hungrier than ever, and to call attention to his plight he was flouncing around on the oak branch from one end to the other. Perhaps the approach of two observers added to his distraction. At any rate he flounced a bit too far and too fancy, somersaulted off the branch and landed on the ground below in a flurry of feathers.

Mary and Mickey stood motionless with shock. Not so Baby Spot, who seemed quite unperturbed as if the experience was nothing new for him. First he shook himself vigorously to get rid of more feathers which had been loosened by his fall. Then, with a gait that was half-waddle, half-swagger, he headed back to the tree trunk and began climbing. (Since learning about the climbing tactics of owls, I have watched a flicker, too young to fly, climb a large palm tree in the same manner, using both beak and claws. And condor expert Ian McMillan tells of seeing these enormous birds ascend to the tops of trees in order to gain the altitude necessary for take-off.) It was a slow, laborious climb but both tree and bird were equipped for it. The owl's sharply curved claws and beak fitted into the deep grooves of the oak bark.

Up, up went Baby Spot and when he had regained his perch in the oak tree he promptly closed his eyes and went to sleep. But within five minutes he was awake again and the whole performance started over, the fidgeting, the flouncing, and finally, to the dismay of his observers, the falling. For the second time in half an hour owl feathers filled the air and littered the ground. And another mystery was solved—the origin of all the feathers we'd found that afternoon. They belonged to Baby Spot, and it seemed probable that if he kept up his present rate he would become the first bald owl in ornithological history.

Once more he began his long, slow ascent of the tree trunk. He was about a third of the way up when through the canyon came a sound that was equally welcome to all three of the listeners. It was a series of notes, higher in pitch than the call of the great horned owl, and not so much a *who, who, who, who,* as a *what, what, what.*

It was almost totally dark by this time, and what took place in the oak tree was a kind of shadow play with sound effects. The parent owls arrived in a fluster of *what-what's* and whistles, and another noise that sounded to the imaginative Mickey like the squeaking of a mouse. Perhaps the other young owl heard it too, for he suddenly appeared out of nowhere, took his place beside Baby Spot on the oak branch—where he had spent the day remained his secret—and the little family was united again. Soon the parents went off in search of more food and the babies were left alone. They sat quietly side by side, looking like twin ghosts resting up after a haunting.

The Hylands and the Williamses kept the spotted owl family under observation until mid-August when the opening of deer hunting season made the canyon too dangerous to linger in. By this time the young owls were ready for independence, with wing and tail feathers well developed. The last I heard of them, they were still haunting their wooded canyon.

I have since had news concerning two other owls mentioned

previously in this chapter. Someone cut the wire of the cage where Tiny lived, the burrowing owl who was a pet at the Museum of Natural History for years. Perhaps it was a senseless piece of vandalism, or perhaps Tiny's escape was engineered by someone of good faith and poor judgment who didn't realize the little bird had been raised in captivity and couldn't survive by himself.

On a happier note, the living quarters under the museum roof which were long left vacant after the death of the screech owl Hermie have been found, approved and occupied by another screech owl. Possibly among owls, as among humans, the dwelling defines the dweller. Hermie Too has developed the same peculiarties and social mannerisms as his predecessor, and most visitors to the museum don't know he isn't the original.

Volumes could be written on the subject of the differences between the sexes among birds. Space limitations permit me only to emphasize that there are no hard and fast rules.

Usually the male is larger and stronger than the female, yet most of the male predators—eagles, hawks, falcons, harriers, buteos—are smaller than their mates and look to them for leadership.

Though singing is the prerogative of the male of most species, female grosbeaks sing, and so do cardinals, robins and mockingbirds. The dipper sometimes joins her mate in a duet, as do the females of several species of owl. Recently a pair of great horned owls put on a concert while sitting, appropriately enough, on our television antenna. Perhaps it wasn't singing in the Metropolitan Opera sense, but I've heard human performances I've enjoyed less.

In at least one species of bird the female not only sings, she can do so with her mouth full. On a February morning I watched a pair of house finches during an early stage of their courtship. The female, who was being fed by the male, several times broke into song, enough like the male's song to be identifiable, but softer and incomplete.

Usually it is the male bird who makes advances to the female, by displaying in various ways or by presenting her with nesting materials. But here too there are buts. Some female birds, like the skua, present grass and twigs to the males at courting time, and mutual display is the rule rather than the exception among sea birds.

One spring I watched a pair of mockingbirds put on what I thought was a mutual display beside the road in front of our house. The stage was an area about six feet square and the mockers stood facing each other, heads and tails held high, so that both birds looked larger than normal and of somewhat different shape. One of the birds hopped into the center of the stage and bowed briskly. The other did the same. The first bird gave a little hop to the left and bowed, the second repeated the movements exactly. This went on for some time, with the birds often meeting chest to chest in a seemingly amorous posture. The performance was both solemn and funny, and an onlooker couldn't help being reminded of the fact that many folk dances originated in attempts to copy the movements of birds.

When I first witnessed this mockingbird exhibition it was during early spring and I assumed the dancers were male and female, and the dance was intended to take advantage of the difference. This assumption was shaken when, the following October, I saw a pair going through precisely the same ritual. Perhaps October eyes are different, unblurred by the winds of March, the rains of April, the wild weather of the heart in spring. At any rate my autumn eyes saw the birds as two males engaged in a bluffing match to decide territorial boundaries.

Since that time I've witnessed many such mockingbird rituals. When the same two birds were involved the arena was usually the same patch of ground and the demonstration occasionally ended with feathers flying, but more often with the dignified retreat of one of the contestants. There can be little doubt that these were territorial disputes, or what Edward A. Armstrong calls "hostility displays, slightly socialised." I say little doubt rather than no doubt because among birds, as among human beings, love-making exhibits some striking similarities to hate-making.

Mr. Armstrong also points out, in *Bird Display and Behaviour,* that among certain birds like terns, cormorants, grebes and band-tailed pigeons, even the climactic act of mounting doesn't belong exclusively to the male.

A friend was recently lamenting that the task of differentiating between the human sexes was becoming more and more intricate, what with males coiffed and perfumed like females and females dressed like males. I suggested that the only really certain method was to wait and see which one of a pair went to the hospital to have the baby. We might do well to apply this to birds: the one that lays the eggs is the female.

Wolves and Waxwings

The western tanager is a symbol for
me of the strangeness and beauty of my first year of bird watching.
It is as effective as a time machine. At the sight of one of these
birds I am instantly transported back to an August morning
several years ago.

It was a summer of extremes. Along the shore the fogs were
thick enough to stop traffic and virtually close the airport, yet a
mile and a half crow's flight away, in the foothills, we were having
a heat wave. Santa Barbara's heat waves are not publicly acknowl-
eged since the official thermometer is down at the wharf. It is
more or less amusing to sit in a 90° living room reading in the
evening paper about how the rest of the nation sweltered while
Santa Barbara remained "cool and comfortable with a midday
high of 70°."

Officially recognized or not, the heat wave, and the drought that
went with it, continued. Most of the streams had long since dried
up, and ours at the bottom of the canyon had only a trickle of
water left in it. This, plus the containers of water we'd put out, in

various sizes and at various heights, attracted a great many birds since water was in shorter supply than food.

The first tanager appeared on August 15, a male still wearing the brilliant red hood of his breeding plumage. I had never seen a western tanager before, and after I watched him drink and bathe and depart, I consulted the local check list of birds. On the check list then in use in Santa Barbara, the western tanager was marked as a local resident. Such a list is practically a bible to the new bird watcher. Certainly I had no wish or reason to question it. So when the tanager appeared again the next day, with a couple of his relatives, I assumed that these were simply birds who lived in the area and were discovering our feeding station for the first time.

The three tanagers, all of them males, sat in the tea tree eating grapes. Since the occasion in early summer when I first put out grapes as substitutes for cherries, every day I'd been fastening a small bunch of them in the tea tree. They were eaten by the house finches, California thrashers, mockers and hooded orioles, but not avidly. There were always some left over for the silver-gray rats that streaked up and down the tree after dark like ribbons of light.

The tanagers seemed hungrier than the other birds. Perhaps they actually were, or perhaps the grapes were a particular treat—a child eating a plate of ice cream can look a lot hungrier than one eating a plate of spinach. At any rate the bunch of grapes was gone in no time. Though the slightest movement at one of the picture windows made the birds fly away, they came back immediately and hung around the tea tree, almost as if they were waiting for others to arrive.

They were, and others did—a mixed group of adult and immature males. I put out the last of the grapes I had on hand. When these were eaten the birds turned to the other edibles in the tea tree: doughnuts, a banana, half a coconut shell filled with peanut butter and corn meal mixture.

At that point Ken and I had no misgivings whatever. We were delighted to be hosts to such beautiful birds and we proved it by making a quick trip to the store for more grapes. The grapes were a little over-ripe and on the way home a large number of them fell off their stems into the bottom of the paper bag. I washed them all thoroughly, as usual, wondering how to serve loose grapes to birds obviously accustomed to picking their own. The tanagers were wild creatures, easily alarmed, quite the opposite of the tame and trustful hooded orioles, though the females of these two species look quite similar to the untrained eye. I doubted that the tanagers would come down to the ledge to gather loose grapes so I had the idea of impaling the grapes on the twigs of a two-foot plastic tree we'd bought the previous Christmas to serve holiday delicacies to guests. I took the tree out of storage. It was still going to feed guests; they would merely be of another kind.

I fastened the tree to the far end of the porch railing. When its crystal-clear boughs were trimmed with blue and green grapes it looked very enticing. The birds agreed. It was picked clean within half an hour. I put out a fresh supply and the same thing happened again, in even less time. As the week ended I began to realize that I had spent the greater part of it sticking grapes on a plastic tree.

I had also succeeded in putting a large dent in my food budget. The band-tailed pigeons were a serious enough problem but at least it was relatively easy to fill a hopper with grain, and the grain used, milo, cost only a little over four dollars for a hundred pounds. Grapes, which had to be tied with twine or fastened with pipe cleaners or impaled on plastic twigs, caused considerably more trouble and expense. Nor was the situation likely to improve. Later in the season grapes, if they were available at all, would be prohibitively priced.

I will make no attempt to estimate our tanager population as the month of September ended. I'll simply confess that I could no longer afford to buy enough grapes to keep the birds fed and I was reduced to asking for discards from the various markets to supplement the grapes I bought. This meant at least one, and often two or three trips a day checking produce departments and being ingratiating to store managers. Patience is not one of my virtues, so I am astonished, on looking over my records, to find the following autumnal note:

"The season for grapes is almost over. When I think of the hours I've spent lugging the things—since August 15—and putting them out in the trees, I begrudge not one minute of them."

Perhaps happiness is a thing called feeding birds.

Meanwhile the tanagers kept coming. The majority of the new arrivals were females and young males, and traveling with them was the occasional Bullock oriole and hooded oriole, the whitish belly distinguishing the former species from the latter. Among the tanagers themselves there was considerable fighting, frontal jabs and pecks on the rump, and a lone male trying to feed with a group of a dozen females was promptly given the bum's rush.

Watching the tanagers in the tea tree was a little like watching a movie made in the early twenties, because there was no sound. The birds arrived, ate, drank, communicated, fought and departed without uttering a note. It seemed unnatural to us, accustomed as we were to the forceful comments of the acorn woodpeckers, the scoldings of the wrentits and the bold exposés of the scrub jays. Our tanagers were as silent as color. A year and a half was to pass before I heard one sing and then it was in the mountains near Flagstaff, Arizona, and I mistook the song for a robin's. W. L. Dawson, whose translations of bird songs I find irresistible, writes the tanager's thus: *piteric whew, we soor a-ary e-erie witooer.* Amen.

As the weeks passed the majority of female and young male tanagers over adult males constantly increased. If, as the check list claimed, the birds were resident in our area, what was happening to all the adult males? I began to suspect that the check list might be wrong and that the birds we were feeding were not the same ones over and over but were different groups stopping to eat and rest for a day or two before moving on. This would explain why they never became any tamer or more friendly toward us.

A phone call to the Museum of Natural History confirmed my suspicion. While the western tanager has been recorded here every month of the year, it is far more commonly known as a migrant. The spring migration begins as early as the second week in March, and the fall migration goes on until the end of October, though the peaks are mid-April to mid-May, and the last three weeks of September. A few pairs stay to breed in the lowlands but the majority favor the pines and firs of the upper altitudes, as do the hepatic tanagers. The other two species of tanager that migrate to the United States from the tropics both prefer lower altitudes, the summer tanager keeping pretty much to the cottonwoods along streams and the scarlet tanager to oak trees.

At our feeding station we have learned to tell at a glance whether a particular tanager is remaining for a while in the area or whether he is a migrant. The bird which has grown accustomed to the station will grab a grape and fly off the way our permanent residents, the mockingbirds, do. Probably, like the mocker, he is aware of the stiff competition and prefers his meals cafeteria style. The migrating bird, on the other hand, usually stays and eats, restaurant style, in the manner of the black-headed grosbeaks.

The rather belated discovery that our tanagers were migrants did nothing to alleviate the problem of keeping them all fed. October arrived. Most of the summer birds had left, the flycatchers and swallows, the grosbeaks and orioles, the Wilson and yellow warblers and the chat; and some winter ones had already arrived, the white-crowned and golden-crowned sparrows, Audubon's warblers, hermit thrushes and pine siskins. Still the tanagers kept coming. My hospitality had deteriorated considerably—the plastic tree was long since taken down, scrubbed and stored away for the next Christmas, to serve less greedy, less numerous guests. Now I simply hurled the grapes by the boxful onto the terrace, unwashed, some mouldy, some brown with rot.

It was in October that we became acquainted with Richard the rat—in fact, it might be said that in a roundabout way the tanagers introduced us to him.

We have a wide variety of wildlife in our canyon, but at that point we had seen little of it beyond the rats in the tea tree. There were clues that couldn't be overlooked, however. Every morsel of food left at night on the ledge or terrace was gone by morning. Sometimes we caught a whiff of musk or there was a sudden rustling in a tree with no wind to explain it. On half a dozen occasions we found the ceramic bird bath on the lower terrace overturned. The last time it broke, and we replaced it with one that was heavier and not so high, and beside it we put a large saucer and filled it with water. I know now that many wild creatures were watching our house every night, familiarizing themselves with us and our dogs and our various routines.

Every wooded canyon attracts rats, and the way the great

horned owls haunted our particular canyon led us to believe we had more than our share. The rat we called Richard was not just a member of the pack. He was different, a loner. That he had a splendid reason for being a loner we didn't discover for some time.

While the other rats were scurrying up and down the tea tree as soon as the sun set, Richard's scene of action was the cotoneaster tree growing beside the porch outside my office. Here I had experimented with hanging half a coconut shell as a sunflower seed feeder for the finches and titmice. I figured that the voracious scrub jays would find it impossible to land on the shell and so the smaller birds would get their fair share for a change. I was partly right: the jays found it impossible to land on, but they didn't find it impossible to try to land on, and their efforts made the shell toss and pitch and bounce and rock so vigorously that within five minutes there wasn't a seed left in it. I abandoned the project and the coconut shell remained empty until Richard discovered it.

I saw him for the first time one night when I was working late. The sky was cloudless, the moon almost full and I could make out the coconut shell in the cotoneaster tree, swaying gently on its wire. Two things were wrong with the picture—first, there wasn't enough wind to fret a feather; second, I saw hanging from the bottom of the shell what appeared to be another length of wire which hadn't been present in the afternoon. Curious, I turned the beam of my desk lamp on the tree. Richard was curled up in the coconut shell, eyes closed, tail hanging straight down. His conscience must have been clear indeed because even when I called Ken and the two of us went right out on the porch, Richard didn't wake up. There was something moving about this wild little creature trusting us enough to go to sleep in such an exposed place. There was something mighty suspicious about it too, though we didn't think of it at the time.

The following night Richard was back again for another long, deep sleep. He fitted so neatly into the coconut shell that it might well have been constructed especially for him. I was reminded of all the old movies with tropical settings provided by a potted palm, an imitation cobra and a couple of wicker chairs, the winged and hooded kind that sort of wrap around you or at least meet you halfway. In one of these chairs the rubber planter or civil servant or visiting cad would doze off after a few belts of brandy. The coconut shell bore some resemblance to such a chair, but Richard bore none at all to a rubber planter or civil servant or even visiting cad, and I couldn't figure out why I was reminded of the old movies. To many people sounds are more evocative than sights— "Darling, they're playing our song"—and smells more evocative than either sight or sound. Probably the novelty of the whole business dulled my sense of smell because it wasn't until the end of the week that I became aware of the strange mixture of odors out on the porch. Half the mixture was what you might expect at a busy feeding station, the rest was definitely not.

We were experimenting with a flashlight to see just how much it took to wake Richard up. He didn't respond to light at all, and didn't open his eyes even when Ken jiggled the coconut shell up and down and back and forth. Richard had either a weak survival instinct or an optimistic nature, since the area had both bobcats and domestic cats as well as great horned owls. The odor on the porch was particularly strong that night and not unpleasant, in fact, a little bit like wine.

"Wine," I said. *"Wine."* I pointed at our unconscious guest. "He's not tame, he doesn't trust us, he's not just sleeping—he's dead drunk. *Stoned."*

"That's impossible. Where would he get any wine?"

"I don't know. But he got it."

We let the situation go at that for the night, since neither of us was sure how a drunken rat would react to being suddenly awakened and evicted.

An investigation the next day revealed the picture. The coconut shell, which contained a few seeds and bits of rotting grapes, was serving as Richard's winery. Whatever grapes the tanagers had left on the terrace to ferment, Richard had been gathering up and depositing in the coconut shell. If wine bottled for humans is aged by the year, Richard's must have aged by the minute. But it had the same effect. For a certain period every night Richard forgot the cares and casualties of life and dreamed of a world where streets were not paved with gold but upholstered with cat pelts and owl feathers.

Unlike many of his human counterparts Richard was harming nothing but his liver. Still, some changes had to be made. The smell on the porch was increasingly bad—even sober rats tend to be a bit casual in their personal habits—and I found myself opening my office windows less and less. Two steps were agreed on: more careful selection of grapes for the lower terrace and removal of Richard's coconut shell winery to a place farther from the house and less exposed to his enemies.

We don't know what happened—whether one or both of these steps mortally offended Richard or whether he succumbed to cirrhosis or less subtle enemies—but we never saw him again, or if we saw him he was merely part of the group and indistinguishable from the rest. The bougainvillaea has long since grown up over the deserted winery.

Richard and the tanagers were only the beginning of what was to be a most unusual fall and winter. New bird watchers don't know what to expect and are unable to tell whether or not something is out of the ordinary. I accepted everything that happened as something that had doubtless happened the previous year and would happen again the following year. When Silk and Satin, the pair of phainopeplas that had nested in the pepper tree, departed in the fall I fully expected them to return the next spring. They'd practically been household pets, spending a great deal of time outside Ken's office windows, eating the berries from the nightshade and the bugs from the tomato plants. The nightshade berries, the bugs, the pepper tree all remain, but the phainopeplas have not come back.

On September 26 a green-tailed towhee arrived, the first of the mountain species to visit us in the lowlands that autumn. We knew him only by his picture in the field guide and were delighted at the lordly way he kept his head feathers raised so that he seemed to be wearing a bright cinnamon crown. The brown towhee too raises his crest but not nearly so noticeably or so often. Green-tail stayed for a week. Perhaps because he was out of his element he acted in a much shyer manner than others of his family we've since seen in the mountains. He kept to the lower terrace, skulking in and out of the wild blackberry vines and poison oak. We never saw him fly.

The green tail, by the way, figures less prominently in the living bird than it does in the scientific name given to it, *chlorura chlorura*, which is Greek for green tail green tail.

Overlapping the visit of the green-tailed towhee was a male Scott's oriole in full lemon-and-black plumage. Once again the scene was the lower terrace, where we had arranged the bird bath fed by a continuous drip from a hose. Such a drip may have seemed like a waterfall to the oriole since he is a desert bird rarely found in our region. We very infrequently see Bullock's or hooded orioles near the bird baths, perhaps because their diet of insects, fruit and flower nectar provides them with sufficient liquid. But the Scott's oriole seemed fascinated by water. He perched on the rim of the bird bath or stood under the drip from the hose for long periods of time. Though this species is noted for its persistent and beautiful singing, our guest was as silent as the tanagers whose grapes he shared for four days.

Many of the birds that visit us are equally quiet. They arrive in the fall, their families raised and songs sung, and depart again in the spring before new songs rise in them. Audubon warblers are among our most abundant winter visitors, yet we must go high into the mountains to hear one sing. This is true of other species. On a June morning in Banff National Park I discovered that the new song I was listening to came from an old friend, the ruby-crowned kinglet, whose ordinary winter rattle we hear from nearly every oak tree. And it was at Jenny Lake in the Grand Tetons where I heard my first hermit thrush sing. Everybody knows the robin's song—except the people who've stayed in Santa Barbara all their lives. (At least one pair of robins has attempted to correct this situation by nesting in a park beside the Woman's Club for the past three years.)

Two of our winter visitors, on the other hand, try to make up for the rest. The white-crowned and golden-crowned sparrows sing every day they are here, at dawn or at dusk, singly or in duet, from tree and thicket and field. To me this is the sound of the California winter, the clear sweet sparrow songs that seem to be rejoicing that our winter is only a pretend one and spring and summer never really leave.

The third week in October brought a varied thrush, shy, melancholy cousin of the robin, to eat the ripening cotoneaster berries, and a Grace's warbler which, unwarblerlike, perched for a long time in one place as if it were exhausted. It was considerably off course since it's a bird mainly of the coniferous mountains of Arizona and New Mexico and the only previous sighting of the species in California dated back to 1881.

A Steller's jay and a mountain chickadee blew in on a windstorm at the end of the month. We couldn't have asked for a better study in contrasts, the affable little chickadee, for whom I cooked special pancakes, and the large belligerent jay whom I ended up chasing off the ledge with a broom.

The jay's name, Big Boy Blue, seemed inevitable—even the "frown" lines on his forehead were sky-blue. He decided soon after his arrival to convert the ledge into a private dining room and he went to work right away, announcing his intention in squawks so fierce that they either frightened or shamed the scrub jays into silence. He would take up his position in the tea tree, well hidden, and wait there quietly until the ledge had attracted a reasonable number of customers. Then he would swoop down with an ear-piercing shriek and fly low the entire length of the ledge, scattering birds in all directions. Ordinarily I don't interfere in bird bickerings but the situation became serious when some of the smaller birds, fleeing in panic before Big Boy's wrath, struck the window. Many were knocked unconscious and two were killed, and I was forced to begin chasing Big Boy off the ledge and out of the tea tree every time I saw him. In similar situations involving the bird world I have found one thing to be true: the bird invariably wins because he can concentrate all his attention on the problem and I have other things to do.

The sight of me wielding a broom may have reminded Big Boy of Halloween but it certainly didn't scare him. He simply waited until the doorbell or the phone called the witch back into the house, then he cleared the ledge as usual. Only once did he get his comeuppance and it wasn't from me. A flock of about seventy-five band-tailed pigeons were perched in the tops of the eucalyptus trees waiting for the descent signal. It was given at the same moment that Big Boy decided to rid the ledge of his competitors. When the sky suddenly opened up and rained pigeons Big Boy must have thought his time of reckoning had arrived because he took flight like a blue bullet and we didn't see him for the rest of the afternoon. But the next day he was back at his old tricks.

Bribery may not be the best way to handle a bird but it's more effective and less time-consuming than wielding a broom. I recalled an occasion when I went to the Museum of Natural History to check a bird and saw one of the Museum's tame scrub jays hopping around the front desk in a welter of peanut shells. If scrub jays liked peanuts it seemed inevitable that Steller's jays would too. The museum jays had their peanuts shelled for them. I decided to remove just enough of the shell to show Big Boy there was a treat for him inside, then let him take over from there. The theory was that if we could keep Big Boy busy with some project of his own at the front of the house he would leave the birds feeding on the ledge at the back of the house unmolested.

Jays, having voracious appetites, are highly adaptable to changes in food. The first day I put out some shelled and some partly shelled peanuts. The loose nuts Big Boy hauled away, two or three at a time—the maximum carrying capacity of his beak turned out to be five whole Virginia peanuts. Though he jabbed at the others he couldn't dislodge them from their shells. Finally he flew down to the side of the road carrying a shell and began dashing it repeatedly on the concrete, the way scrub jays beat caterpillars on the ground to remove their unpalatable fuzz. Eventually the peanuts rolled out. This method worked only as long as the shells were partly removed. Big Boy tried the same thing with peanuts whose shells were intact and nothing at all happened. The shells didn't crack open because they were too resilient. Big Boy made a very funny picture beating them on the concrete and then hopefully searching the roadway for loose peanuts.

He caught on pretty quickly, though, and changed his tactics. He would carry the shells to the garage roof, which was made of rough shingles and offered sure footing for him. Various crevices held the shells tightly while he jabbed holes in them big enough to allow him to get at the nutmeats. This gentle drumming punctuated the rest of our winter days. Hearing it we would be reassured that the smaller birds were eating unmolested and that Big Boy was flinging himself into his new hobby.

When he departed in February I missed his noisy company and looked forward to his return. Like many of the unusual birds of that unusual year, the green-tailed towhee, the mountain chickadee, the Grace's warbler, Big Boy was a creature of the mountains. Other mountain species were seen elsewhere in Santa Barbara during late fall and early winter, a Clark's nutcracker on Mission Ridge Road, a Townsend's Solitaire in Montecito, a flock of mountain bluebirds in a field near Goleta slough. Of the seven species only the mountain chickadees have returned. And this is good news because it means that the drought of 1961, which brought the mountain species down to us, has not been repeated.

There were other uncommon birds arriving that fall who made their visits yearly events. I have previously mentioned the yellow-breasted chat who comes at the end of August and remains until the end of September and who, during all that time, never opens his mouth except to eat bananas and grapes. It's difficult to believe that this is the same bird whose springtime repertoire is so varied that many people believe he is a true mimic like the mockingbird. If this were the case, the chats found in southern Alberta would have different sounds from the ones found in our Refugio Canyon because of the different kinds of birds and animals to imitate. I haven't found this to be true.

On the other hand, the mockingbirds that sing from our television antenna and the top of the neighbor's sequoia tree are easily distinguishable by ear from those around the house where my bird-watching niece, Jane, lives. Her house, over the hill toward the sea, is in an area of open hills with few large trees. Jane's mockingbirds imitate, as ours never do, the red-tailed hawks and ash-throated flycatchers and green-backed goldfinches, while the notes that characterize our mockers of the woods are missing, the scold of the titmouse and the acorn woodpecker, the lisp of the bushtit.

On October 6 a white-throated sparrow arrived to spend the winter. Though Easterners are well acquainted with this bird he is rare in California and usually seen only at feeding stations. Two days later a lively little band of pine siskins flew in for a stay of two weeks. The comings and goings of these engaging creatures are usually described as erratic, yet every fall they appear here, darting in and out of the feed boxes and hopping and splashing in the bird baths. So completely do they make themselves at home that it is hard for me to believe my eyes when I look out one morning and find them gone. Often in the case of migrating birds the main group will move on leaving a straggler or two behind. This never happened with the siskins, who arrived together, ate together, bathed together and left together. I am told that they sometimes carry their communality to the extent of nesting together in one tree, though I have no direct knowledge of this. Like most of our other guests that fall, they perform their most important function in the mountains: Santa Barbara is a nice place to visit but they wouldn't want to love here.

October also brought our first robins and cedar waxwings. In spite of the large number of berried shrubs on our property, cotoneaster, toyon, eugenia and pyracantha, we have never had huge flocks of robins such as I've seen in nearby areas. That winter we were hosts to a pair of robins, one of whom, after Big Boy Blue was lured around to the front of the house with peanuts, tried repeatedly to take over the ledge. He didn't succeed. Short-tempered and peremptory as he was, he lacked Big Boy's substantial voice and personal force and as soon as be began driving the birds off one end of the ledge, they began congregating at the other end. Perhaps the explanation is simply that birds recognize members of the jay family as their enemies. For all his pomposity the robin is a thrush, no stealer of eggs or eater of nestlings, and he was more of a nuisance than a threat to the other birds.

The arrival of the waxwings presented an entirely different problem. These inoffensive little creatures, gentle as silk, were responsible for more havoc among the other birds than the robins and jays combined. The trouble was caused by their numbers and their gregarious instincts. One waxwing on a bird bath or a food perch still leaves plenty of room for a purple finch, a slaty fox sparrow, a brown towhee and a couple of Audubon warblers. In the world of birds, however, a single waxwing is very rare and seen only at the beginning of the fall season when one is scouting an area in advance, or at the beginning of the spring season when a crippled or diseased bird is left behind by the departing flock.

A hundred waxwings on a ledge, fifty in a bird bath, ten on a doughnut, will drive non-waxwings away more effectively than the tactics of birds twice the size and a dozen times more aggressive. What it boils down to is a matter of room. When there is no more room, other species of birds will simply depart, but the waxwings keep on coming even if they have to land on each other's backs. Instinct tells them to follow their leader and follow they must, usually with good results but often with disastrous ones. We have had a dozen strike a window in as many seconds, most of them fatally, this in spite of the fact that I was standing at the window, waving them away with a newspaper.

Many similar events have made me a reluctant student of window kills—which of the dozens of species around our house actually hit the windows; what birds are killed, what ones are knocked out but survive, and what ones are tough enough to fly away uninjured, at least in any obvious way, and which birds are repeaters who have impaired faculties from previous strikes or other accidents.

The species that fits every one of the above categories and has more strikes to its discredit than all the others combined, including the waxwings, is the mourning dove. Doves also account for the most fatalities, though the percentage of these is low compared to the great number of strikes. It is a simple matter to keep track of the number because birds of this family have a gray powdery coating on their feathers which adheres to any surface they touch. If a window of our house goes unwashed for a month it becomes a showcase for a parade of glaucous ghosts. More than a dozen outlines of doves can be counted, each as clear as a photocopy. Band-tailed pigeons rank second in number of strikes but do not leave such complete or such distinct impressions on the glass, only half a wing sketched here or a bit of head there.

On any day in winter the mourning doves and band-tailed pigeons make up about ten percent of the birds feeding on our ledge. When ten percent of the population is responsible for over ninety percent of the window strikes we must be concerned with the reason why. All birds are believed to have superb eyesight. Experiments with pigeons have shown that they can differentiate as many as twenty shades of color, and since their eyes are at the sides of their heads, they have a field of vision of about 340°; in other words, they can see everything in their environment except the space occupied by their own bodies (Welty, *The Life of Birds*). In spite of all this I'm tempted to think that members of this family have some organic or functional weakness of the eye. (Perhaps I should explain at this point that the lighting in our front room is arranged so that no bird can mistake it for a flythrough: when the north window is open, the south one is draped, and so on.)

A few of the less serious window strikes involving pigeons and doves may be accounted for by their awkwardness in handling themselves at close quarters, landing or taking off. Most of the fatalities, however, occur when a bird, starting in another part of the canyon, comes at full speed toward our windows in what appears to be nothing less than a suicide attempt. For some time we preserved on glass an example of this kind of strike. It happened in the fall of 1964. While talking to a friend on the telephone I saw a mourning dove fly out from the top of a eucalyptus tree about two hundred feet away. The bird's flight was very fast and very direct, straight toward our window. It hit head on, its wings raised for the next beat that never came. The sound of the impact was so loud that my friend on the other end of the telephone thought it was some kind of explosion. Certainly death must have been instantaneous, for the dove ricocheted into the heavy underbrush on the canyon slope, leaving behind on the window a perfect record of the last episode in its life.

Of the ghosts on our glass this one was the clearest: feather and foot, head, beak and eyes—in fact, the outlines of its eyes, we discovered, were not outlines at all but the actual eyes themselves which had been jolted out of their sockets and adhered to the glass like glue. For several months we left that part of the window unwashed and while the eyes very gradually shrank in size, the rest of the dove's memorial remained unfaded by sun, unerased by rain and fog.

The speed of the bird's flight indicated that it was attempting to escape man or hawk. But it had other and safer directions to take, and plenty of time to alter course. Why did this dove, and many others before and after it, fly directly to their deaths when a lift of just a few feet would have allowed them to clear both the window and the roof?

Hermit thrushes and fox sparrows were responsible for a much greater percentage of window strikes than their small numbers would lead us to expect. Conversely, some species struck rarely or not at all. For seven months of every year there were as many Audubon warblers feeding on our ledge as there were house finches. It might reasonably be assumed that the finches, who spent their entire lives around buildings, would be sophisticated about windows, and that the tree-dwelling warblers would not. The opposite turned out to be true. One Audubon warbler, an immature, died in this manner compared to dozens of house finches. In the winter of 1964–1965 we had seven kinds of sparrows at the feeding station—Lincoln's, song, golden-crowned, white-crowned, Harris', English and fox—and only the last named ever struck any of our windows. The record of the icterid family is even better: no strikes among the hundreds of cowbirds, red-winged and tricolor blackbirds, hooded and Bullock orioles. Jays, woodpeckers, mockers and thrashers also have perfect records.

Young birds were more likely to hit the windows than older ones. That spring three baby grosbeaks struck, and only one survived after about a twenty-minute period of semi-consciousness. The experts tell me, by the way, that when a bird is injured by a window strike it should be left strictly alone. Handling it, no matter how gently, may result in a fatal stroke or heart attack caused by fear.

During the past year we tried a system for preventing window kills which has worked very well for the smaller birds but has had no appreciable effect on the doves and pigeons. After the windows are washed on the outside we deliberately "spot" them, either with a hose or with one of the water pistols we keep around the house to discourage dog fights. The resulting stains mar the windows somewhat, but serve as caution signals for birds without interfering too much with the pleasure of watching them.

As the month of October continued I began to notice not so much a decrease in the number of tanagers as a decrease in the number of trips I had to make to the market for grapes. By the middle of the month the females and immatures going through were drably dressed for travel and the few males had lost all trace of their red heads of springtime. On October 22, I counted only five tanagers, and the following day, none at all. A lone bird appeared November 5, either a late migrant arriving, or a bird who hadn't been able to keep pace with his group and had come back for more rest and food. He stayed for two days. His departure marked the end of the tanager migration. It had covered a period of eighty-three days and involved countless birds. The word countless is the only applicable one since we had no way of knowing which birds ate and departed, and which stayed for a day or two, or a week, or even longer.

Without the tanagers the terrace looked strangely colorless and still. Grapes rotted and mildewed in the shade, and shriveled to raisins in the sun. At the market I would be asked how all the tanagers were, and I would have to say I didn't know, they had gone. Where? I wasn't sure but the book said they wintered from Mexico to Costa Rica. Would they be back? Of course, I replied, and I believed it. Tanagers migrated every year, there was no reason why they shouldn't visit us again the next fall and the one after. As a new bird watcher, I had no way of knowing that what brought the tanagers our way in the fall of 1961 was an unusual set of circumstances which probably wouldn't be repeated in our lifetime.

The first reference I found to such a migration was in *Birds of America,* edited by T. Gilbert Pearson:

> *The tanagers are in California every year, and every year they migrate to their nesting grounds in spring and return in fall, but only at long intervals do they swarm in prodigious numbers. Evidently the migration ordinarily takes place along the mountains where the birds are not noticed. It is possible that in some years the mountain region lacks the requisite food, and so the migrating birds are obliged to descend into the valleys. This would seem to be the most plausible explanation of the occurrence—that is, that the usual line of migration is along the Sierra Nevada, but some years, owing to scarcity of food, or other cause, the flight is forced farther west into the coast ranges.*

A. C. Bent, in the tanager volume of his *Life Histories of North American Birds,* gives an account of a large migration in southern California, from April 23 to May 16 in 1896, and of another in 1903, in Pasadena, with the greatest number occurring the last three weeks in May.

In *Birds of California,* W. L. Dawson mentions the spring of 1912 as a very unusual one, when the birds "fairly swarmed," and "one could have seen a hundred adult males in the course of an afternoon's drive." In the next paragraph he tells of a lady in Montecito—the part of Santa Barbara where we live—who during that spring had an arrangement for feeding halved oranges to the tanagers and as many as twelve birds would feed at the same time. Dawson adds, "Never was a more distinguished array of beauty at a single function—not in Montecito even." I think we did as well in 1961 but it was much too late to invite Mr. Dawson.

The three heavy migrations mentioned took place in the spring and covered a period of less than a month. Ours was a fall migration and from the first arrival to the last departure a period of nearly three months elapsed. Why? The passage I quoted previously from T. Gilbert Pearson, in *Birds of America,* suggests that the mountain areas may be short of food in certain years and the tanagers have to move down into the lowlands. A study of our rainfall figures supports this theory.

The lush and varied foliage of Santa Barbara proper gives no indication that ours is a semi-arid region with an average yearly rainfall of 17.7 inches, all but a trace of which falls between November 1 and May 1. Our total rainfall for the last hundred Julys, for instance, measures a little over two inches, and for the same number of Augusts, less than two and a half inches. *Total,* not average. The native plants have adapted to this schedule and survive and even flourish throughout the dry summer months if they have received enough moisture during the winter and early spring. A flood year, 1958, brought nearly twice the normal amount of rain and more than the total rainfall of the three drought years that followed. Mere figures don't give an adequate picture, however. For instance, in the season of 1960–1961 we had 9.99 inches of rain. This wouldn't be so bad if it had been distributed fairly evenly over our six-month rainy season, but nearly all of it fell in November. By the middle of August, 1961, the third of three drought years, creek beds were as dry as the Mojave Desert, and in the mountains all but the toughest shrubs and trees were blighted, their leaves crisped and their fruits withered by unmitigated sun. What was worse still for the birds, insects were in short supply, especially the wasps and other hymenoptera which make up a much larger percentage of the tanager's diet than fruits of any kind.

So the tanagers came down from the mountains. And came and came and came . . .

A Tempest of Tanagers

The flood began in February. It was as if some well-intentioned but muddleheaded weatherlord had made a belated study of the low precipitation figures for the last three years and decided to even things up a bit for Santa Barbara. More rain fell, eighteen inches, than during an average year, and the month became the wettest since weather records were started in 1867. The birds were also the wettest since 1867. Differences seemed to dissolve in water and one soggy bird looked very much like another. Even those distinctive dandies, the waxwings, could be identified from a distance only by their dumpy little legs. Their crests looked like water-flattened cowlicks and their sleek beige coats were black and blotched.

The only birds that didn't change in looks were those colored mainly black and white. The acorn woodpeckers were so unique in appearance that no mere foot and a half of rain could alter them, and the bold stripings of the white-crowned sparrows simply became exaggerated, with the black turning blacker and the white whiter. The same was true of the little black-throated gray warbler who had decided to spend the winter with us. Every now and then he would forage in the cotoneaster outside my office door and I would see the glitter of his golden eye jewel like a tear caught before it fell.

Readers familiar with our area will perhaps wonder why I omitted mentioning blackbirds in the preceding paragraph. The fact is, though it seems incredible to me now, the only blackbird we had then was a Brewer's male who would come and perch quietly in a tree to watch the other birds eat. Weeks passed before he himself flew down to feed, and weeks more before he brought a friend and then a friend's friend. The red-winged blackbirds didn't discover our feeding station until June of 1962 when it had been established for a year, and another year was to elapse before we had our first brown-headed cowbird. The English sparrows too were mercifully slow in discovering us. That winter we had a grand total of five—and didn't have sense enough to appreciate how grand it was! These last four species, depending somewhat on the season, now make up about seventy-five percent of our bird population and their sheer numbers have become a problem, especially the English sparrows. It is rumored that the breeding season of these birds begins on March 1 and ends on February 28, with a one-day holiday every leap year. My own observations lead me to disagree—our English sparrows don't observe the holiday.

That month of February marked the first time that I saw the orange crown of the orange-crowned warbler. During or right after a heavy rain this crown is visible because soaking flattens the greenish feather tips that normally conceal the burnt-orange color underneath. There was another first that month: on the 20th, John Glenn took three very quick trips around the world.

The rain continued, interrupted every now and then by an interlude of dazzling sun that turned the eucalyptus leaves to silver and made golden balls out of the pittosporum pods. The waxwings, as usual, had their own idea of how to make the best use of these dry interludes—they bathed, as any chronicler of waxwing eccentricities should have guessed. They bathed as if they'd just been released from some desert prison.

While our creek turned into a roaring river and our yard into a swamp, while we were bailing out our lanai and piling furniture on furniture trying to keep half of it dry, while bridges disappeared, and fences and sections of road, the waxwings fluttered down into the bird baths like wet autumn leaves and fluttered back up again to the tops of the eucalyptus trees whose blossoms they shared with the Audubon warblers. If I opened the dining-room window while they were using the bird bath just below it, I could hear the flock communicating with each other in their continual whistles so high that many people are unable to register the sound. Of the birds I've heard, only the blackpoll warbler reaches as high a pitch. Another of the waxwings' familiar noises was made not by their vocal chords but by the rush of air through many pairs of wings as they rose in a body to the tops of the trees. It consisted of a long, drawn-out *phew*.

As the rains went on and on, even the waxwings had to dry out sometimes. I would find them roosting all over the place, on the rafters in the garage, under the eaves, in the woodpile, and once I even found a row of them perched on the handlebar of my bicycle, looking for all the world as if they expected to be taken for a ride. In a fit of compassion, untempered by common sense, I arranged a shelter for them on the porch, an old-fashioned wooden clothes-drying rack left over from the prelaundromat days. I had long since switched from grapes, which were not available, to apples, which were, and during the period that the clothes rack remained on the porch I learned one equation well: apples + waxwings = applesauce.

Other birds discovered the rack too, and it soon became a popular hangout. I counted ten species on it at one time: band-tailed pigeons and mourning doves, waxwings, mockingbirds, jays, English sparrows, house finches, purple finches, white-crowned sparrows and golden-crowned sparrows. Such a close and peaceful assemblage would have been unlikely to occur in good weather when its members had more freedom of choice. In fact, the change in attitude brought about by a prolonged period of storms was apparent not only in the birds' relationship with each other, but in their relationship to me. In a four-inch rain I was the kindly purveyor of seeds and doughnuts and peanut butter sandwiches, and the birds perched on window ledges and porch railings waiting for a handout, and peered in at me over the edge of the roof. A day of sun, however, shrank me down to size. The same creatures who'd almost eaten out of my hand now looked at me as if they had never seen me before and expected the worst.

During the storms we had our first and most intimate experiences with purple finches. Some of these birds, which usually breed at the higher altitudes, come down to the southern California coastal areas for the winter, their numbers varying considerably from year to year according to the availability of food in the mountains. That winter they were almost as common as our permanent residents, the house finches. The two species resemble each other physically, but there are striking differences in behavior. It would, in fact, make more sense if it were the purple finches who pursued a close association with dwellings and people. They are calmer in deportment, quieter in voice, and in general seem more adaptable to human beings.

House finches are nervous, noisy birds, always chipping and chirping and on the move. Their fright reaction to a door opening for the five thousandth time is the same as their reaction when the door opened for the first time. Such behavior is instinctive, but in the case of the purple finches it was quickly modified by experience. They learned that the opening of a particular door meant doughnuts, not disaster, and while instinct always made them fly away, experience kept shortening the distance. By April 23, when the last of them migrated, the flyaway distance had become the merest token foot or two.

The purple finches showed a pronounced weakness for sweets. When I put out the doughnuts in the morning, they avoided the plain kind and went immediately to the ones coated with icing. Instead of pecking at them here and there the way all the other birds did, the finches carefully proceeded to eat every trace of icing off, barely touching what lay underneath. We could always tell which doughnuts had been finch food: they hung naked in the trees like Christmas ornaments with the tinsel worn off.

Purple finches were more numerous at the feeding station that winter than any year since. This was also true of fox sparrows, represented by the three main subspecies, the dusky brown, the rusty and the slaty—by the end of the season a total of about fifteen birds. Subsequent winters have brought no more than one or two fox sparrows at a time and none of them stayed for the season.

In recent years other local birders have found fox sparrows in short supply. On the last five Christmas counts, for instance, a total of only fifty-eight were reported. Contrast this with the estimate, made by W. L. Dawson in the early twenties, that there were present "on a winter day in California anywhere from 20 to 200 million fox sparrows." Perhaps the reason for the difference can be deduced from another set of figures: in the early twenties the human population of California was three and a half million, today it is nearly twenty million.

Some species, like the mockingbird, have adjusted so well to human intrusion that they are usually seen only in inhabited areas. Mockers appear to be more at home on a T.V. antenna than on a tree top, and better able to cope with cats and dogs than with hawks and owls. Such an adaptation is a much more complicated procedure for birds as innately shy as the fox sparrows. However, another species noted for its shyness is proving surprisingly adaptable. This is the wrentit.

At quite a number of feeding stations in this area, wrentits have become as sociable as titmice. Ours serenade us from the porch railing, their long expressive tails vibrating in rhythm with each note, and in the spring the young ones learn to sing in the lower branches of the ceanothus or elderberry bush. The song, among the easiest of all bird songs to identify, must be difficult to perfect. The summer air rings from dawn to dusk with the sound of wrentits practicing. These music lessons remind me of all the little boys who ever sawed away at a violin and all the little girls who ever blew earnestly into a woodwind.

The wrentit, which used to be our state bird, has been replaced by the California quail. People who deplore the change point out that the California quail is only one of 165 members of the family of *Phasianidae,* whereas the wrentit is the only member in the whole world of his family, the *Chamaeidae.* His scientific name, *Chamaea fasciata,* means "fastened to the ground." Because of his weak flight and home-loving nature, the name may almost be taken literally. Indeed, the porch railing of the second floor of our house is a veritable Matterhorn for the wrentit.

The uniqueness of the little bird is further emphasized by the fact that he inhabits only the Pacific coastal area from southern Oregon to Baja California. This makes him a more strictly regional bird than the California quail, which has been introduced widely throughout the West.

Perhaps the quail was chosen as replacement because he is more easily seen and more colorful than the wrentit, or perhaps because his greeting sounds so hospitable. On almost any hike you can hear the quail's cheerful throaty voice urging everyone to "sit right down, sit right down." Birders new to our area are advised not to take the invitation too seriously—it is frequently issued in a canyon overgrown with poison oak. (Poison oak offers quail some protection which they badly need at nesting time. Surely one of the funniest and most touching sights in the avian world is that of newly hatched quail tagging along behind their parents. One fellow birder, Neva Plank, is responsible for what seems the perfect description of them—"walking walnuts.")

The adjustability of the innately shy wrentits to human conditions can probably be explained by the fact that these birds are not migratory but live out their entire lives in a small circumscribed area. When your world measures only an acre, you can take better stock of it, get to know what's poison and what's meat, where the seeds are and where the cats aren't, when to fly, when to freeze. The bird that must cover hundreds of miles every spring and fall has no chance for such careful scrutiny. If, in spite of this, he adapts easily and well to the presence of people—like the hooded oriole, the black-headed grosbeak, the white-crowned sparrow—we must attribute it to his inborn good nature. In *The Life of Birds* Welty states that "tameness, shyness and belligerence commonly run in families and are very likely based on hereditary behavior patterns. Phalaropes, puffbirds, kinglets and titmice are relatively tame, confiding birds, while oyster catchers, roseate spoonbills and redshanks are shy, wild species."

This brings us back to the cedar waxwings. Watch a large flock of them feeding in a pepper tree and you get the impression that they are the most fidgety and nervous of birds. This impression quickly disappears after you've had some experience with them. They show little suspicion and fear of either humans or the various contrivances humans have rigged up to protect their ornamental fruits and berries—dangling twists of metal, strips of cloth, plastic windmills from the dimestore, colored discs and Japanese glass chimes. Several times during that winter I put food out as usual and then, instead of going immediately back into the house, I sat down quietly on the ledge. The length of time I had to wait until the waxwings arrived depended on whether the birds were near enough to see the fresh food. If they were, they came down to the ledge without hesitation—either ignoring or accepting my presence, I'm not sure which—and fed themselves within touching distance of me.

Several accounts have been written of how young or injured waxwings adjust to captivity and become as tame and sometimes as mischievous as parakeets. Their amiability toward human beings extends to other birds as well as to each other. They are courteous and affectionate and they never fight among themselves the way most species of birds and mammals do. A probable reason for this is suggested in A. C. Bent's *Life Histories of North American Birds*. Dr. Arthur A. Allen is quoted to the effect that cedar waxwings "have nothing to gain by fighting, for their food is of such a nature that there is either more of it than they could consume before it spoils or else there is none at all. Since they can fly long distances to feeding places, they do not need to defend a feeding territory about their nests." This, perhaps, might also account for their lack of song.

Writing in the same volume, Winsor Barrett Tyler refers to the waxwing as the perfect gentleman of the bird world. Certainly this is true as far as dress and deportment are concerned, but at the table the waxwing most resembles a high-spirited child, alternating serious eating with playful antics like tossing food into the air and catching it, at the same time keeping up an incessant noise.

I used to share with many other people the impression that these birds were strictly berry eaters. During the winter of 1961–1962 I learned that berries were not even their favorite food when more exotic items were available. The berries on all our cotoneaster and toyon trees were untouched as long as I kept the ledge supplied with apples and doughnuts and waxwing pudding and a mixture we called raisin-mess. The recipe for the latter was given to us by Mr. Rett, who said he'd used it successfully on the museum grounds to attract warblers. A pound of ground raisins was stirred into a pound of melted beef fat—it took a heap of stirring because the two didn't want to mix—and when the whole sticky mess was cold and set it was put into suet feeders or into various crannies and crevices in the bark of a tree. I don't recall that the mixture attracted many warblers but it was an instant hit with the waxwings as well as the opossums, raccoons and rats.

Waxwing pudding was served in three old ice trays kept out on the ledge. It was a general name we used for any mixture which had moistened bread as its basis, with various other things added according to what was available—sugar, cornmeal, canned fruit, eggs, raisins, leftover mashed potatoes, spaghetti, stuffed green peppers, suet, peanut butter—no combination was too wild for the waxwings, who ate stuff even the omnivorous scrub jays wouldn't go near.

As to their manner of eating this mixture I can only say that they wolfed it. Since early childhood I've heard this expression but I never really understood what wolfing your food meant until a couple of years ago when Pete and Adu Batten acquired a pair of timber wolves, Thomas and Virginia. I happened to be around at feeding time one day. Virginia was about the size of our German shepherd, Brandy, who weighs 105 pounds; Thomas was considerably larger. Both wolves received a large bowl of horsemeat and kibble, but within a fraction of a minute every scrap of food was gone. It was an unbelievable performance on the part of two animals born and raised in captivity and well fed from the beginning.

Naturalists used to believe that this manner of eating on the part of wolves was necessary to ensure their survival, since in their native environment, the Arctic tundra and the boreal forests of Canada, they often had to go for days without capturing any large prey. Therefore, when such food was available it had to be eaten quickly, before it froze in winter or spoiled in summer. It seemed a beautifully logical theory until Canadian biologist Farley Mowat took up residence with wolves in the wild and learned they lived mainly on mice in summer and rabbits in winter. So much for logic.

Meanwhile, some three thousand miles to the southwest our waxwings wolfed their food.

Paul Vercammen is a local bird fancier who at one time in his aviary kept four cedar waxwings in addition to more exotic species like Lady Amherst and golden pheasants. The latter were fed a scientifically balanced mixture in the form of pellets while Paul went to considerable lengths to supply the waxwings with pyracantha berries. People who have kept more than one pet simultaneously, canine, feline, avian or any other, should be able to guess what happened: the pheasants took a liking to pyracantha berries and the waxwings thrived on pheasant pellets for five years. They'd probably still be doing it if Paul hadn't given them to the Museum of Natural History where they're back on a more conventional diet.

There were only a few items of food which our waxwings refused that winter. One of them was dark bread, rye, pumpernickel and the like, and another was chocolate in any form—both of these were also turned down by the other birds unless absolutely nothing else was available. Chocolate doughnuts, and those merely iced with chocolate, were the last to be eaten, and pieces of rye bread were often left around for days. The aversion didn't extend to wheat bread, no matter how dark, or to ginger cake, which rules out the possibility that the birds were reacting to the color. Since they're supposed to have a poorly developed sense of smell and taste, I'm at a loss to explain why our birds exhibited the same dislikes year after year.

Apples cut in halves were particular favorites of the waxwings. Every atom of pulp and seed would be eaten until only a spine of core remained holding together the paper-thin shell of skin. When the wind blew, these shells would move back and forth on the ledge like little riderless rocking horses.

In some parts of the country waxwings are known as cherry-birds because of their fondness for this fruit. But in California waxwings are winter birds and their favorite fruit is the firethorn, or pyracantha berry, which resembles not so much a cherry as a small red apple with a soft yellowish pulp. We have pyracanthas planted for the birds as well as toyons, eugenias, cotoneasters and pepper trees. In 1964–1965, a normal year in climate and vegetation, the pyracantha berries were all gone by February 20, the toyons, eugenias and peppers were untouched, and the cotoneasters were dragging on the ground with the weight of their fruit. During the first week of March, the waxwings started in seriously on the cotoneaster outside Ken's office. By March 5, an estimated 250 to 300 pounds of berries had been consumed and the limbs of the tree had risen off the ground, back to their usual position.

The waxwing appetite is notorious in the bird world. Audubon mentions their eating so heavily that they were unable to fly, and John Tyler writes of numbers of them, in the vineyard regions of northern California, choking to death trying to swallow too many raisins at once. I've never witnessed such extremes, even during that wet winter of 1962, though I saw many a bulging beak and distended throat, and many a batch of waxwing pudding disappear within a minute or two.

One Sunday morning in early March, while we were having a respite from the rain, my brother-in-law, Clarence Schlagel, decided to take some pictures of the waxwings feeding on the ledge for his collection of nature slides. He arrived early with all his equipment: technical assistants wife Dorothy and daughter Jane, one plain and one fancy camera, tripod and telescopic lens. After the usual photographer's fussbudgeting, he ended up dispensing with everything except the plain camera and simply shooting the birds through the plate-glass window. The results, he phoned later in the week to tell us, were fine as far as the waxwings were concerned, but the old ice trays we used as feeders had ruined the pictures aesthetically. Didn't we have something prettier and more photogenic?

I explained, somewhat sharply, that when you were feeding hundreds of birds daily, you had little time to worry about aesthetics. But my pride was injured, and that afternoon I searched through some cupboards and came across a candy dish I'd been given in my pre-birding days. It was made of Italian marble in the shape of a pedestal bird bath decorated with doves. Clarence dropped in to inspect my discovery and pronounced it perfect—the whiteness of the marble would emphasize the tawny shades of the waxwings grouped picturesquely around it.

I knew enough about waxwings by this time to doubt that they would group picturesquely around anything if someone wanted them to. However, I agreed to try and arrange a more artistic setting, substituting the marble dish for one of the ice trays and putting in it something pretty and colorful instead of the rather repulsive-looking waxwing pudding.

After checking what was available in the house my brother-in-law decided on maraschino cherries. I opened a jar, put half a dozen cherries in the miniature marble bird bath and set it out on the ledge. It looked irresistible, but beauty is in the eye of the beholder and evidently the waxwings weren't seeing eye to eye with either Clarence or me. For the balance of the day they came as usual, ate their repulsive-looking waxwing pudding and flew off, paying no attention to the beautiful cherries in the elegant dish. I was not only disappointed, I was downright shocked. A newcomer to the bird world, I innocently assumed that things would be more rational there than in other worlds I already knew. Here were cherries and here were cherrybirds—something should be happening.

I told myself that it was probably a matter of the birds getting used to a new object on the ledge and all I had to do was wait. I waited for the rest of the week. Every now and then I'd see three or four waxwings perched on the marble dish or sitting beside it.

The following Sunday, Clarence returned with his photographic paraphernalia and his two assistants to have another try. He wanted to know whether the waxwings had become accustomed to the marble bird bath by this time and were grouping picturesquely around it. I assured him they were.

"They must make a colorful sight eating the cherries," he said.

"They might if they were but they're not," I said. "They're eating the bird bath."

I pulled open the drapes. Most of the waxwings flew off in protest at the interruption, but at least half a dozen remained where they were on the bird bath. Each of them was carefully and vigorously honing its beak, first on one side, then on the other. The little marble doves used as decoration along the rim of the dish had already been honed into oblivion as had part of the base.

Birds, ornithologists point out, are adaptable. But you never know to what.

On April 2, I wrote in my notebook:

> *Spring has arrived and those gay gluttons, the wax-*
> *wings, have left us, except for one sad sick little one. His*
> *neck is unfeathered and the exposed skin looks raw, and*
> *his plumage is almost black. I've tried to find out what*

*ails him but no one seems to know. His flight is weak
and it's obvious he couldn't have kept up with his
northbound friends.*

*Speaking of whom, I find their departure has dis-
turbed the other birds as much as their arrival did. They
seem nervous, leery at the idea of landing on the ledge
as if they sense something is "wrong" because there
are no waxwings in sight. I share their feeling to a certain
extent, but mine is tempered by relief.*

*Waxwings are not noted for their territorial fidelity.
Still, I'll bet a dozen doughnuts and a peck of apples
they'll be back on the ledge next year, come October or
November. . . .*

I would have lost the bet. October arrived, and November, but
no waxwings. By Christmas I had seen two flocks in the neighborhood, neither of which paid any attention to the ledge with its
bird bath, its doughnuts, apples and waxwing pudding. January
brought a small flock or two every day and this continued through
March. They ate our cotoneaster berries, our toyons, pyracanthas,
eugenias and eucalyptus blossoms. During the next three winters
we must have seen many thousands of waxwings from our house,
yet not a single one of them came down to the ledge to bathe, to
eat, to hone its bill.

My fellow birders have suggested possible reasons:

It may have been a fluke that the waxwings started eating off the
ledge that first winter. A group leader, his curiosity aroused by the
sight of other birds eating there, might have decided to come down
for a taste. Then, once started, the waxwings simply continued
throughout the season.

Possibly the waxwings of 1961–1962 did not return in the other
years. (Why not?) Or, if they returned, they forgot about the
waxwing pudding. (I wish I could. I tend to remember it most
vividly just as I'm setting out to sea in a small boat.)

Perhaps the real reason is the simplest: waxwings are as unpredictable as people.

The Winterlings

Some newcomers to the coast of southern California confess a certain nostalgia for the changes of season they knew back in Pittsburgh or Providence, Peoria or Butte. True, we have summer days in winter, and flowers bloom all year and the reason we find it difficult to grow certain plants is that our climate won't allow them a time to rest. We have birds all year too, yet it is the birds who differentiate the reasons most clearly for many of us.

The warbler departing from the New England states at the end of summer leaves a vacuum. In California his place is taken almost immediately. With the coming of autumn we substitute Audubon, myrtle and Townsend warblers for yellow and Wilson and black-throated gray. Summerlings like the black-hooded grosbeaks and western tanagers give way to the winterlings, the ruby-crowned kinglets and purple finches. The hooded and Bullock orioles are replaced by the fox sparrows and the whitecrowns and goldcrowns, the turkey vultures by the sharp-shinned hawks. The path of the departing Swainson thrush crosses that of the arriving hermit. On one occasion these two species actually met on our ledge, with no sign of being much interested in each other. Perhaps the traveler was too tired and the embarker too eager to be gone.

The return of birds year after year to the same nesting area has been widely discussed and researched. Not so much has been done on the subject of territorial fidelity to winter quarters, yet almost every Californian with a feeding station is aware how strong this fidelity is among most species. The Audubon warblers and the white-crowned and golden-crowned sparrows come first to mind since they are the most numerous. It is easier, however, to keep records on the less numerous species, the Lincoln sparrow, for instance, which is quite rare in our area.

Every October a pair of Lincoln sparrows appears on the lower terrace and for the next five months they divide their time between the terrace and the ledge, doing their best to dispel the widespread rumors that they are shy and retiring and given to skulking in the underbrush. These birds have not been banded but it seems likely, both from their behavior and the scarcity of the species locally, that they are the same birds year after year. Many of our bird watching friends have come to the house in order to compare the Lincoln with the song sparrow. The two frequent the same area and can often be seen side by side. At these times the differences show up quite clearly—the Lincoln's ochre-washed chest, finely streaked with black, is distinctive. Younger song sparrows resemble Lincolns more closely than the older birds do.

Another of our regular winter visitors is unusual not because the species is rare here—we list hundreds of Oregon juncos on every Christmas count—but because these birds are gregarious creatures, always in flocks, and our junco, a female, arrives in October alone, spends the winter alone and leaves again in mid-April, still alone. I frequently see groups of juncos on the adjacent property foraging under the avocado trees, so there are obviously many of them in the neighborhood. Yet, as far as we can tell, only this lone female comes to feed on the ledge.

A ranger-naturalist at Jenny Lake in the Grand Tetons National Park told us of a similar experience he had and showed us the female junco involved, a member of the pink-sided subspecies. She was nesting where she had in previous years, under a small bush right beside the main walk into Jenny Lake Museum. She allowed herself to be lifted off the nest so that we could see her moss-lined bowl of little speckled eggs. As soon as we entered the museum she returned to her eggs, displaying no signs of rancor or nervousness. Since Grand Tetons Park comprises over 300,000 acres it is difficult to understand why she chose a spot where dozens of pairs of feet passed every day. Perhaps she depended on the presence of human beings to discourage enemies of hers that reached much further back in time than man. The ranger said she showed up every June alone, and built her nest and raised her young alone. He and other employees of the park had watched carefully for signs of her mate but no one ever caught sight of him and his existence has to be presumed on the evidence of three lively children.

Our own Oregon junco was responsible for a misunderstanding which probably caused many a raised eyebrow in local circles. It happened one day in November, a time when severe winds often sweep down the canyon, shaking the crowns of the palm trees as if they were feather dusters, and twisting the eucalyptus into frenzied contortionists. We'd been having trouble with our extension phone and had arranged for a repairman to come and look at it. Returning home from downtown I found that the wind had blown open the door of my office. Birdseed was scattered all over the carpeting and in the middle of it, peacefully foraging, was the little female junco. She seemed quite at home, choosing a seed here and a seed there and then flying up to inspect the desk and lamp and bookcase and my writing chair. When I tried to persuade her to go back out the door she merely hopped into the living room. Here she continued her inspection tour of the house, showing signs of uneasiness only when she discovered that the picture window was made of glass and offered her no means of exit.

Birds, like some people, have a tendency to panic when they realize they're trapped. The junco was more phlegmatic than most but I was afraid this wouldn't last and I wanted to coax her out of there in a hurry. I opened all openable windows and removed the screens. Her only response to my attempts to help her was to keep fluttering her wings against the same picture window.

At this point the doorbell rang announcing the arrival of the telephone repairman. Since birds are much more sensitive to movement than to noise I stayed where I was and shouted through the door: "Wait on the porch for a minute. I have a junco in here I'm trying to get rid of."

"Can I help?"

"No thanks, I'll manage."

And I finally did, by slowly drawing the drapes across the picture window. The junco proved she knew the exits perfectly and had been just playing a game with me. Pausing only long enough to send me a that's-not-fair look she made a beeline for the nearest unscreened window. When I opened the drapes she was already back in her place on the ledge.

I let the repairman into the house. He stared around the room with a rather disappointed expression. "I see you got rid of him O.K."

"Yes. She went out the window."

"A female yet. Which window?"

I pointed to it and he crossed the room and looked down at the patio below.

"Say, that's some drop, must be twelve to fifteen feet and solid concrete underneath. How about that, eh? These junkies will try anything."

He was so keen and excited that I didn't have the heart to set him straight. It has probably become part of his family legend— how he was present the day the dope addict jumped out of the bird addict's window.

Under special circumstances records of territorial fidelity to winter quarters can be kept without banding the birds. This applied in some degree to our pair of Lincoln sparrows. It applied even more to a bird well known to people living in the East and Midwest, though there had never been a California record of it.

The bird appeared in a willow tree in the yard of Jewell and Russ Kriger about the middle of October, 1961. The willow leaves were still very dense, and at first Jewell was able to catch only a glimpse of the bird, but it was enough to convince her it belonged to a species new in the area. When she finally saw it clearly, she couldn't believe her eyes and didn't expect anyone else to believe them either. She spent more than a week studying the bird before she confessed to me on the phone that she had a Baltimore oriole in the willow tree beyond her balcony.

I said what I had to say: "That's impossible."

"I know. It's a male, in perfect plumage, head solid black, belly and rump oranger than oranges."

I told her I'd be right over, bringing along all my reference books on birds.

When I arrived at the Krigers' some twenty minutes later, the oriole had left. Jewell was confident though that he would return because his friend was still in the willow tree. She showed me the "friend," a red-breasted sapsucker, a rather uncommon winter visitor in this region and well worth the trip over just by himself.

The friendship was strictly a one-sided affair, the sapsucker's opinion of orioles being low, and regrettably, quite justified. As almost everyone who feeds hummingbirds is aware, orioles have a weakness for sweet syrup. So do sapsuckers. But there the similarity ends, for the sapsucker works for his syrup. The oriole, whose beak is not equipped to drill into the bark of trees, does the next best thing—he follows the sapsucker as the jaeger follows the tern and the gull the pelican.

While we were waiting for the Baltimore oriole to rejoin his friend in the willow tree I checked the various books I'd brought with me for references to the species. It was not mentioned at all in Ralph Hoffman's *Birds of the Pacific States*, W. L. Dawson's *Birds of California*, or Brown and Weston's *Handbook of California Birds*. *Birds of America*, edited by T. Gilbert Pearson, limited the range of the Baltimore oriole to east of the Rockies, and Roger Tory Peterson, in his *Field Guide to Western Birds*, wrote that any appearance of the species in California or Arizona was accidental. I began to have serious doubts about Jewell's eyesight.

Through binoculars I watched the sapsucker drill another hole in the already riddled tree—these birds are partial to willows because the wood is soft and juicy. He was young and tousled-looking as if he'd just blown in on a high wind, and the red of his upper parts was duller and darker than in any pictures I'd seen of him. (A year later he was a much sleeker and more beautiful bird.)

Suddenly the sapsucker paused, turned his head, shook himself all over as though in a rage, and flew off. Almost instantly his place at the newly drilled hole was taken by the Baltimore oriole. There wasn't the slightest doubt about the bird's identification, every feather was perfect. The solid black head and the orange of the undertail reversed the colors of the hooded oriole, and a thin white wing bar supplanted the broad white patch of the Bullock oriole.

I called Mr. Rett at the Museum of Natural History, told him I was watching a Baltimore oriole in the Krigers' yard and asked him to send someone from the museum to come and check it.

He sounded quite exasperated. "I can't send the members of our staff charging off every time a crackpot call comes in. You know what kind of reports we get?—condors perched on rooftops, coppery-tailed trogons fluttering around gardens, cactus wrens in pine trees. . . ."

He went on to what I assumed was his standard lecture to crackpot callers: birds often didn't look exactly like their pictures in the field guides; size was always, and color usually, very deceiving, yellow and orange, for instance. The bird I was watching might well be a Scott's oriole since one had recently been reported in Montecito.

"I know," I said coldly. "I reported it. And yellow and orange are no more alike than lemons and oranges."

"All right, all right, all *right*. I'll see if Waldo can make it out there later in the day."

Arrangements were made for Waldo Abbott to come at two o'clock since the oriole's time of arrival in the afternoon averaged about two-thirty according to Jewell's records. Meanwhile the word had spread. Pat Higginson arrived hoping to add a new bird to her list, Mary Hyland staggered in with half a ton of photographic equipment, and shortly before two Waldo arrived, looking like a man determined to be underwhelmed.

Waldo is a very active, restless man, and as long as he was helping Mary move photographic equipment around and set it up, he was content. But the instant he had to sit down quietly in a chair and wait for the oriole he began to show signs of wanting to bolt. We couldn't risk losing him at this critical juncture so Pat and I had a conference in the kitchen. She suggested that since Waldo was a man who loved food and birds—not necessarily in that order—we should ply him with food and bird questions. Waldo was a born teacher and he could no more walk away from a question than an actor could walk away from an audience. Pat supplied the cookies and coffee, I supplied the questions.

The oriole picked that day to be late. Three o'clock came and no bird, and Waldo was fit to be tied. In fact, Pat and I were seriously considering tying him if nothing else worked. Fortunately we didn't have to. At three-thirty the red-breasted sapsucker flew into the willow tree, closely followed by his orange-and-black "friend."

Cameras clicked, and the Baltimore oriole became part of Santa Barbara's bird history. The colored slides taken by Mary and Waldo that day, of the Baltimore oriole alone and with the sapsucker, were burned in a serious fire started by chemicals in Mr. Rett's lab, but Mary still has all the negatives. Subsequently, Waldo wrote an article about the oriole which appeared in *Condor* magazine and which, as far as I know, was the first official report of the bird in California. Since then, this species has been sighted in the state on many occasions. Two years after the appearance of Jewell's Baltimore oriole, which stayed in her yard all that winter and every winter since, ten members of this species were seen at various places in southern California: Santa Ana, Rancho Park and Point Loma in addition to Montecito.

No single wild bird has become more popular with nature lovers throughout the state than the Krigers' Baltimore oriole, which came to be affectionately know, at Pat Higginson's suggestion, by its initials. During fall and winter, birders, in fact whole bird clubs, arrive at the Krigers' house equipped with binoculars, field guides, sandwiches, and in at least one instance, a sleeping bag. As Easterners prepare for the winter by having their furnaces checked, the Krigers prepare for it by buying up extra quantities of coffee and bracing themselves for a series of telephone calls that usually begin: "Do you still have your B.O.?"

Long-time residents of Santa Barbara know that Olive Mill Road was named for its olive mill, which is still standing and used as a residence; that Parra Grande Lane, in the 1800s, was the site of the world's largest single grapevine, covering a trellis 100,000 square feet in area; and that Salsipuedes was one of the old town boundaries and meant, "Get out if you can." Newcomers find out for themselves that Conejo Road has rabbits, Las Encinas oaks, Nogales walnuts, that Overlook Lane overlooks and that in the early spring the Monarch butterflies swarm like bees in the Monterey cypresses of Butterfly Lane.

Local bird watchers were puzzled by the fact that one small area of Montecito, as soon as the Krigers moved into it, should produce such a number and variety of orioles, both in and out of season. (On one November morning in 1963, for instance, I saw there four kinds of orioles, a hooded, two Bullocks, the adult male Baltimore with a younger male in tow and a male orchard oriole.) It was a happy accident that I discovered, less than a block from the Krigers' back yard, a small private lane almost hidden by its own lush foliage. A wooden sign indicated its name, Oriole Road. Evidently orioles had been frequenting the neighborhood for a long time, but what kind? Were they merely our rather common summer visitors, the hooded, or the somewhat less common Bullock? Or was it possible that Baltimore orioles had been coming there every winter for years and were simply not spotted by competent observers? Shortage of such observers is underlined by the fact that these flashy, vivid birds, visible half a mile away, have wintered in Montecito since 1961 but have not been reported from any area except the Krigers' back yard.

On the same November day that the male orchard oriole visited the Krigers, I learned from Mary Hyland that another male of the same species had been in the yard of Neva Plank, on the other side of town, since the beginning of the month. Mrs. Plank, a bird watcher, had identified it immediately but hadn't told anyone except Mary about it because she didn't want news of the oriole's presence to get around to any collector. Mary assured Mrs. Plank of my strong anti-collecting stand and I was invited to her house, along with Jewell Kriger and Nelson Metcalf. The orchard oriole, while not as gaudy as Jewell's B.O., was easier to see because he hung out close to the house in the tecomaria bushes, along with several Allen's hummingbirds who should have been gone by the end of August.

Tecomaria is also known to gardeners by its scientific name, *Tecoma capensis,* and by its nickname, cape honeysuckle. Grown either as a vine or a shrub, it is a plant every backyard catering to birds should contain. With its delicate dark-green leaflets that glitter in the sun, and its vivid orange-red flowers that bloom almost all year, it looks like an exotic which requires much care and water. In fact, it thrives on neglect. Like the tree tobacco, another great attraction for birds, especially hummers and orioles, it grows anywhere, reseeds like mad, and needs no summer watering. Credit should be given to the three T's—tobacco, trumpet and tecomaria—for the part they play in enabling increasing numbers of migrants and breeding birds to remain here all year. But the most credit must go to the eucalyptus trees, of which there are almost a hundred kinds growing in the Santa Barbara region. On a late winter or early spring day the crowns of the larger eucalypts are literally alive with Audubon warblers, hooded and Bullock orioles and cedar waxwings, and in midsummer, when the red-flowered varieties are in bloom, each tree can be heard a block away, so many hummingbirds and bees are battling for its honey.

The orchard oriole, a common nester in the more southerly parts of the East and Midwest, had been seen in California only a few times and Mrs. Plank's bird was the first record for Santa Barbara. He was dubbed Mr. Chocolate and almost immediately he became as popular as his name. He never failed to show up for visiting birders and pose for his photograph, and he obligingly stayed around for one Audubon Christmas count. I visited him quite frequently during the winter and early spring until his departure in mid-April. This coincided almost exactly with the departure of Jewell's adult Baltimore, the young Baltimore having left the last week in January, probably out of frustration: he had spent two and a half months trying to imitate the way the adult drank out of the oriole syrup feeder and he never got the hang of it.

The record books for birds are changing year by year. It is difficult to assess how many of these changes are real, caused by variations in climatic conditions, and how many are apparent, caused by an increase in the number of observers and people who attract birds by feeding and appropriate plantings. In the winter of 1964, according to *Audubon Field Notes* (Vol. 19, No. 3), the following summer species were reported in southern California: fifteen hooded orioles, twenty-nine Bullock orioles, twelve western tanagers and a black-headed grosbeak. The grosbeak and four of the tanagers were at our feeding station. The two species arrived within a day of each other during the first week in December and left a month later. Where they spent the rest of the winter is anybody's guess, but on March 17, three western tanagers returned, two males and a female, accompanied by a female summer tanager and a male just acquiring his manly plumage—he was the same yellow-green shade as the female except for an orange-pink wash across his chest and orange-pink patches beside his shoulders and on top of his head. It was a day of vicious weather, severe winds, rain, thunder and hail, hardly an ideal occasion to watch birds. But birds often do the unexpected— we had thirty-two species in our yard that day. Some of them must have been rather astonished at the California weather.

The continual presence all winter of Mr. Chocolate, Neva Plank's orchard oriole, and the way he stuck so close to the house until mid-April, made Santa Barbara birders confident that he would return every year just as Jewell's B.O. did. In early summer we got the bad news: the Planks' property had been condemned to make room for a new road connecting the mesa area with the city proper, and the Planks were being forced to move. It was painful for me to picture such a busy and lovingly tended feeding station crushed by bulldozers, and I stayed away from that part of town.

In the fall, preparations began for the annual Christmas bird count. The previous year, 1963, Santa Barbara with its 166 species ranked fifth out of 688 counts made in the United States and Canada. None of us entertained much hope of equaling this figure in 1964. Too many things had happened—a disastrous fire, encroaching subdivisions, disappearing green belts. The reduction of Stow Lake and pond was further complicated by a new housing project and meant virtually the elimination of this region as a good area for waterfowl and shore birds. The Bird Refuge, at the southeastern end of the city, was in poor shape, and while the Santa Barbara Audubon Society was working toward the gigantic task of freshening and aerating the water and landscaping the part adjacent to the railroad tracks, little had been accomplished so far.

Count day arrived, cold and cloudy, with wind and rain in most sections of the prescribed territorial limits. At noon I got in touch with Nelson Metcalf by prearrangement. We were both discouraged by the morning's results; it seemed unlikely that we would see more than 140 species. A large portion of the area Jewell and I had covered was devastated by fire and we'd found the number of birds ordinarily common there, like quail and Bewick wrens and wrentits, had decreased; only the Oregon juncos, foraging on the ground among the burned oaks and the skeletons of little mammals, seemed to have increased. Nelson too was having bad luck and hadn't turned up one unusual shore bird or warbler or a single tanager or oriole. During the week an orchard oriole had been reported at Carpinteria, but it was the wrong time and the wrong place as far as the count was concerned since it was seen outside the fifteen-mile-diameter circle and on the wrong day.

It brought us, however, to the subject of Mr. Chocolate and the Planks, who'd moved to a new house on the north side of town. What about the road that had dispossessed them? Was it already built, still under construction, or perhaps not yet started? This last possibility offered a mere wisp of straw but Nelson clutched at it.

He called me late that night. The road remained on the drawing board, and the tecomaria was still untouched by the bulldozers. Fluttering among its glistening leaflets, looking good enough to eat, was Mr. Chocolate. And, as if he alone were not enough, in the same tecomaria was a western tanager and a short distance away, a Bullock oriole. Our count day ended with a total of 155 species, considerably fewer than the preceding year but more than we had anticipated. Santa Barbara was credited with only 154 species in the published report in *Audubon Field Notes* (Vol. 19, No. 2) due to the omission of half a dozen myrtle warblers—a mistake undoubtedly ours rather than that of the meticulous editor, Allan D. Cruickshank.

The Christmas count always has its surprises and moments of suspense, its triumphs and failures, and most important of all, a new batch of devotees. People who've taken part in one count seldom want to miss the next. And the chances are they won't have to, no matter what area of the United States or Canada they happen to be in when December rolls around. In 1964, over 750 counts were submitted, and some twenty-five were turned down because of rule-breaking, illegibility and other reasons. The number of people participating in a count varied from one, such as Ramon Burron of Cambridge Bay, N. W. Territories, who spent four hours walking five miles in 50°-below-zero weather to record a single species—eleven rock ptarmigans—to the eighty-six counters of Coot Bay–Everglades National Park, Florida, who covered their balmy region on foot, by car, by boat and by airplane to record 174 species.

Dedicated birders frequently participate in more than one count, some in as many as half a dozen. This is especially true in Texas, and I must mention here what birders from other parts of the country learn for themselves, that for sheer verve and vigor the members of the Texas Ornithological Society cannot be surpassed.

Many bird watchers traveling in December will stop to take part in the nearest count and find themselves in the company of complete strangers, wading through mud flats, climbing cliffs and crossing rivers they didn't even know existed. Thus, Brooks Atkinson, a New York bird watcher who used to dabble in drama criticism, was with one of our Santa Barbara groups in 1963. So was retired Navy Captain Elgin Hurlbert with his wife, Wini. They live in Pacific Grove, California, and after taking part in the Monterey Peninsula count, they came down for ours a week later, prior to starting out on a long trailer trip across country. We lost track of them until more than a year later when the 1964 Christmas count edition of *Audubon Field Notes* was published, and we found their names listed among the counters both at Bentsen State Park and La Sal Vieja, Texas. A number of birders, wanting to be members just once of a champion count team, have journeyed to Cocoa, Florida, around Christmas time to join Allan Cruickshank's group, which at one time held the record of 204 species. This record fell in 1966, when Cocoa upped its count to 206 and was tied by San Diego, California.

There are no rules concerning how the prescribed territory is to be covered in a Christmas count. The commonest ways are by car and by foot, but many other modes of transportation have been listed including skis, snowshoes, canoes, horses, airplanes, jeeps, trucks and motorboats. I have bicycled over part of my territory and on one occasion, when sea birds were blanketed by a deep fog, Ken swam three-quarters of a mile in a 52° ocean to get us a pair of horned grebes for our list.

The Audubon Society's insistence that the Christmas bird count is not a competition seems a bit like claiming that human nature is not human. Of course it's a competition, even if you're only competing with your own record of last year or the year before. If you want to go beyond this and compete with Cocoa, Florida; Tomales Bay or San Diego, California; Freeport or Houston, Texas, good luck! You'll need it.

Old-timers in the field are astonished—some of them disgusted—by the fact that bird watching has become an accepted form of recreation. Credit for this must go to one man in particular, Roger Tory Peterson. He has made bird watching respectable and it has made him famous. A fair exchange.

Mnemos

The bird arriving here in the spring is dominated by one great purpose. He must find a place to breed, a nesting site safe from predators, with food and water available and suitable singing posts to announce his identity and intentions, his charm and vigor and the fact that he has title to a nice piece of real estate. The bird arriving in autumn to spend the winter has only himself to consider and is less affected by changes in his environment. The Krigers' Baltimore oriole and red-breasted sapsucker have returned to the same willow every winter for six years, though there is now a large house practically on top of the tree and a lively family with a dog and cat in the yard.

The land bird population of our area in the winter remains fairly constant in spite of the encroachments of people. This is due partly to the emerging adaptability of the birds themselves and partly to the fact that every new development, whether it's an apartment complex, a housing tract, a shopping center or even a parking lot, must be appropriately landscaped. This is, of course, done for the sake of people, not birds, but the birds get the benefit. It is a happy example of serendipity.

If similar arrangements could be made which would indirectly benefit shore birds, their future would look less dim. Every year some wetlands disappear, more sloughs are turned into marinas, more beaches become parking lots, more lakes and rivers are polluted with wastes and pesticides, yet California must provide winter food and sanctuary for thousands upon thousands of shore birds. The hummingbird who has lost his favorite patch of wild tobacco to the bulldozer can easily settle for the fuchsias in the garden of a condominium or the melaleucas planted along a new street. But the egret, deprived of his pond, cannot switch to a swimming pool.

The concept of green belts has been widely accepted, at least in theory. The concept of wet belts, however, is a different matter. We have no local ordinances which guarantee the preservation of a certain percentage of each wet area for the benefit of wildlife, and proposals for such an ordinance have not been seriously considered. To the person blinded by ignorance and fear, a slough is not a place of wonder, it is a breeding ground for mosquitoes, a source of odors and a temptation for children to get their clothes muddy. To the birder a slough is where the great blue heron stands motionless, waiting for a minnow, where the kingfisher rattles from a tree stump and the Forster's tern hawks for dragonflies or dozes on a piece of driftwood. It is where the snowy egret shuffles through the mud on his big yellow feet and the phalarope spins for her supper like a hungry ballerina; where the black-necked stilt and the greater yellowlegs fold up like jackknives to rest, and the sora rail, silent as a shadow, tracks a frog through the salicornia.

With few exceptions, the birds of the Pacific Ocean and of the shores bordering it are seen by local birders only in the fall and winter. They become so familiar to us in their non-breeding plumage that the first time I saw a dunlin in breeding plumage I thought, for one glorious moment, I'd found a new bird. Sometimes in the spring when the plumages are changing we catch a glimpse of a black-bellied plover in the midst of dressing for the most important occasion of his life, or an avocet just assuming his bridegroom's blush or a royal tern his black nuptial cap. But in the main we're accustomed to shore birds at their drabbest and most difficult to identify.

Among birds, as among people, for every rule there's a rule breaker, and in this case it's the willet. He looks exactly the same in June as he does in January because he carries his breeding plumage under his wings and all he has to do is raise them in order to be known, and, presumably, loved.

Just as the willet is the exception, so there are exceptions among willets. Some do not develop the hormonic stimulation necessary to instigate migration to the breeding grounds and consequently will remain here for the summer. We became well acquainted with one of these lone birds through our German shepherd, Brandy. Brandy was born in May and in July we took him on his first trip to the quiet beach which he was to visit every day from then on. The shore birds were long since gone and I was surprised to be greeted by the shrill cries of a willet protesting the invasion of his privacy. Brandy too was surprised. In his limited experience birds were inoffensive creatures that sat in trees or ate quietly on ledges or porch railings. This squawking fury baffled him and he turned and ran back to Ken for protection.

My bird records for the next few months are interspersed with reports on Brandy's development. Watching a German shepherd grow is much like watching a time-lapse sequence in a nature movie, only there's no trick photography needed to improve on nature. The Brandy that got up in the morning was noticeably larger than the one that had gone to bed the night before. At the end of July he weighed in at twenty-three pounds, a month later he was thirty-six pounds and by the end of October, sixty pounds. (Now, at maturity, he weighs 105 pounds and at low tide he leaves tracks in the wet sand like those of the Abominable Snowman.) These changes did not go unnoticed either by Brandy, who became increasingly bold, or by the willet, who kept a more respectful distance.

Every day our visit to the beach began in the same way. The willet, much keener-eyed than mere dogs and people, would spot us getting out of the car and acknowledge our arrival with a scream of outrage. Hearing it, Brandy would respond with a bellow and go charging down the stone steps in pursuit, taking me with him if I happened to be attached to the other end of the leash.

At first both bird and dog played their parts with wild enthusiasm. The chase was intense and earnest, the escape hairbreadth, the sound effects ear-shattering. But as the weeks passed and the game remained a scoreless tie, the players began to show signs of flagging interest. In the middle of the chase Brandy would catch a scent and go ambling off to investigate a dead sand shark or a decayed lobster claw; and the willet, no longer pursued, would stop to probe for a sand flea or stalk a hermit crab; and the game would be over. The willet could then proceed with his bird business, and Brandy with his dog business, each aware through experience of the other's habits and capabilities. Eventually the whole thing boiled down to the merest formality.

The willet, catching sight of Brandy at the top of the steps, would shift his feet and open his bill slightly as if to say, *Ho hum, here comes that hairy beast again.*

And Brandy would answer with the smallest excuse of a bark: *I see that feathered fool is still around. Well, so be it.*

Left alone to cope with problems of adjustment, animals often do a better job than humans.

Bird watchers coming to southern California for the first time invariably arrive with a list of birds they most want to see. Some of these most-wanted species, like the acorn woodpecker and Anna's hummingbird and band-tailed pigeon, are all over the place and could only be missed if you kept your eyes closed and your ears plugged. Others can be found in the right places in abundance, such as the yellow-billed magpie and Laurence's goldfinch. Still others must be searched for in particular habitats, but can usually be located. Among these are the white-tailed kite, California condor and phainopepla. Others are completely unpredictable and among them I would include most of the pelagic birds.

These creatures have the remoteness and mystery of an element alien to us. Some Sierra Club members are as familiar with Santa Barbara County's back country as they are with the city—they know every peak and potrero in that vast, rugged wilderness, and every roadless valley and barranca. But even the keenest sailor is a stranger to the sea. A thousand things happen under his keel which he will never know about. The wave he passes which floats a marbled murrelet he will never pass again, and once the ashy petrel fluttering in a water furrow disappears from his view, he could spend a year looking for it and never find it.

It seems impossible for anyone to write as intimately about the pink-footed shearwater or the pigeon guillemot as about the kingbird or the house finch without adding sea water to his veins and eel grass to his diet. (I suspect R.M. Lockley of meeting both these conditions while he was doing his marvelous book on shearwaters.) Simply locating them is chancy enough. We have gone out after shearwaters and found half a million, and we have gone out another year, at the same time, to the same place and under the same conditions, and found none.

Once a pelagic bird is located, the business of identification arises. If the seas are rough—and in our channel they often are—it's not easy to hang on to the railing of a boat while focusing binoculars, balancing a field guide and trying to keep both them and yourself dry.

There are additional problems. If a black-footed albatross is in the vicinity he can readily be seen since he's about three feet long and has a seven-foot wingspread. But a great many of the pelagic birds are tiny and the boat has to be practically on top of them before they're visible floating in the trough of waves or barely skimming the surface of the water to cut down air resistance and conserve their energy. The sailor's old prayer, "O God, Thy sea is so large and my boat is so small," should have a bird watcher's addition, "and Thy sea birds should be a lot bigger." The least and the ashy petrels are the size of myrtle warblers and white-crowned sparrows, respectively. Our rare winter visitor, Cassin's auklet, is no larger than a kingbird. Murrelets and puffins range from the size of towhees to the size of flickers.

A male red-shafted flicker, at fourteen inches, may look pretty large and conspicuous perched on top of a telephone pole. Surrounded by a 63,985,000-square-mile expanse of water he would change considerably in relative size and visibility. He would also, if he were to become a sea bird, lose his fetching red whisker marks and his handsome wing and tail linings. The plumages of sea birds are confined to somber grays and whites and blacks, and brilliant colors appear only in the hard, horny parts like the red-orange-yellow beaks of puffins and the carmine feet of pigeon guillemots.

For some time I wondered if the albatross, which was the nemesis of a certain mariner, was destined to be mine too, but after a dozen pelagic trips I finally found one. Meanwhile, my real nemesis has been identified. He is nothing so imposing as an albatross, being only ten inches long and not noted for any special display either in the air or in the water. I have seen all the other members of his family which frequent our area. I have even been on boats when my nemesis was spotted by practically everyone on board, but I missed him by a fraction of a second, the blink of an eye, a sudden lurch of the boat, a binocular lens fogged by salt spray, an ill-timed sandwich in the galley or snatch of conversation in the stern. Whatever the reason, I've repeatedly missed seeing the ancient murrelet.

I am prepared for him. I know, without consulting the field guide, exactly what he looks like and how I can instantaneously distinguish him from the two brothers he closely resembles. Even if I sincerely wanted to forget this information, I couldn't. I am the lifetime victim of my own mnemonic devices.

Bird watchers used to begin their hobby at a very early age. They had to. In the absence of adequately illustrated field guides and moderately priced, easy-to-carry binoculars, learning about birds was a lengthy process, not unlike learning in general before the invention of the printing press. Then the second quarter of the twentieth century brought vast improvements in color photography and reproduction and in the uses of lightweight metals; the Japanese started manufacturing precision optical instruments within the average man's price range, Roger Tory Peterson introduced the first of his field guides, and suddenly it was no longer necessary to begin bird watching at seven or eight. You could begin at forty-five. As I did.

Well aware that I had many years of study and observation to make up, I decided to avail myself of all possible memory aids. I've always used mnemonic devices, especially those involving rhyme, so when I was confronted with two pages of warblers to memorize I did the natural thing. From the check list of local birds I picked the warblers seen in our area, omitting those easy to remember, like the yellow, the orange-crowned and the black-throated gray. The rest I put into a poem:

> *Myrtle has a white throat,*
> *Audubon a yellow,*
> *Townsend has black throat and ears—*

What a dirty fellow.
Wilson wears a beanie,
Black to match his eye.
Yellow throat a black mask,
Though females don't comply.
Yellow head and white chest
Is little Hermit's chief test.
MacGillivray's hood is greenish blue,
Just like Nashville's head in hue.

Since these literally deathless lines were written I've seen many thousands of Audubon warblers and there is no need to remind myself that they have yellow throats. Yet the warbler ditty is so strongly fixed in my mind that whenever I hear the word Audubon, I silently and automatically add "a yellow."

Will I, in the next thirty or forty years, be freed from "Audubon a yellow?" It seems unlikely. Getting rid of a mnemonic device requires much more ingenuity than acquiring it—more, in fact, than I have currently in stock. The sight of an egret, a bittern or a heron may inspire other people to compose works of art or to commune with nature, but I find myself repeating the words branded on my cortex:

The eager bitter heron
Is short of neck when airin'.

On the theory that sharing a load lightens it, I would like to pass this couplet along to all new bird watchers to help them remember that bitterns have naturally short necks, egrets and herons fly with their necks folded, and, by inference of omission, ibises and cranes fly with their necks extended.

Sharing may well be the only answer to my problem. What I need is a dozen or so people going around muttering to themselves:

"It's Nutty to have a dirty neck." Or perhaps, "It is common to be half-bald, but poor Forster is all bald." Or, "Wred wrump, wrock wren."

The last is self-explanatory. The first refers to the fact that the Nuttall woodpecker has a greater expanse of black around the neck than has his almost-twin, the ladder-backed woodpecker. The second applies to terns in fall plumage when the common tern loses half his black head covering and the Forster's tern all of it. It helps to remember this if you know, as I do, a man called Forster who is as bald as a tern egg.

"Black-capped Hutton rang his solitary bell." That sentence could be the beginning of a somber English mystery that takes place in an isolated country house. Actually it's a list of the vireos which have wing bars, the black-capped, Hutton, solitary and Bell.

> *Downy has lots*
> *More white spots.*

I find this an easy way to distinguish the downy from the hairy woodpecker when I don't want to put my trust in the difference in size.

> *"The cuckoo can converge his eyes*
> *On things in front and things behindwise,"* is not going to

help you identify a cuckoo, but you might use it as a conversational gambit some day when you're desperate. Another along the same line goes,

> *Shearwaters, petrels and fulmars smell*
> *Like musk, which isn't very well.*

With this tucked in a corner of your mind, if you should ever find yourself on an uninhabited sea island and detect the odor of musk, you'll be able to deduce that there must be a shearwater, fulmar or petrel somewhere upwind. Conversely, if you don't know what musk smells like and want to find out, go look for an uninhabited island with shearwaters, fulmars, or petrels on it. In either case you are prepared. If you'd rather just forget the whole thing, do so. I can't.

The preceding memory aids were based on rhyme, alliteration, plays on words and allusions. Once in a while I've managed to use a combination of methods, as in:

> *Gamble, you silly cuss,*
> *On a black umbilicus.*

This is just another way of saying that Gambel's is the only North American quail which has a black bellybutton, a piece of information not eagerly sought after, perhaps, but useful to a new birder caught in quail country without a field guide—possibly the same birder who goes to the uninhabited sea island to locate a shearwater, fulmar or petrel in order to find out what musk smells like.

> *Rock ptarmigans sound like frogs,*
> *White-tailed ptarmigans sound like woodpeckers.*

For the sake of the rhyme it would naturally be much better if white-tailed ptarmigans sounded like dogs or hogs. But they don't, so this has to stand as an example of a mnemonic device, or mnemo, that works because of its defect: it has no rhyme where one is expected.

Sometimes I must resort to a mnemo when, in spite of repeated studying, I find it impossible to distinguish between two birds of similar appearance. This was the case when Ken and I decided to take a trip to southern Arizona in May of 1965. Our plans were along the same lines as those of other birding trips but a little more elaborate. All available books were consulted, check lists were sent for, and Mary Hyland lent me the journal she kept when she and Tom covered the area. From these various sources I made a list divided into two sections: birds I'd see simply by keeping my eyes open, and birds I'd be likely to find only with patience, luck and good weather.

In the latter group were two species of sparrow, Cassin's and Botteri's, found in the same arid habitat and almost identical in appearance. The situation demanded a mnemo. I hereby share it with any reader who might find himself confronted by two look-alike sparrows in a patch of sacaton grass in the southwestern desert:

> *Whether a son or a daughtery,*
> *Cassin is grayer than Botteri.*

While most of my mnemos are applied to birds, I've also used them on bird watchers. I recall my initial meeting, at a Western Audubon Conference at Asilomar, with that delightful pair of birders, Captain Elgin B. Hurlbert, U.S.N. Ret., and his wife. The name, which was uncommon enough, was complicated by the fact that Captain Hurlbert was called by a most unusual nickname. Drastic measures were called for. I wrote on my mnemo pad: "If the ox whinnies, hurl it, Bert." The picture of the great beast flying through the air is so vivid in my mind that I know I'll never be able to avoid seeing it every time I meet Oxy Hurlbert and his wife, Wini.

Mnemos are of special importance in the case of pelagic birds because the watcher is already at a disadvantage trying to focus on a moving object from a moving object. If he has to stop and look up a picture in a field guide, he is doubling the disadvantage. It is much easier to use a mnemo, one that will call your attention immediately to that aspect of the bird which distinguishes him from all others.

The murrelets are a case in point. Three species are seen in local waters in the winter, Xantus', the marbled and the ancient. They appear mainly in pairs or small groups, floating in the furrows between waves or skimming along the surface or diving into the water in alarm at the sight of a boat. All are towhee-sized and colored dark above and white below. I had no trouble with the first two species:

> *Marbled type—*
> *Sides have a stripe.*
> *Xantus by name—*
> *Very plain.*

My mnemo for the ancient murrelet is different from any of the others in that it's in the first person, as if I unconsciously knew, when I made it up, that this murrelet was very special, was, in fact, destined to be my nemesis.

Each time I board a boat the words go through my head—and every ancient murrelet in the channel heads for the open seas:

> *My ancient cap is black,*
> *Gray is my ancient back.*

Hanky-Panky

Spring was on its way.

By mid-February the blue gums were in full bloom. Their whitish fuzzy blossoms blew in gusts across our windows and covered the vacant field next-door like hoar frost. In the tops of the trees Allen and Anna hummingbirds fought with noisy abandon, and restless flocks of cedar waxwings fed on the bugs and nectar in the flowers as well as the petals themselves. These three species show no seasonal change in plumage, so they were no different from the way they'd been in the fall, except that possibly the waxwings looked a bit sharper after the addition of the marble bird bath to their diet. (The final sliver of the bird bath had been thrown in the trashcan.)

It was in the Audubon warblers, occupying the same eucalyptus trees, that real changes were occurring. During the last two weeks of February and the first two of March they were busy donning their traveling togs, dark gray topcoat with black stripes and a white sidepatch, dashing little yellow cap and solid-black scarf draped with careless elegance across the chest. Mature birds retained their yellow throats and younger birds acquired theirs. This solved one of my problems: during the fall and winter I'd had to strain to differentiate the young Audubons from the myrtles, since both have white throats. The white of the myrtle's throat extends to outline the cheek somewhat and this species also has a light eyestripe, but neither of these field marks is very noticeable and I had to look at a hundred Audubons to find a myrtle, much rarer in our parts.

The passage of time changed all this. Myrtle and Audubon assumed strictly individualistic plumage, one of nature's devices to ensure the continuation of the species and prevent hybridization. The myrtles also assumed a characteristic quite funny in such small birds—they became noticeably more aggressive and would go to considerable trouble to clear the ledge of Audubons before settling down to eat. I've never seen a myrtle act this way toward any bird except an Audubon or another myrtle. Over many thousands of years he has learned a lesson in survival: the species seeking the same food that he seeks is his enemy, and he has more to fear from a tiny warbler than from any cast of hawks or gathering of eagles.

At the beginning of March the oak trees too came into bloom. From a distance they appeared to be covered with dark pink blossoms, but the binoculars revealed that these were actually the new leaves, as yet unfurled, and the real blossoms were the catkins hanging down. These catkins proved a popular food with the white-crowned and gold-crowned sparrows, and later, the brown-headed cowbirds.

The pittosporum undulatum was also in full bloom by now and whole sections of the city were permeated by its poignant sweetness which is to me the loveliest of all flower scents and the one that evokes California and home more than a hundred thousand orange blossoms. The flowers and seeds of this kind of pittosporum, which can grow forty feet in height and nearly that in width, are not particularly attractive to birds but its dense, deep foliage provides excellent cover for them. They use it for protection from weather and predators, and as a safe roost at night. Often at twilight I've seen whole flocks of birds disappear into the largest of our pittosporums with scarcely the telltale flutter of a leaf. At this point I wrote in my notebook:

The season of hanky-panky is upon us—male linnets on the porch railing feeding willing females, red-winged blackbirds posturing and singing oo-ka-lee *at the Bird*

*Refuge, green-backed finches whistling all over the Botanic
Garden, song sparrows calling from the acacias down by
the creek, press, press, press, Presbyterians, sometimes
giving the Presbyterians one less press. All over town the
doves are nesting, the bandtails and the towhees, the
mockers and hummingbirds. And so on . . . ad, one
hopes, infinitum.*

One does, indeed.

We put out nesting materials, strips of cloth and short lengths of
twine hung on the clothesline, yarn unraveled from an old sweater,
balls of cotton tied in the trees, or piled in tiny wicker cornucopias
left over from Thanksgiving, pieces of kapok placed in the venti-
lated plastic boxes fresh berries are packed in. The hummingbirds
preferred to hover while pulling out shreds of cotton through the
interstices of the wicker. Some birds grabbed and flew off before I
could raise my binoculars, and others perched on the side of the
plastic box or on the clothesline and made their selection with the
careful gravity of engineers about to try a new kind of building
material. Some particularly fussy linnets, dissastisfied with what I
had to offer them, took their business to a house across the canyon. In due time Renée Westermeyer, the lady of the house, reported that the large umbrella she kept on her patio no longer had
any tassels on it.

The behavior of a male green-backed goldfinch caused quite a
few comments on the part of my bird-watching friends. The goldfinch always brought his industrious little bride with him, and for a
very good reason: she did all the work. He would lead her to the
clothesline, which was hung with bits of string and colored yarn,
and she would begin meticulously testing them for size and texture
and color, since she wanted nothing too large or gaudy or rough.
Meanwhile, he perched on a twig in the nearby tea tree and
preened his feathers. The most he contributed to the proceedings
was a lively snatch of song now and then, probably intended to
assure her that he was manning the lookout post while she was
womanning the nest.

The titmice and orange-crowned warblers were steady customers for the cotton balls in the cornucopia. So was the hooded oriole, but for an entirely different reason. Over a period of about a week I'd watched this bird, a female, gathering the long tough fibers from the leaves of a Washington fan palm in the neighborhood. (Hooded orioles in southern California have such a predilection for building their nests in these trees that they were once called "palm-leaf orioles.") At the same time, the cornucopia in the tree outside my office was being emptied of cotton balls as fast as I could replenish the supply. I naturally assumed that the balls were being used to make a soft lining in various birds' nests and I was surprised to find a dozen or so scattered around the patio and at least that many more caught in the boxwood hedge and the bougainvillaea. It was as if some bird, perhaps a flicker, whose weight the cornucopia couldn't support, had been awkwardly trying to land on it anyway, spilling the cotton balls each time I put out a new batch.

Then one morning, as I was sitting down to write, the culprit appeared. It was the female hooded oriole. She landed gracefully on the rim of the cornucopia, picked up a cotton ball in her beak and deliberately dropped it over the side to the ground. When the cornucopia was empty she flew off. I filled it up again. Half an hour later she was back to repeat her performance. No one witnessing it could believe it was anything but a deliberate and well-motivated action—only what was the motivation?

Once the cotton balls were tossed on the ground she showed no further interest, so it was clear that she didn't want them as nest-lining. Two theories occur to me, but until some form of oriole communication is discovered they'll very likely remain theories.

There is a certain family of insects, *Aprophorinae,* sometimes called froghoppers, whose young are hidden in a spittle of white froth which protects them while they live by sucking sap. I've often watched orioles go after these spittle insects in the conifers in our canyon. The foamy masses bear considerable resemblance to cotton, so it's possible that the female oriole was testing the cotton balls in the cornucopia to see if they contained food, and discovering that they didn't, chucked them out. This theory seems to me to insult the little lady's intelligence. Birds may not be the smartest of God's creatures but where food is concerned they learn fast, and I can't believe it would have taken that many cotton balls to convince the oriole she was on the wrong track.

What is more, she gave no sign that she was investigating the balls. She grabbed one after another and without hesitation chucked them out as if she was getting rid of them as fast as possible because they represented a threat to her and her family. Most people know the trick of sticking pieces of cotton into the screen of a door or window in order to repel houseflies. The idea behind it is that the houseflies will stay away from the cotton because they mistake it for the nest of a certain wasp that likes housefly meat. Perhaps the hooded oriole was acting under a similar misapprehension. We must give her credit anyway for knowing her business—she successfully raised three broods that spring and summer. And I went through an awful lot of cotton balls. Every bird's nest in the neighborhood, except the hooded oriole's, must have been lined by Johnson and Johnson.

The sight of a band of bushtits twittering and tumbling from bush to bush makes it difficult to believe that they could ever settle down to the sober business of raising a family. Yet the bushtits were among the first birds to nest. As early as the middle of January, I'd noticed that the flocks passing through the canyon were getting smaller as the birds were beginning to pair off. One particular couple we came to know very well since they chose one of our oaks as the site for their elaborate nest, the cornucopia as their home-furnishing store and the porch railing as their restaurant.

The bushtit is an insect-eating bird and no garden could have a better friend, especially since scale and aphids make up about one-fifth of his diet. I'm sure our little couple would have been content with this fare if they hadn't seen so many other birds eating doughnuts and decided to try a taste. One bite and they were addicted. Almost any time of the day I could look out my office window and see them pecking happily away at a doughnut, often at the same time as the yellowthroat and the Bewick's wren, the Audubon warblers and song sparrows. These are all tiny creatures but none is so tiny as the bushtit. His thumb-sized body and vivacious movements make other birds seem large and clumsy.

On February 13 the bushtits began gathering cotton from the

cornucopia. On February 24, I watched them shredding a piece of Kleenex in the front yard, and on March 6, I saw one of them carrying leaves in his beak. While they were engaged in relatively quiet pursuits like these, the difference in the eye color of the male and female was much more noticeable than when the birds are seen only in constantly moving flocks. Getting close enough to bushtits to study them is no problem since they usually ignore the presence of a human being, with good reason—they present no challenging target for the gun or slingshot, no taste treat for the palate, no handsome trophy for the den wall, and so they are indeed fearless of men. Getting these lively little devils to stay still while you study them is another matter.

I'd been watching the flocks in our canyon every day for a long time but it wasn't until the pair came to taste doughnuts that I became aware of the noticeable difference in eye color, and even then I wasn't positive which color belonged to which sex. The Peterson field guide simply stated that "females are said to have light eyes, males dark." I knew this was true of the black-eared bushtit found in New Mexico, but the female of this species is different from the male in plumage as well. In the common bushtit of our area, eye color is the only noticeable difference between the sexes.

The little birds told me which was which, in a very simple and direct way. On March 10, I heard the saucy chatter of a chipmunk from the tangle of ceanothus trees and I picked up my binoculars to look for him. A pair of bushtits wandered into my field of vision, gleaning among the leaves for bugs. At least one of them was gleaning. The other evidently had different things in mind, for he quickly and precisely mounted the first bird, hopped away, returned and mounted again. The whole business didn't take half a minute, during which time the female showed no reaction whatever. She didn't stop eating or even turn her head, surely a unique example of sang-froid.

The male's eyes were as black as beads of jet, the female's as tawny as topaz. They gave her a look of continual curiosity, like that of a wide-eyed child. It suited her to a T, for nothing in our yard could be kept a secret from this diminutive creature.

She knew where the earwig hid by day beneath a rock, under which leaf the whitefly had laid her eggs and where the young of the black scale crawled along the limbs of the olive trees. She spotted where the spider had hidden his dinner fly in the brush pile, where a gopher's digging had brought a batch of bugs to the surface and which loquat tree was the scene of a fruit-fly orgy. She knew which citrus tree the ants were using to herd their aphids and from which rosebush the leaf roller had borrowed a leaf for his pupa to occupy in privacy. But all this was insignificant compared to her really important piece of knowledge—where the doughnuts were.

At this season I was putting out a dozen doughnuts at a time in various places around the house and yard. If the bushtit found a purple finch or gold-crowned sparrow already occupying the doughnut in the tea tree, she simply went on to the next one in the cotoneaster, or the next hanging from a nail on the porch or a clothes hook under the dining-room window. Until March 25 she brought her mate with her. After that she came alone. For more than a month, almost every time I looked out a window, I would see her on one doughnut or another and it became obvious that she was eating for two, or five, or even more. Many birds which subsist on seeds and vegetable matter will, when their young are hatched, feed them insects, since the protein is more nourishing and fewer feedings are necessary. But this was my first experience with an insect-eating bird feeding vegetable matter to its young.

As time passed and the female kept appearing alone I began to suspect that her mate had met with some disaster and left her a widow with a family to raise by herself. Male and female bushtits under ordinary conditions share equally the duties of incubation and gathering insects to feed the young. Deprived of assistance, perhaps the female was feeding them what was readily available—doughnuts. I had visions of a weak and sickly brood raised entirely on carbohydrates.

Then, during the third week of April, I happened to see the male and female together gleaning in an oak tree. I like to think that this was the same male and that all the times I waited for him to show up at the doughnuts, he was in fact gathering bugs to provide his children with a more conventional and healthful diet.

Whether or not it was the same male, the same procedure started again: the lady began gathering cotton and shredding leaves and bits of paper, and on May 10 she brought the male to the doughnut. They ate together for a couple of weeks as they had in March, then she began coming alone. During the raising of the second brood her visits weren't nearly so frequent, probably because our place was one vast nursery by this time and so many young of the larger species were being fed there that the little bushtit was intimidated. In the middle of June she stopped coming altogether.

During the summer, flocks of bushtits began to form again, starting with family groups—the young being recognizable by their shorter tails and less skilful acrobatics—and getting larger and noisier as the weeks passed. Their constant twittering, which is the way the members keep in touch as they forage from bush to bush, changed only when the sparrow hawk from the adjacent canyon came over to visit. I've never seen any sparrow hawk in this area show the slightest interest in catching a bushtit, but evidently he represents an old and respected enemy, for at the sight of him the tiny birds began issuing their alarm cry, high, shrill, pulsating notes that seemed to be coming from anywhere and everywhere, like the singing of tree frogs. Our visitor was apparently offended by such an unfriendly greeting and he never stayed more than a few minutes, long enough for a short bath and a quick shake.

That fall and winter, watching the bushtits as they went through the front yard combing the arbutus and eugenias and pyracanthas, I would look at them and wonder which one was the little lady I had seen so often and so intimately for a third of the year. When the little birds passed through the back yard, however, I had no need to wonder. The flock would forage as usual through the cotoneaster and the tea tree, but then, as it passed my office window on the way to the elderberry bush, one small gray form would detach itself from the group. Having been alerted by the sound of the birds' twittering, I was always ready to catch the first gleam of two golden eyes and watch as the little female lit on the doughnut in the soap bark tree. There was a kind of furtive joy in her manner. Aphids and scale were all very well for the ordinary bushtit, but not for one who has known the delights of doughnuts and even passed them along to her children.

On these gastronomical side trips she never brought any members of her family or the group; they were strictly private and solitary excursions. Nor in all my weeks of watching did I see any member pay the slightest attention either when she left the group or when she hurried to catch up with it again. Certainly no attempt was made to follow her, although at least one male, possibly two, knew that doughnuts were available and how to reach them. I can offer no explanation for this. Perhaps there isn't any and we must simply accept the word of the ornithologists who state that the bushtit is an impulsive bird given to whims and fancies. This describes our little female rather well: she had a fancy for doughnuts and a whim of steel.

Birders in bushtit country should not merely be content with identifying a flock of these birds. They would do well to observe each individual carefully, since one or two may turn out to be not bushtits at all but other tiny birds who've joined up with the flock to forage. In our area these others are mainly warblers. In the company of bushtits I've found Townsend warblers, Audubon, myrtle, black-throated gray, orange-crowned, Wilson, yellow and hermit.

Winter arrived and the visits of our small gourmet friend became less frequent. Unlike some species of birds which have a regular routine you can set your watch by, bushtits are spasmodic foragers. When the flock passed quite close to the house, our friend would pause for a bite of doughnut; when the foraging was too far away to permit her to rejoin the other members of her group easily, she played it safe and stayed with them.

In midwinter the roving bands of bushtits began to get smaller as pairs formed and left the group. The first week in February, I caught sight of a male bushtit cocking an inquisitive black eye at the cornucopia. The next morning, in a heavy rain, two of them arrived together, male and female. And high in the air the red-shouldered hawk was screaming at his mate, ordering her to *come here, come here, come here.* From the acacias down by the creek the song sparrow was pressing for Presbyterians and the Hutton's vireo whistling for sweets, sweets, sweets.

". . . All over town the doves are nesting, the bandtails and the towhees, the mockers and hummingbirds. And so on . . . ad, one hopes, infinitum."

Life in the Worm Factory

What distinguishes a bird from all other living creatures? Feathers. And what distinguishes an acorn woodpecker from all other birds? Practically everything.

Acorn woodpeckers are the characters of our part of the bird world, the true uniques, in appearance, voice, mannerisms, feeding, nesting and care of young. So it was natural enough, I suppose, that they should have been the ones responsible for our going into the worm business.

The word "togetherness" usually conjures up a picture of a large family group celebrating Thanksgiving or Christmas. To me it conjures up the telephone pole beside our driveway, for in it lived a family group that celebrated every day in the year. I don't know exactly how many members constituted the group—an acorn woodpecker census, as I'll show later, is not simple, and estimates of numbers tend to be too high since the birds are so noisy—but I would say between seven and nine.

Our road in Montecito is a circle, half a mile around. Three families of woodpeckers lived on this street, approximately equal distances apart. The first family had its headquarters in the top of a dead palm tree. I had almost nothing to do with this group except to watch for it in passing. The second group I came to know better. It used a telephone pole located beside the creek that ran through the neighboring canyon, an area of numerous mature live oaks, any one of which would have made an excellent storage tree, in my opinion. But the woodpeckers didn't invite my opinion. For their storage tree they had chosen the attic of a pretty little white frame cottage whose owner, Miss Holbrook, fortunately for the birds, was both a nature lover and somewhat deaf.

The third family was ours—or we were theirs, depending on point of view. Less than fifty feet separated the window beside my bed from the excavation in the telephone pole where they slept, if so mild a word can be used to describe the deathlike coma into which they fell with the darkness. I heard their guttural goodnights as they squeezed and squashed into the hole, and in the morning, their throat clearings as their metabolism quickened after the torpor of the night. Their temperatures rose, their bodies warmed, their senses became alert as they returned to life. With life came hunger, and with hunger, the hope that the Millars would be serving breakfast al fresco, as usual. They chose a sentry to keep watch.

Acorn woodpeckers are not the earliest risers in the bird world —based on the records I've kept, I would have to give this distinction to the brown towhee—but they were well ahead of me. By the time I opened my eyes the sentry was already perched on a dead branch of the eucalyptus tree, loosening up his voice box with a few rolling notes now and then. The instant I stepped out on the porch, he let go:

Jacob, Jacob, wake up, wake up!
Jack up, Jack up, get up, get up!
Yack up, yack up, yack up, yack up, yack up, yack up, yack up, yack up, yack up.

This last sequence is like a crescendo and decrescendo, reaching its height of volume and pitch on the fifth *yack up,* then decreasing. It sounds so much like a carpenter sawing through a board that I actually mistook it for just that. When we first moved here I used to wonder how our neighbor, a professional man with a demanding job, could afford to spend so much time at home building things.

The sentry's calls brought immediate responses. Pretty soon the canyon was an echo chamber of noise, for if there was one thing the acorn woodpeckers liked it was a loud and lively family conference. They seemed ready to confer at any time from dawn to dusk, on any subject from soup to sunspots. At least that's the impression a listener might get from their variety of noises and their range of pitch and volume. They talked to their relatives and friends and to the other species of birds who'd responded to the breakfast call, especially the scrub jays, their chief competitors for acorns, or in this case, doughnuts and bread. They also talked to themselves. Under ordinary circumstances this was done quietly, rather like a person muttering to himself while he tries to solve a personal problem. But there was one bird, a hotheaded male, whose soliloquies could be heard all the way to City Hall. He will be formally introduced later.

Breakfast was served on a corner of the porch railing, in a wooden dish that had once been a salad bowl. A large nail had been driven through the dish to keep it steady and to serve as a spear for two doughnuts. This left room for a couple of pieces of bread, broken into bits, and a few grapes when they were in season. I have never seen woodpeckers go after grapes on the vine—it would be difficult for them to find a proper landing place —but they ate them readily out of the wooden dish, frequently flying across the canyon to hide them behind the loose bark of a blue gum eucalyptus which also served as a hiding place for other choice tidbits. Remembering our little wine-making friend Richard the rat, I used to watch the woodpeckers carefully for signs of tippling. I never saw any. Either they ate the grapes before the process of fermentation started, or, more likely, they forgot about them since they invariably store much more food than they can possibly eat.

Nature has been generous to the acorn woodpecker. He is not dependent, as his relatives are, on the vagaries of insect life, nor is it necessary for him to fight for seeds or vegetation that are in short supply. Our part of California is filled with oaks and acorns, and living has been relatively easy for the woodpeckers dependent on them. Their abundance so testifies. Santa Barbara's Christmas bird census always lists several hundred of them. In last year's Christmas bird census Santa Barbara listed 456—the highest count in the nation.

As soon as the sentry had issued the call for breakfast, he himself came down to the wooden dish to eat. I knew it was a male because he lacked the broad black forehead band that marks the female and is noticeable at a considerable distance. (For some reason this sexual dimorphism is not often mentioned in bird books.) I wasn't sure whether it was the same male who acted as sentry all the time. On some mornings I noticed a decidedly pink cast to the normally whitish eye, which led me to believe that more than one male bird was involved. I still believe it—not, however, on this evidence. Dr. Mary Erickson, an ornithologist at the University of California at Santa Barbara who has been doing field work on these woodpeckers for a long time, tells me that this pinkish cast is not due to pigmentation but to a suffusion of blood caused by stress or excitement. She has observed it frequently in the eyes of woodpeckers who are being banded.

I knew from the sleekness and brightness of his coat that the sentry was an adult bird. Young birds often show dark eyes—perhaps because their pupils are expanded after time spent in the murkiness of the nest hole—and considerable red in the underplumage of the chest, neck and head, a reminder of their close relationship with the red-headed woodpecker of the East and Midwest, *Melanerpes erythrocephalus*. The acorn woodpecker's scientific name, *Melanerpes formicivorus,* meaning creeping black anteater, was based on inadequate or faulty information. Ants constitute such a small percentage of the diet that it seems likely they're ingested by accident while the birds are eating acorns or other nuts and fruits.

The number of these woodpeckers feeding from the wooden dish varied according to the time of year. In spring and summer there were a great many—I didn't attempt to count individual birds since this was impossible without banding; I simply kept track of how often they monopolized the feeder—and in the fall there were absolutely none. I used to think this was due to post-breeding dispersal, families splitting up and moving from one pole or tree to another pole or tree when the groups became too large and the quarters too unsanitary. These movements did occur every summer, but the birds never went far. When the family in the telephone pole beside our driveway moved, for instance, it was only to the large dead eucalyptus tree on the edge of the property. This location was no further away from the wooden dish than the other, yet in September the birds stopped coming. I would see them hurry past our porch railing as if it were a bird trap and doughnuts were poison bait and I a sinister stranger; I, who for months hadn't been able to step out of a door without evoking a canyonful of clangorous "good mornings."

It was as though our house had suddenly been declared off-limits. Perhaps a single woodpecker stopped for a rest, a quick grape or a bite of doughnut during that autumn and the early part of winter, but if he did, I failed to see him. No mere moving from one headquarters to another could account for such a complete reversal in behavior pattern. There had to be another explanation. And there was—staring at me from every twig of every coast live oak tree in the canyon. In September the acorns begin to ripen and fancy tidbits that can't be properly stored must be forgotten in the interests of the future.

The group worked busily and harmoniously together. New holes were made in the storage tree, in this case a sycamore, and the acorns were pounded in, usually lengthwise, very occasionally sideways, if this was the way they could best be fitted in. I have seen a woodpecker try a particular acorn in a dozen or more different holes until one was found that was the exact fit, an essential part of the proceedings since the hole is intended to serve as a vise to hold the nut securely while they hammer the shells open with their beaks. Anyone skeptical about the skill and efficiency of these birds would do well to visit a storage tree and try to remove an acorn with his hands. Many ancient California Indian tribes, like the Chumash, Yokut and Shoshone, who shared the territory of these woodpeckers before the arrival of the Spaniards, undoubtedly obtained their method for cracking the nuts from watching the birds. The Indians used a hole in a rock instead of a tree, putting the acorns in securely, pointed end down, and hammering open the wider, exposed end. After the nuts were cured and ground, the tannic acid was removed with hot water and the meal was left to harden into cakes. A friend who has tasted one of these cakes, still made by the Yokuts, claims the Indians would have done better to have copied the woodpeckers entirely and eaten the acorns right out of the shell.

Every day when I passed Miss Holbrook's small white cottage I could hear the woodpeckers at work. Sometimes I stopped to watch them drilling under the eaves as industriously as if the lady of the house was paying them carpenters' union wages.

Work sessions were sometimes silent, sometimes accompanied by loud and spirited conversation which may have sounded to an untutored ear like quarreling. Actually they were good-natured, gregarious birds. For all their crowded living quarters and communal breeding—things which would have driven the human animal to distraction—I never saw them fight with each other. Although there appeared to be a pecking order at the wooden dish, it was maintained merely by a polite exchange of words:

"That's my doughnut you're eating, dear chap."

"Really? I'm terribly sorry. I'll leave immediately, old sport."

They could fight when they wanted to, however, and they often did, their usual adversary being their fellow consumer of acorns, the scrub jay. In battle the woodpeckers took advantage of their proclivity for group action. A single scrub jay eating on the porch railing was, to mix birds and metaphors, a sitting duck for a trio of acorn woodpeckers who took turns dive-bombing him from the roof. No actual physical contact was involved but the harassed jay would nearly always retreat to a more peaceful foraging area. I didn't waste much sympathy on him. He himself used the dive-bombing technique on other birds whenever he had the chance.

In the meantime the scrub jay too was gathering acorns and storing them. His storage method—burying them in the ground, then often as not forgetting where—seemed much inferior to that of the woodpeckers, but was, in fact, a neat piece of ecology. Some acorns would be found and eaten, enabling the jay to survive, and some would be forgotten and reseed, enabling the oaks to survive.

Scrub jays are natural-born buriers. Even when the adobe soil was so dry and hard they had to chisel it like stone, they carried away everything that wasn't nailed down—bits of bread, potato chips, grapes, peanuts, chunks of apple, pretzels, cheese crackers, cookies, hard-boiled eggs—and used every inch of bare ground they could find. Ours would have been quite a unique neighborhood if all the items they buried had sprouted and grown. Only one did, the sunflower seeds. By June the lower and upper terrace and the adjoining field had turned into a forest of the things. Nor did the jays confine their activities to our property. In fact, a stranger visiting our street for the first time would have thought that half the people living on it had decided to go in for commercial sunflower growing. Where the sunflowers stopped marked the territorial limits of the jays who patronized our feeders.

Give these birds a decent-sized piece of bare earth to work with and their planting is as neat and symmetrical as any human gardener's. The man living next door had, at the rear of his house, a dirt road which was no longer in use. The jays took on the job of landscaping it. Down the middle of each tire track they planted sunflower seeds, exactly five inches apart.

Something of a more reasonable size might have escaped detection, but as the sunflowers reached five, six, seven feet they practically forced themselves on the property owner's attention. He was not known as a nature lover, and had, in fact, been somewhat critical of my bandtails landing on his T.V. antenna and *cahooing* too early in the morning. When we met at the mailbox one noon he mentioned that sunflowers were coming up in his avocado orchard and lemon grove and even in his cutting garden, and he asked me if I'd noticed. I had a choice of admitting that I'd noticed or confessing to total blindness, so I said, yes, I'd seen a few sunflowers coming up here and there.

He gave me a suspicious look. "They're all over the place. What do you suppose is at the bottom of it?"

"Sunflower seeds," I said, and retreated before he could pursue the subject further.

People familiar with these noisy, colorful jays might wonder how the man could have missed seeing them at work. The fact is that when a scrub jay is doing something important like burying food or looking for other birds' nests to rob, stalking a lizard or spying out the acorn caches of the woodpeckers, he is absolutely silent and moves with a practiced stealth which makes him almost invisible.

Planting sunflower seeds became such an obsession with our jays that we rarely saw them eat one. When they did, they anchored the seed firmly with their feet and hammered it open with their beaks, in the manner of titmice, quite different from the way the house finches ate. The finches didn't use their feet; they simply held the seed in their beaks and sawed it right down the middle. Every few days I had to sweep their neatly halved hulls off the ledge.

All that cool, moist winter the jays planted, and in the sunny spring the sunflowers grew, and in the hot, dry summer they died. None reached fruition and the diligent but luckless farmers never harvested a single seed. Some of the plants were toppled by wind or their own weight; some couldn't compete with the sturdier natives for what small amount of moisture was available; others were knocked down by dogs and cats or trampled by possums and raccoons and bush bunnies. With the sunflowers died my hope, never too robust, of saving a little money at the feed store. (Not long ago a visiting Easterner was complaining of having to pay fifteen cents a pound for the California-grown sunflower seeds he fed his birds at home. I told him that we Californians paid exactly twice that amount. There are many similar inequities in the price of produce. I once asked an agronomist why, and he replied in about ten thousand words that he didn't know. He seemed delighted when I suggested the reason might be sunspots.)

While the sunflowers were dying, the baby scrub jays flourished. Perched on the porch railing, waiting their turn at the wooden dish, they were fat and fluffy and oddly quiet. In appearance they resembled the Mexican jay of Arizona and New Mexico more than they did their parents. They lacked the scrub jay's eyebrow stripe and half-necklace and cobalt-blue head.

Their innocence and docility was quite touching. Soon they would learn that this is not the way of a jay, but for a little time they were gentle creatures bossed around by nearly all the other birds. They were dive-bombed by woodpeckers, crowded out by blackbirds, pecked by towhees and mockers, pushed off the railing by thrashers, even jostled by sparrows, and they never fought back or let out a single squawk of protest. The only noise they made was a very infrequent sound, loud and shrill, that reminded me of a flicker's. I have heard it no more than a dozen times in our years of operating the feeding station.

There are a number of sounds that can be heard only when you live right in the midst of birds. An excellent example is the good-night of the acorn woodpeckers, a low-pitched, sleepy mumbling made about half an hour after they've disappeared into the telephone pole for the night. The interpreting of bird language, at this stage of our knowledge, must be subjective, so I can only claim that to me this mumbling sounds like the response to a question: "Yes, everything's fine, now settle down and go to sleep."

The acorn woodpeckers provided me with another example of special semantic effects, at least one of them did. He was a mature bird, perhaps the head of the clan, certainly old enough to be set in his ways. In his case this meant that he had very strong likes and dislikes in the food department. One afternoon when I was dusting in the living room I saw an object fly over the porch railing that seemed too small to be any bird I knew. Hope, the poet said, springs eternal in the human breast. And if the breast happens to belong to a birder, the hope is often wild and wonderful: a green-backed twinspot or locust finch from Africa—blown a few thousand miles off course—a red avadavat from the East Indies, a yellow-tailed diamondbird from Australia. I was ready to settle for something found a bit closer to home, like the bee hummingbird of Cuba. The new bird watcher, and I suspect a few old ones as well, lives in a beautiful world where anything is possible! I grabbed my binoculars and rushed into my office on the track of the unidentified flying object.

The male acorn woodpecker was perched on the rim of the wooden dish which I had had to fill three times that day with bread and doughnuts and grapes. I now understood why. My UFO was no twinspot from Africa or avadavat from the Indies or diamondbird from Australia, it was a piece of bread from the corner bakery. Our crochety guest had decided not only that he would refuse to eat bread, which satisfied the rest of his family, but that he wouldn't even tolerate its presence in the same container as decent food. Before taking so much as a peck at the doughnuts or grapes, he tossed out of the dish and over the porch railing every single scrap of bread. It reminded me of the hooded oriole chucking the cotton balls out of the cornucopia, except that the oriole did the job quietly while the woodpecker informed the neighborhood at the top of his lungs what he thought of peasant food like bread and the barbarians who dared serve it to him. Every time I filled the dish that spring he repeated his performance, until he tired of it or else finally accepted the idea of bread. His nickname, B.T., in the beginning stood for Bread Tosser.

One morning as I was gathering together all the bird food, I came across a tin of salted cashews no longer fresh enough for people to eat. Thinking the woodpeckers would be delighted at such a treat I put ten or twelve cashews in the wooden dish instead of grapes. The male sentry flew down and ate as usual, paying no attention to the nuts. The next two woodpeckers, both females, hesitated a few moments over the new item of food, like very good shoppers. Then one took a nut and flew off, the other departed carrying a piece of bread after several pecks at the doughnut.

Then came B.T. Crouching low over the wooden dish he let out a "Jacob?" whose meaning couldn't have been clearer if he'd spoken it in Harvard English: "What's this?"

He turned his head to the right and studied the cashews with his left eye, he turned his head to the left and studied them with his right eye. Both eyes agreed: the new stuff was bad.

He told me all about it, me and everyone else in the canyon, shouting at the top of his lungs and moving his body violently up and down and from side to side like a drunken sailor trying madly to compensate for the pitch and toss of the ship under him. His performance lasted nearly five minutes. It didn't earn him an Academy Award or even a new name. It simply changed the meaning of his old one. B.T. no longer stood for Bread Tosser but for Bad Temper.

Everyone who has watched birds has seen and heard them express anger at the intrusion of people or animals or other birds. B.T.'s anger—rage might be a better word—was different. No other creatures were present: he was reacting entirely to an unfamiliar food. One of our scrub jays reacted in a similar way to a comparable situation involving food. Since the acorn woodpeckers had ganged up to drive him away from the wooden dish on the porch railing, he had taken to eating off the ledge. Every now and then he was unable to resist the sight of a nice fresh doughnut practically asking to be buried and he would attempt to pick it up in his beak and make off with it. Since a whole doughnut weighed almost as much as he did, it simply dropped out of his beak and rolled across the ledge and down onto the patio below.

When food disappears off the ledge, by accident or design, some birds, the house finches for example, adopt an easy-come, easy-go attitude and show no curiosity or further interest in it. Our friend the scrub jay was much too intelligent to believe that doughnuts can disappear into thin air and he immediately hopped to the edge to investigate. When he saw the doughnut lying on the patio he launched into a violent tirade against the offender, and when that failed to evoke a response he dropped down and pecked at it furiously between squawks. It was very much like watching a man curse a hammer that had struck his thumb or break a golf club that had missed a putt or shake his fist at a bowling ball that had zigged instead of zagged. If a bowling ball, a golf club or a hammer can be considered culprits, we can hardly wonder at the jay assigning this role to a doughnut which had escaped from his beak and "flown" off the ledge onto the patio.

Jays are adept at vocal self-expression and their tirades were often triggered by other things. I could expect a brisk tongue-lashing when I was half an hour late putting out breakfast or if I turned on a certain sprinkler that interfered with their foraging or if I let the dogs out at an inconvenient time. The only occasion when it really snowed in our area, a pair of jays sat in one of the Monterey pine trees and squawked from the first snowflake to the last.

Among zoologists there is a tendency not to allow for individual differences of temperament and mentality among members of a species. Yet anyone who runs a feeding station for birds and animals becomes keenly aware of many such differences even if the explanations for them aren't apparent. Why did one acorn wood-pecker readily accept a new food which caused another to throw a fit? Why did some woodpeckers put useless things like stones and eucalyptus pods in the holes that had been drilled for acorns? Why did most of the rats eat the grapes on the spot while one hoarded them to start a winery?

Why, after a dozen Bewick wrens furnished their nests without incident, did the thirteenth wren attempt repeatedly to push into the nesting hole material that was too bulky, and fly into a fury when his efforts were unsuccessful? Why, of all the California thrashers who've passed our windows and eaten our food, should there have been one who habitually talked to himself?

These thrasher monologues bore no resemblance to the frenetic protests of B.T. and the scrub jays, and little to the normal voice of the thrasher which is loud and droll and vivacious. They consisted of a series of soft notes, a kind of gentle, absent-minded mumbling that sounded oddly human. I heard it a number of times before I found out who was responsible. When I finally caught him in my binoculars he looked oddly human too. He was an older bird, as indicated by the curvature and great length of the bill which, some ornithologists suggest, may keep growing throughout a thrasher's lifetime. He reminded me of an elderly uncle, fussy but benign, making some well-chosen remarks as he went about the complicated business of terrestrial living. He would take a few little running steps—he resorted to flying infrequently and for short distances only—and then he would pause to glance around him, probe a clump of earth, examine a patch of grass, peer under a dead leaf. All this time his throat was vibrating and his beak was opening and closing as he rambled on to himself. Am I sure it was to himself? Well, there was no one there but me, and I prefer to think that thrashers talk to themselves rather than to people. If people overhear, that's their problem.

During April no psychic powers were needed to make us aware that among the acorn woodpeckers more was going on than met the eye and that it was going on inside the hole in the telephone pole. We had no way of determining whether one or two females laid their eggs in the nest, but on the basis of numbers of different woodpeckers seen entering and leaving we suspected the presence of a double clutch of eggs, and a couple of weeks later, a double batch of young.

These were certainly well attended and fed frequently, though not the kind of diet considered ideal for baby woodpeckers since it was made up entirely of doughnuts and bread, grapes being out of season and unobtainable. The female bushtit had brought up both her broods on doughnuts, but the male had supplemented their diet with insects. On the few occasions that our woodpeckers flew from the pole to catch an insect in midair, the maneuver seemed more like a game than serious foraging; what's more, the insect was eaten on the spot, not carried into the nest cavity.

I began to worry that the baby woodpeckers, stuffed with carbohydrates but starved for protein, would fail to develop properly and that the parents would abandon them the way the Hylands' pigeons, Morgan and Dapplegray, had abandoned their ailing offspring. I decided to improve their diet by adding peanuts which I shelled myself. Theoretically, and from the human point of view, this was a great idea: peanuts were close enough to their natural food to be acceptable, as well as richer in oils and protein, so the babies would grow up strong of leg, clear of eye and sleek of plumage. It would probably have worked out fine if the woodpeckers hadn't had their own idea of how to treat a peanut.

And just how did a woodpecker treat a peanut? He stored it, of course; not where he stored acorns which had to be shelled, but where he stored ready-to-eat food like grapes, in the large blue gum eucalyptus tree across the canyon. Behind its peeling bark went the peanuts I carefully shelled and put out for the baby woodpeckers, who never got so much as a sniff of one. Obviously more drastic measures were called for if I wanted the babies to get enough protein to develop normally. (By the way, that baffling bird B.T. showed as positive a liking for peanuts as he had a dislike for cashews.)

It was about this time that Ken and I were invited to visit for the first time the large aviary operated as a hobby by Paul Vercammen. A partial list of some of his more unusual species included black-cap and great reed warblers, gray wagtails, bullfinches, yellow buntings, stonechats, Mexican flycatchers, white-rumped shamas, golden orioles, saffron and lavender finches, nightingales, Pekin robins, purple sunbirds and emerald tanagers.

We were allowed inside while Paul gave the birds their morning feeding. It was holiday fare, indeed: quartered oranges and apples, peeled bananas, fresh ripe figs, raisins soaked in hot water to make them tender and plump, bread and cake crumbs, pieces of cheese, various cooked vegetables and of course, seeds of all kinds. But the favorite of most birds was what Paul fed them by hand for dessert, meal worms.

Meal worms, chock full of protein and obviously a bird favorite, seemed like the perfect food for our baby woodpeckers. On the way home we stopped at a pet store. Here we learned that meal worms were not worms at all but the larvae of darkling beetles, which were a dime a dozen except in pet stores where they were fifty cents a dozen. During their life cycle these beetles destroyed large quantities of flour and cereal; nevertheless they were bred commercially as food for birds. Some animals, like the smaller monkeys, were also fed meal worms to prevent or to cure arthritis. At the going price of four cents for a one-inch worm, medicine for monkeys seemed to have reached more dizzying heights than medicine for humans who could still get an aspirin tablet for a fraction of a penny.

Used medicinally meal worms were expensive enough. Offered as daily fare at a large feeding station they would have been prohibitive. Even I, who obstinately refused to face the economics of our bird feeding, had to concede that much. We couldn't put out meal worms for the woodpeckers without the other birds demanding and getting their share. If, as Marie Beals had told me, a single robin consumed sixteen feet of earthworms in a day, he could be expected to consume an equal amount of meal worms, or 192 inches. At four cents an inch this would amount to $7.68 a day for each robin, or $2,803.20 a year—definitely not chicken feed.

There seemed only one reasonable solution: I would become a commercial breeder of darkling beetles. Ken took a very dim view of this idea, but Harry, the man at the pet shop, explained that it was as easy as rolling off a log. The beetles did the work; all I had to do was provide them with suitable living arrangements and food.

The initial equipment was simple and very cheap, considering what stupendously expensive little creatures—pound for pound in the same class as emeralds—were supposed to emerge from it. I washed and dried a ten-gallon tin can that had once contained beef fat for the birds. It had a tight-fitting lid in which I punctured some small holes for ventilation. Meal worms don't require much oxygen, they do some of their best work in the middle of hundred-pound sacks of flour. On Harry's advice I used as a flour substitute duck bran purchased at a feed and grain store for sixty-five cents. I added the meal worms and a large piece of burlap for them to cling to and a quartered apple for moisture. Then I clamped on the lid and put the whole thing down in a storage room on the lower floor where I figured the little creatures could go about their business, and mine, undisturbed.

Like many people new to a commercial venture I had dreams of glory—perhaps eventually I would become known as the meal worm queen of the Southwest—but the dreams were promptly undermined by labor troubles. Because what happened inside that ten-gallon can for the next month was nothing, absolutely nothing. I checked it every day—and every day, nothing. Ken suggested that the creatures might be inhibited by my surveillance, but I began to suspect more basic problems.

I phoned Harry at the pet store and accused him of giving me all-male or all-female stock. He explained that meal worms weren't fussy about such things but they failed to develop sometimes if they were lonesome. What was probably the matter was that the can was too large for a mere dozen meal worms and they'd probably lost contact and couldn't find each other.

"They can find each other," I said coldly. "They're just not trying."

Harry had a solution: not a smaller can, of course, but more meal worms. If I could stamp out meal worm loneliness I would be back in business.

I drove down to the pet store. Harry had four dozen meal worms packed in a cardboard carton waiting for me. He assured me he'd picked the liveliest ones he could find and I could expect quick action provided all his instructions had been followed. Did I buy the right kind of bran? Yes. Did I remember the burlap and the pieces of raw apple or potato? Yes. Was I keeping their quarters warm and cosy at about 80°? No. The storage room was about as warm and cosy as the catacombs. I didn't tell Harry. I just got out of there as fast as possible—before he could sell me a meal worm heater.

The big question then was, where would be the best place in the house to keep a ten-gallon can rather conspicuously labeled "Hoffman's Pure Rendered Beef Fat"? Two rooms were eliminated immediately. Ken said that much as he liked to share things with his fellow creatures, his study and the lanai adjoining it were too cold. (And, his tone implied, they weren't going to get any warmer if he could help it.) The kitchen, which seemed a logical place, was eliminated because it was hardly bigger than an orange crate and every nook and cranny was already filled with containers of bird seed, stale bread and doughnuts. For aesthetic reasons the living room was excluded, and since a can of meal worms would, in spite of their name, do nothing to enhance meals, so was the dining room.

The choice finally narrowed down, as I should have known it would, to my office. The meal worms, presumably no longer lonesome with the arrival of four dozen of their friends, were ensconced on top of a bookcase, just above a heating outlet, and my office was known from that time on as the Worm Factory.

Meanwhile the baby woodpeckers who were the reason for the factory's existence had grown up. They showed no obvious signs of protein starvation or of malnutrition in general. They were fat, contented little creatures as they sat, often three and four at a time, around the rim of the wooden dish on the porch railing. They weren't easily alarmed; in fact, their confidence in me distressed their parents, who tried to squawk some sense into their heads from the telephone pole or the eucalyptus tree, "Watch out, watch out, watch out!" In this imperfect world we share with the woodpeckers, maturation must include the learning of fears.

If I'd been informed that meal worms were slow and uncooperative and demanded a great deal of heat, I would never have started the project. I was already heartily sick of staring at that big ugly can on top of the bookcase and working in a room that was ten degrees too hot. But I was also reluctant to give up and admit defeat. If the protein was too late for this generation of woodpeckers, it would at least be ready for the next.

In late spring my niece, Jane, came to spend a weekend. She slept in my office, which doubled as a spare bedroom, and I overheard her describing the experience to a friend over the telephone: "It's called the Worm Factory. No, they don't crawl all over you, but even if they did it would be O.K. because they're pets."

Thus it was Jane who was responsible for the only good thing ever said about my meal worms: they didn't crawl all over you. It was Jane too who doomed my future as the meal worm queen of the Southwest. She came into the kitchen while I was preparing lunch and announced that B.T. was on the wooden dish again throwing another fit. Since I'd started to keep records of the intensity and duration of B.T.'s fits, I hurried into my office. I saw immediately that the roof was missing from the worm factory. There was no need to ask what had thrown B.T. into a frenzy.

Whether B.T. was simply venting his spleen or whether he was issuing a genuine alarm to warn the other woodpeckers in the canyon against the newfangled poison, I will never know. I do know this: of the meal worms Jane put out, the scrub jay carried away three, the black-headed grosbeak ate one and the rest just disappeared.

That afternoon I dropped in on Adu and Peter Batten to see the latest additions to their household. The most unusual was a week-old lion which Adu was bottle-feeding and which she let me hold. His coat was finer than silk and his paws like velvet pincushions. The only slightly rough thing about him was his tongue. Someday it would have the texture of the coarsest grade of sandpaper and his affectionate kisses would not be so popular.

Another addition was a margay, a spotted wild cat of Central and South America, which looked like a small ocelot. The resemblance almost cost the margay his life since he'd been purchased by some imbecilic woman to attract attention: she intended to parade him on a leash when she wore her ocelot coat. She knew nothing whatever about the care and feeding of animals and made no effort to find out. By the time the Battens got hold of the margay, he was so weak and crippled with rickets he couldn't even stand up. They treated him with vitamin shots and a special high-nutritive formula made for humans and he was already showing improvement. By the end of summer he was active enough to make a real pest of himself because of his boundless curiosity.

The third new member of the household was a little African bush baby, or galago, a primate about twelve inches long, half of which was tail. Like his nocturnal cousins, the lorises and pottos, he had huge round eyes that gave him a look of continual amazement. In the wild, a bush baby spends the daylight hours sleeping in trees, sometimes in abandoned birds' nests, but at night he comes alive. He can climb like a monkey and use his front paws the way a human child uses his hands, he can leap like a kangaroo, chirp like a bird, and furl and unfurl his ears like nothing else I know of in the animal kingdom.

The bush baby was shy and disinclined to eat, so Adu was trying to tempt his appetite by offering him his favorite food, grasshoppers. Unfortunately she wasn't as well equipped as he was for locating and catching grasshoppers, and feeding the bush baby was taking a disproportionate amount of time when she had so many other animals to look after. I suggested that since meal worms were used both as food and medicine for other small monkeys, the bush baby would probably accept them as a substitute for grasshoppers. She agreed and I delivered the worm factory to her that same afternoon.

It is commonly stated that the two happiest days in a couple's life are the day they acquire a boat and the day they get rid of it. I've experienced both of these and neither can compare to the beautiful day that the Hoffman's Pure Rendered Beef Fat can was removed from the bookcase, the thermostat was turned down to 72° and the Worm Factory became once again my plain and simple office.

Besides a taste for acorns, the acorn woodpeckers share with the scrub jays the ability to live at close quarters with human beings. There is, however, a big difference in their approach: the jays are aggressive and fearless, the woodpeckers simply don't give a darn. Evidence of this is the fact that Tucker's Grove, a small oak-studded park where nearly every weekend hundreds of people go for company barbecues or club outings, is a favorite woodpecker haunt. I sat at one of the picnic tables recently and started to count the storage holes in the bark of the ancient live oak above me. I gave up at a thousand. There are probably thirty or forty times that many and the storage tree is still used.

Estimates of the number of woodpeckers living in Tucker's Grove ran from thirty to sixty. But Jody Bennett, then a graduate student at the University of California at Santa Barbara, who was doing research in the grove on the communal life of acorn woodpeckers, was convinced that these estimates were exaggerated because the birds were so noisy and conspicuous, and that the actual figure was close to twenty. She asked the members of the Santa Barbara Audubon Society to help her take a census. A pair of observers was stationed at each storage tree and nesting site within the eighteen-acre area and an automobile horn signaled the counting to begin and to end. The results surprised everyone but Jody—there were only nineteen woodpeckers in the park. In a subsequent census the figure was the same.

On the days after a large barbecue or picnic at Tucker's Grove the woodpeckers will fly down to the ground for bits of food, and when the creek is dry they perch on the fountains to drink, but in my experience they can not be readily tamed like some of the other birds. Their indifference to people is partly a result of nature's bounty. B.T. knows I am the source of his breakfast doughnut, but he knows too that there is an abundance of other food available and that he can afford to keep his freedom and independence, and his inalienable right to rage.

The Younger Generation and How It Aged—Us

All spring and most of the summer the ledge served as a nursery. The personnel changed from week to week as babies grew up and departed voluntarily or were forcibly removed to make room for other babies. Many of the birds in our area have two or more broods. The championship in this department must go to the mourning dove, who lays up to five clutches in a year—although poorly constructed nests on or near the ground result in heavy losses among both eggs and young.

It is a common summer sight to see mated pairs of birds feeding the first batch of babies while building a new nest or fixing up an old nest or otherwise preparing for a second or third batch. One afternoon I was watching a female brown towhee feeding her offspring on the dead limb of an oak tree. A male towhee suddenly appeared, and with the full cooperation of the female, he mounted her quickly and flew away. This was repeated four times at intervals of about ten seconds. Both parents seemed to have forgotten the baby bird who eventually left the scene with some of his bloom of innocence rubbed off.

During the last week of May the hooded oriole, that most patient of fathers, was pestered from dawn to dusk, from pine to pepper, from eucalyptus to eugenia, by his tenacious green daughter. Whenever he managed to elude her for a fraction of a minute she would deftly spear a grape or take a bite of doughnut, but the instant she caught sight of him again she became a quivering, helpless, starving infant. If he was annoyed by her silly posturings he didn't show it the way many parent birds did, with a swipe of the wing or a sharp peck. He certainly had reason to be annoyed—waiting for him in the nest were two babies who were truly helpless.

They made their debut on the ledge in the middle of June and the sight of them sent me scurrying to consult the bird books: they resembled their drab little mother, as they were supposed to, except that each of them wore an orange skullcap. I've been unable to find a reference to such a color quirk in any of my bird books but I saw another example of it that same week when I visited the Krigers' house. The hooded orioles had nested, as usual, in the banana tree outside their living-room window and one of the second-brood birds was marked exactly like the two at our feeding station.

Our young orioles departed early, still capped in orange and mystery. Was their unusual plumage temporary or permanent? Was it caused by genetic mutation, or some factor like diet, or a substance they came in contact with, like pollen? Were all three of the birds I'd observed males and was the orange color the result of premature activity of the hormones? I suspect this was the case but as an amateur I can afford the luxury of simply saying that I don't know.

On April 7 the first brood of house finches appeared on the ledge, and about a month later, the second brood. Each young bird wore tufts of feathers that looked like horns. This was appropriate enough, for they were veritable devils, sometimes actually attacking the mother in their attempts to prove they were still babies and needed food and attention. In between broods I watched an interesting little scene which proved to me that the human female isn't necessarily the only determined woman.

The action took place at B.T.'s feeder, the wooden dish. When the larger birds were busy elsewhere, the smaller birds ate here, in this case a male and female house finch. Some male house finches show a wide color variation and this one was a dingy pumpkin color whereas the majority of his relatives were red. Pumpkin showed no evidence of special appeal or, in fact, of any interest in the little lady eating opposite him, but this didn't faze her. She had chosen Pumpkin, he was it, and that was that. She quivered seductively in front of him. He looked baffled, then nervous, and finally flew away in alarm. She flew after him, and a few minutes later they were both back and she resumed her attempts to make him think she was irresistible.

She did turn out to be irresistible, but not to the right bird. A second male, Red, watching from a nearby cotoneaster, was enchanted by her performance and indicated as much by swooping down on the feeder and driving Pumpkin away. Instead of taking this as a compliment, the lady was furious. She turned on Red and pecked at him violently until he flew off. Then she set out after Pumpkin again and brought him back to the feeder.

This scene was repeated twice. The third time another female got into the act and made it clear that she too had fallen for Pumpkin's well-hidden charms. In the animal kingdom it is the peculiar-looking mammal who is shunned, the odd-colored bird who is at the bottom of the pecking order. Pumpkin's difference only made him more appealing to the ladies. Affairs of the heart, in man, beast or bird, are not always easy to comprehend.

Every April we watched the blackbirds courting. The redwings, their epaulets almost fluorescent, whistled in concert from the tangles of ceanothus their mad and merry *Oo-long-tea, whee!* The Brewer blackbirds, bodies inflated and wings raised, looked like comical little Draculas as they pursued the females around the ledge. The cowbirds, heads glossy as milk chocolate, sang the gurgling notes which sounded so much like water trickling down a drain that I checked the kitchen plumbing half a dozen times before I discovered that the noise was coming from a bird, not a leaky tap.

In mid-May the baby Brewers appeared and used our ledge as the place where they learned the rudiments of living—how to fly, how to drink and bathe, how to forage for themselves. The ledge made an ideal kindergarten or, more accurately, Brewery. It was high, but with shrubs below and nearby in case of falls; it was safe from daytime predators since the sharp-shinned hawks had moved north to breed and our three dogs kept the area clear of cats and boys with BB guns or slingshots; and there was an abundance of food and fresh water. Most baby blackbirds took their lessons in stride and wingbeat, but a few were unlucky, some were timid and some slow to learn.

The unluckiest of them all struck the wooden gate that separated the ledge from the porch. It was a bad strike. I heard it in my office and I was amazed when I rushed into the living room to see that the bird was still alive on the ledge. He lay on his back, silent, trembling all over. During the next five minutes that were to be the final ones of his short life I witnessed a most touching exhibition of the group solicitude of these birds for their young. More than a dozen blackbirds assembled in as many seconds, most of them males. They surrounded and fussed over the injured baby, trying to coax him to sit up. Even after he died they kept coming back to him to make sure he couldn't use their help.

Other babies had better luck—and needed it. One afternoon when Ken and I returned home from lunch downtown we heard a commotion on the ledge before we even opened the front door. Its source was a baby Brewer taking his first lesson in flying. How he'd gotten as far as the ledge I don't know, but one thing seemed absolutely certain—he didn't intend to go any further. He had taken up his position as close as possible to the wall and was bleating loudly and piteously to be rescued. Meanwhile his father kept talking to him in a reassuring way and swooping back and forth in front of him to show him just how easy flying was. *Here's how it's done*—swoop—*Nothing to it at all, really*—swoop—*Watch this and you'll get the picture*—swoop.

Baby Brewer was not interested in how it was done; he didn't get the picture and he didn't swoop. He wanted only to be back in that nice, safe, cosy nest and he so stated clearly, lustily and several hundred times. For the entire afternoon Dad coaxed and swooped while his diffident child clung stubbornly to the ledge. It began to look more and more like a battle of wills than a flying lesson. Whoever won the battle, I knew who'd be the loser. By six o'clock my nerves were cracking and I'd already made a trip to the storeroom and another to the garage in a futile search for a container that would adequately house a baby blackbird. The ledge, safe enough in the daytime, became a different place at night. Rats scampered up and down it, opossums crossed it on their way to and from the tea tree, raccoons climbed it to claim their share of the bread and doughnuts, great horned owls watched it from the television antenna. There was nothing whatever to recommend that ledge to a baby bird and I wished to heaven I had some way of conveying the message to him before the sun went down.

Perhaps it was the sun itself that conveyed the message. As it started to sink behind the eucalyptus trees the little bird mustered all his courage and strength and flew into the privet hedge five feet away. The Wright brothers couldn't have enjoyed their moment of glory more thoroughly than Baby Brewer. Carried away by his success he swooped across to the tea tree, and from there, about a hundred feet to the neighbors' roof. The last I saw of him was just before the sun disappeared completely. He was strutting up and down beside the chimney and he looked as though he was congratulating himself: *I made it in one swell foop.*

The devoted attention the young blackbird received from his father contrasted sharply with the parental treatment the young English sparrows received. They were sent out to fend for themselves at so tender an age that they still showed nestling-yellow at the corners of their mouths. Their flight was weak and wobbly and it often seemed a miracle to me that they could cover as much as a few yards. But it was a case of fly or die, so they flew.

The childhood of these birds was brief and bleak. For most species of animal and bird, playing is a part of growing up for the young, and of staying alive for the middle-aged and old. But I've never seen an English sparrow engaged in play. For them, life is real and earnest, and not much fun. Its purpose is simple—more life—and they have no time or energy to waste on anything not directly connected with their purpose. Playfulness, whether the puritans approve or not, is a quality much admired in bird, animal or man, and the reason the English sparrow is so widely despised is probably not because he's common or has particularly bad habits, but because of his grim, cheerless assembly-line reproduction.

One of the first things I noticed about these sparrows at the feeding station was their lack of relationship with any of their fellow boarders. When they came to the ledge to eat, there were no preliminaries, polite or impolite. If other birds were already feeding, the sparrows didn't try to drive them away, they merely squeezed in beside them and began eating. If the sparrows were there first and other birds arrived and attempted to drive them away, the sparrows, even the very young ones, ignored them. They seemed, in fact, not to comprehend the meaning of the other birds' actions. Bluff is the main weapon in the arsenal of most birds. They use it and are, in turn, used by it. The sparrows neither used it nor recognized its use. A Brewer blackbird inflated to twice its size and with his white eye glaring may have looked awesome to the finches and tanagers, but to the English sparrows he looked like an inflated blackbird with a white eye. They had no time or taste for bluffing, which is, after all, a kind of game.

In scientific circles it was fashionable for a while to believe that play was confined to the young and that it was merely an exercising of the muscles and a practicing of the skills that would be necessary in adult life. This theory has had to be modified considerably as it became obvious that not all players were young, and not all playing constructive. Play seems to me a natural activity of birds and animals who have energy left over after the necessities of living have been attended to. The chief necessity is food and the kind of food a bird eats regulates the amount of foraging that must be done every day. The mourning dove, whose diet consists mainly of weed seeds, has to spend a great deal of time and energy getting the same amount of nourishment as a scrub jay gets from one meadow mouse or a few protein-rich caterpillars. How the scrub jay uses his consequent leisure is well known to every chronicler of mischief.

All flying looks like fun to the earthbound, and so we must be cautious in singling out a particular action of a bird and calling it play. Yet in some cases play is unmistakable.

One September, Ken and I drove with the Hylands up to Morro Bay to look for some of the birds that require a wilder and rockier coastline than our area provided—wandering tattlers, black oystercatchers, black turnstones and surfbirds. Sometimes a single rock in the Avila region will provide all four species, and one year a very rare American oystercatcher also took up residence there. Going along the bay we stopped to watch the tide coming in across the mud flats. A certain stream was running quite rapidly and on it were a dozen northern phalaropes having the time of their lives. They would ride down the stream for thirty or forty yards, twirling around now and then like little toy boats caught in an eddy. Then they'd fly back up and start over. This was repeated again and again until the stream gradually slowed and stopped and the tide was in and the phalaropes settled down to the serious business of foraging.

Helen and Nelson Metcalf witnessed a similar performance on one of the Columbia River rapids in Washington. The birds on this occasion were four white pelicans. They would rise in the air and fly single file to the head of the rapids, then ride four abreast all the way down to the quiet water. The Metcalfs watched for half an hour. When they departed, the pelicans were still riding the rapids. Brian Roberts has written an account of common eiders repeatedly riding a tide current in a fjord, and R.A. Stoner tells of an Anna's hummingbird who kept floating down the stream caused by a garden faucet that had been left running. I wonder how many other species of birds indulge in similar games that are unseen or unreported.

Almost all birds fly, but only a few aerial geniuses can soar—that is, rise skyward without wing-flapping, using only winds or thermal updrafts. The white pelican is one. These huge silent birds, which share with the California condor an enormous wingspread, more than eight feet, and a reputation for gentleness and quietness, are capable of fantastic feats of soaring. At the slightest invitation of the wind they will rise high in the air and put on a performance that looks not like mere play but like an inspired and exuberant romp of angels.

White pelicans do not, like condors, cover great distances in the search for food, nor do they have the brown pelican's habit of spotting a fish from the air and diving down into the water to catch it. They feed while swimming leisurely along the surface, finding small, delicate tidbits which their greedy brown brothers would disdain. It is the simplest and easiest way to forage and the energy they save can be, perhaps must be, used for the kind of activity we call play.

Wood storks are masters of the art of soaring. These large shy birds are normally seen in flocks in regions where there is shallow fresh water like the Florida Everglades and the Louisiana bayous. In late summer, post-breeding dispersal brings a number of them to the Salton Sea in California where they stay for a limited time. They rarely appear as far north and west as Santa Barbara, but one individual threw the rulebook overboard and came here to spend two consecutive winters.

His time was divided between our main sloughs, Goleta and Sandyland. He was an excellent example of the way many birds will adjust quickly to such things as air and highway traffic, while remaining extremely wary of people on foot. At Goleta his favorite hangout was below a bluff between the airport and the busy road leading to the university. At Sandyland he stayed as far away from the beach houses as possible, which put him right next to the Los Angeles–San Francisco Freeway. At both sloughs he had for company great blue herons and black-crowned night herons, snowy and common egrets, avocets and the occasional black-necked stilt. He was particularly attracted to the egrets, perhaps because they were white and most resembled his family and friends from whom he'd been separated. The attraction was not mutual.

Wood storks are very gregarious birds and he obviously missed his own kind. In the early morning and late afternoon he foraged; when there were thermals to ride, he rode them. But the times between, when he had nothing to do, were lonely and hard to fill. It was then that he made his advances to the egrets.

The grace and beauty of the wood stork was apparent only in

flight. On land, with his naked gray head and neck showing, he took no prizes, but there was a certain awkward dignity about the great mute bird as he plodded earnestly across the mud toward the egrets. They invariably gave him a look-what-the-tide-brought-in stare and walked away. He followed, they walked away again. Often, after a series of overtures and rebuffs, he would spring into the air on his long black legs and begin circling around the slough, rising higher and higher until he was out of sight. Audubon had a peculiar notion about such flights: he suggested that they were intended to aid the bird's digestion.

All that winter the wood stork tried and failed to establish a relationship with the egrets. He left in early spring, destination unknown. The following October he returned, once again dividing his time between Goleta and Sandyland sloughs. Though he was still no beauty he looked glossier and whiter than the previous year, and his manner was somewhat more self-assured when he pursued the egrets. As Christmas approached I seemed to detect a slight softening in the attitude of the egrets: their rejection of him seemed not so swift or so final. But this may have been merely a subjective and seasonal piece of sentiment on my part. Peace on earth, including the wet haunts of storks and egrets.

Aerial games are also played by albatrosses, frigatebirds, condors, ravens, vultures, kites, buteos, eagles, falcons, gulls, and terns. Some owls are well equipped to soar, but unable to do so because they are active at night when there are no thermals.

Group play includes the formation flying of gulls and white pelicans and the berry-passing of cedar waxwings, so baffling to those ornithologists who used to demand a rational explanation for everything. (For a long time play was considered no explanation at all, let alone a rational one.) The game of passing the berry is practically self-explanatory: a berry—toyon, pepper, eugenia, cotoneaster, pyracantha, to name only a few varieties they eat—is passed along a line of waxwings perched on a telephone wire or the bare bough of a tree. In one such flock I counted over a hundred waxwings, and my hat went off not so much to the birds as to the toyon berry which survived the perilous passage to the end of the line and back again. I have also seen a flock of waxwings chasing and catching snowflakes. Perhaps they were doing it for the moisture, perhaps they were doing it for the heck of it.

The thieving games played by Melanie, the raven described in an earlier chapter, are also played by her crow and magpie cousins, and part of the extracurricular activity of every red-blooded scrub jay and mockingbird is the teasing of dogs and cats.

One of our mockers had a daily rendezvous on the roof with the neighbors' ginger cat. The cat would stalk the bird around the chimney and through the overhanging branches of the oak tree until the cat tired and lay down to rest. Then it was the bird's turn. He would swoop down on the sleeping cat, almost grazing its head, and repeating triumphantly, *yah, yah, yah*. In that *yah, yah, yah,* I hear echoing the voices of all the small bullied boys who are finally getting their say.

Though the mockers and scrub jays occasionally pestered Brandy, our big German shepherd, and Rolls Royce, our cocker spaniel, it was John, the Scottie, built low to the ground and slowed by age, who was the prime target of their dive-bombing game. But John, canny Scott that he was, had figured out a means of protecting himself, using the principle of If you can't lick 'em, go where they can't follow. Whenever he had to make a sortie into jay or mocker territory, he avoided the open spaces and stuck close to the dense, low-growing shrubbery where he was likely to meet only the occasional wrentit, brown towhee or golden-crowned sparrow.

It is always amazing to me how birds and animals, and to a certain extent the young of the human species, can take faster and more accurate measure of each other than human adults can. Mr. Smith may require a year to discover that Mr. Jones is no friend of his, a fact that had been apparent to the Smith kids for 364 days. Birds learn very quickly not only the difference between a dog and a cat, but the difference between a hungry cat and a well-fed cat, and between a nervous dog and a calm dog. I have seen white-crowned sparrows, house finches, Audubon warblers and California thrashers bathe no more than five feet from where Brandy lay chewing a marrow bone, and on one occasion he actually nudged with his nose a purple finch who was busy eating a doughnut. Wild birds do not accept stroking as a form of friendliness and affection the way domestic animals do. To them such physical contact means extreme danger or death, and so the purple finch, unafraid up to this point, at the touch of Brandy's nose, went into a state of shock. Puzzled, Brandy picked the bird up and brought it over to me for an explanation. He carried it so carefully that when it recovered its wits a few moments later, it flew out of my hand without a trace of injury. I wish all large creatures could be so gentle, all small ones so confiding.

We were still waiting, though with little hope, for the return of the phainopeplas which had nested in the large pepper tree in the adjacent canyon. The new crop of pepper berries had meanwhile been discovered by the young of the band-tailed pigeons, recognizable by their non-iridescent, unmarked necks. They ate like the cedar waxwings, greedily and in flocks, but they were, at about three-quarters of a pound apiece, considerably larger, so that the delicate, graceful boughs of the pepper tree hung low under the weight of several dozen bandtails.

About this time two things happened which did nothing to raise my rather low opinion of the common sense of band-tailed pigeons and mourning doves.

The first incident concerned a dove. Eight or ten of these birds had taken a special liking to a new hopper-type feeder Ken had hung in the Monterey pine outside the kitchen window. The feeder, which held some twenty pounds, was made of redwood with glass on two sides so you could see when more seed should be added, and it was filled through a hole in the flat roof. This hole was an oblong measuring 1½ by 2½ inches and the plug for it had long since gone with a wind.

There are households where such small repairs or replacements are made immediately, but ours isn't among them. One morning a hungry house finch arriving at the feeder and finding it completely taken over by doves tried to reach the seed through the hole in the roof and either accidentally fell in or purposely dropped in. I suspect the latter because he certainly didn't panic, he just started eating, and when he had breakfasted he made his way out again without any trouble. Several of his friends learned the trick by watching him and we would often see two or three at a time feasting inside the glass walls. With their legs lost from sight among the seeds, they appeared to be floating on top of the grain like tiny sea birds.

The hole-in-the-roof trick was a good one, but like many good tricks its success depended on timing. In the early morning when the feeder was full to the top, the finches came and went as they pleased. As the seed level dropped throughout the day they had increasing difficulty getting out, and by late afternoon any finch foolish enough to enter, had to be rescued. Quite a few of them spent the night inside the feeder before we learned to check it every evening at dusk and make sure it was free of uninvited guests. If it wasn't, rescue operations were started.

These rescues were complicated by the fact that the feeder had been placed fairly high in the pine tree and the ground underneath was sloping, and if there was any moisture, extremely slippery like all adobe soil. But the chief difficulty turned out to be the feeder itself, which we had bought because it seemed sturdily built. Sturdily built it was, alas. The roof had been put on to stay on, through Atlantic coast hurricanes, Midwestern tornadoes or California earthquakes, and the glass walls had been set in more firmly than our plate-glass picture windows. Faced with our initial rescue, we thought of using a pair of tongs to take hold of the finch and pull him up through the hole in the roof, but the hole was too small, or the tongs too big. Nor was any bird likely to cooperate in such a maneuver.

It was Ken who conceived the idea of reversing the procedure that had caused the trouble in the first place. A bird that had been trapped by the falling of the seed level could very likely be untrapped by raising the seed level again. And so it came to pass, on a dozen occasions or more, that the twilight scene I saw from the kitchen window included a large man slowly and carefully pouring seed into the roof hole of the feeder while inside the glass walls a small finch gradually rose higher and higher, with a kind of stately dignity that reminded me not of a bird at all, but of a ship passing through one of the locks of the Panama Canal. It seemed to take about the same amount of time too, especially if I had dinner waiting on the table and Ken had an eight o'clock meeting to make.

People familiar with these nervous, fidgety finches will be puzzled, as we were, by the fact that they didn't panic. Perhaps they were sodden with food, I don't know. I do know that four of the rescues involved the same finch, a male easily identified by the peculiar mustard color of his head and chest. The Panama Canal system was fine for rescuing finches. One afternoon, however, I looked out and saw a most improbable sight—a mourning dove sitting inside the glass walls of the feeder, contentedly pecking away at the seeds. He had managed to squeeze his corpulent twelve inches into an opening that measured 1½ by 2½ inches, a feat that surely made him the chief contortionist of the dove coterie.

I called Ken and he went out immediately and started pouring more seed into the feeder. It soon became obvious that this method wasn't going to work. Even when the bird was raised to the level of the roof hole he just sat there, lacking the same inducement to squeeze himself out that he'd had to squeeze himself in. The sun began to set and still he gave no indication of wanting to depart. Perhaps he recognized the sound construction of the feeder and thought it was a good place to spend the night, in spite of the man rapping on the glass walls and exhorting him to leave in language that would have been clearly understood by any creature on earth except that symbol of purity and innocence, the dove.

There are times in every marriage when it behooves a wife to walk away, stay out of sight and not answer when her name is called. When I walked back again, half an hour later, the feeder had completely disappeared, the dove was recuperating on the ledge, smoothing his ruffled feathers, and Ken was sweeping off the patio. He glanced up when he heard me coming.

"Funny thing about that feeder," he said calmly. "It wasn't as sturdy as it looked. We should try one of the new plastic kind, don't you think?"

I thought.

Shortly afterward, another event lowered my opinion of the common sense of the dove family. Ken was working one evening in his study when he heard from the adjoining lanai a noise that sounded like the fluttering of wings. We'd had birds in the lanai before—Brandy could open any door in the house and never bothered closing them again—but when Ken went to investigate, there were no birds in sight and the noise had stopped. The same thing happened twice the next morning. By this time Ken was sure that the noise was coming from the chimney of the fireplace. When he looked up the chimney, however, all he saw was a patch of blue sky.

The next afternoon he heard the fluttering sounds again, and again he checked the chimney and found nothing. In spite of his insistence that it was a bird, I said it had to be something else, a bat for instance, since no bird could survive in that chimney for two days and nights without food or water.

I myself could probably survive for a month on the words I've had to eat, the preceding statement being a good example. By the use of a flashlight and a few acrobatics Ken discovered the bird hidden in a kind of small alcove inside the chimney. It was a young band-tailed pigeon. The ordeal had left him frazzled and blotched with soot, but he was still strong enough to fight his rescuer and peck him vigorously on the hand before flying off toward the adjacent canyon.

The visit of our uninvited guest raised many questions. Had he gotten into the chimney accidentally or on purpose? If on purpose, what reason could he have had? Was he escaping from something? Birds normally avoid going into any place unless they're certain of an escape route; and the only local predators I've seen attacking bandtails are the sharp-shinned hawks who had gone north two or three months previously. Why didn't the pigeon simply drop down into the fireplace—less than a yard separated the alcove from the firepit—and try to escape via the lanai? And after he was rescued what did he do first? Eat? Search for water to drink and bathe? Fly as fast and as far away as possible? Attempt to find his friends? Settle down to roost for the balance of the night?

Only one conjecture seems sure to be correct: after two days in a chimney, life in the pepper tree must have looked very good indeed. The small rose-red berry of the California pepper tree consists of a seed surrounded by an almost paper-thin layer of fruit which affords little taste or nourishment. Yet it is a favorite among birds. Some, like the phainopeplas, waxwings, mockingbirds, jays, magpies, blackbirds and finches, eat the berries right from the tree. Others, like the thrushes, thrashers, towhees, white-crowned and golden-crowned sparrows, sometimes even flickers, wait until the berries fall and eat them from the ground.

Visitors occasionally ask if the seeds of the California pepper can be processed and used as a food seasoning like the seeds of South American peppers. They aren't, but I'm not so sure they can't be. I know of an instance when an attempt was made, though I wasn't informed of the results. Every autumn the Botanic Garden offers the public a course on "Trees About Town," conducted by its learned and lively director, Katherine Muller. At one of these classes I met a woman who was engaged in processing California pepper berries which she intended to experiment with as a condiment. I never saw her again, a fact which I prefer to think of as coincidental rather than consequential.

People who intend to plant a pepper tree to attract birds must be sure they purchase one that will bear. For three years Ken and I nurtured a pepper tree in the hope of eventually attracting another pair of phainopeplas. It thrived but produced no fruit. When I contacted our nurseryman about the situation he said he thought he was doing us a favor by selling us a male tree "which wouldn't clutter up the yard with those messy berries."

Of all the baby birds that spring and summer, the most endearing were the black-headed grosbeaks. The first male grosbeak had arrived on March 23 in full breeding plumage, cinnamon and black, with a lemon patch in the center of his belly and under each wing. A week later there were half a dozen males in the neighborhood and two females, more modestly clad than the males, but still vivid with their striped heads and peach-and-coffee bodies. The birds were quiet at this time. There was no singing or sexual display or territorial fighting. They seemed to be calmly sizing up the situation and one another. By what mysterious means they came to an agreement among themselves, biologists will perhaps never know. But a decision was reached: six of the grosbeaks departed, leaving one male and one female.

Then the singing began. There are people who sing and there are others who can be called songsters. And so it is among birds. G-man, our grosbeak, was a true songster. He sang for love and wonder, for pride and joy and to serenade a sunny day, greet a rain, welcome a wind. He sang so often that his lady love was moved to respond with a song of her own, and it was difficult to tell who was singing to whom about what.

Eventually the reasons for the singing appeared, a trio of Baby G's, bodies fat and round as tennis balls, heads striped brown and beige like their mother's. Right from the beginning they showed their musical heritage. As they tagged along after their devoted parents in search for food, they did not make a terrible racket like the baby blackbirds or cheep incessantly like the sparrows and house finches. Their soliciting sound was a soft, plaintive, gently aggrieved "Hey, you!" Every shrub and tree in the yard seemed to be equipped with its own music box which played over and over, "Hey, you! Hey, you! Hey, you!"

The red-shafted flicker normally lays a clutch of half a dozen eggs or more, but that year only one survived to fledgling size. He had two sounds as he followed his parents to the doughnut in the wooden feeder. One was soft like the grosbeaks', a plaintive and questioning, "Yup yop? Yup yop yop?" The other was a shrieking that can't be described in words. When I first heard it I thought a murder was taking place on the porch railing. It looked like a murder too, with the mother flicker thrusting her formidable one-and-a-half-inch beak down the baby's throat while he screamed like a banshee. This noise, as far as a mere spectator-auditor could tell, was caused by nothing more than excitement.

At intervals throughout the day, one or other of the parent flickers, sometimes both, would bring their son, Yup Yop, to the wooden feeder. He was enormous compared to the other young birds, but he was a terribly spoiled baby. The little wrentits and song sparrows and Wilson's warblers and goldfinches all fended for themselves while Yup Yop sat helplessly on the railing, refusing to try even a bite of doughnut or bread or a single grape or peanut. As two weeks passed and Yup Yop still clung to his dependence, his parents were at the end of their wits. They had tried coaxing, prodding, pecking and pushing. Now they tried the only other thing they could think of—they flew off and left him.

Watching Yup Yop's initial attempts to feed himself was like watching a human infant's introduction to solid food. He wasn't used to the texture and he did considerable head shaking and bill wiping before he showed signs of enjoyment. But he soon became our best customer, and as time passed, the boss of the feeder. This lofty position was strictly the result of his size, since his disposition was like that of his parents, mild and unaggressive. He was extremely wary, though. No matter how often he watched from a distance while I took food out to the ledge or worked around the garden or in my office, I could never get close to him. Perhaps it was because in the not too distant past flickers were shot as game birds and had learned the destructiveness of man. Fifty-five species of birds have been observed using that particular feeder, and of them all, only the crows showed more wariness than the flickers.

Yup Yop was also cautious about planes. If one approached the canyon at what he considered too low an altitude he flattened himself in the wooden feeder and stayed there, looking like a feathered turtle, motionless except for the once-a-second blinking of his eyes. I've seen acorn woodpeckers assume this same posture when alarmed, but instead of blinking they moved their heads slowly in a circle the way owls do when they want to examine something.

The month of May was nearly over and we still hadn't seen hide or feather of the new batch of brown-headed cowbirds. We knew cowbirds to be brood parasites whose eggs were hatched and young were raised by other birds, usually a smaller variety, and we were curious to find out which of our neighborhood species had been so used, or misused. At the Botanic Garden we'd watched a newly fledged cowbird being fed by a tiny orange-crowned warbler and another by an Oregon junco. (The beginning bird watcher is apt to be thrown for a loss by the appearance of immature cowbirds, particularly since they are seldom pictured in books. Their color is misleading—a sort of lead laced with platinum.) Also near the house of Alice and Charles Richardson in Montecito we'd seen a Hutton's vireo struggling to feed a cowbird twice its size. But our Oregon junco was gone, there were no nesting vireos of this kind in our immediate neighborhood, and our orange-crowned warblers had already raised a family.

On the ledge, at the other feeders and in the adjoining field, the adult cowbirds associated almost entirely with red-winged blackbirds. No interrelationship between the two species was discernible, they simply showed up in the same place at the same time to eat the same things. With the arrival of the young, however, a baffling picture began to emerge.

The first week in June the baby redwings and cowbirds appeared on the ledge, more than three weeks later than the Brewer's blackbirds. The close association of the adult cowbirds and redwings and the simultaneous appearance of their young led me to believe that the redwings, in spite of their greater size, were being used as the host birds, and so I paid particular attention to the actions of the young cowbirds.

It turned out to be a disappointing and inconclusive study. In my hours of watching every day for a period of two weeks I didn't observe a single instance of an adult redwing feeding a young cowbird, or of a cowbird soliciting a redwing or, in fact, of a cowbird soliciting any kind of bird at all, including its own kind. From the moment the young arrived on the ledge they seemed completely self-sufficient, while the redwings were still in the soliciting stage. This suggests that if a host-parasite relationship existed between the two species, the cowbirds' eggs were laid several days before the redwings'.

In the final week of May the mockingbirds began the first of their nocturnal serenades. The night of May 26, when I was particularly restless, or they were particularly loud, I was awakened at midnight, one thirty, two, three, four and five thirty. To those who insist that it is the brightness of the moon which evokes nocturnal song, I can only report that it was foggy all night and that the following morning all planes were grounded until nine thirty. I have heard many replies to the question of why mockingbirds sing at night. The simplest and perhaps the most satisfactory was given by Ken: "Why not?"

During the hours of darkness the mockers had no vocal competition, but at dawn every baby bird in the neighborhood began sounding its hunger notes. Yup Yop, the flicker, alternately whispered and shrieked, the hooded orioles clucked, the blackbirds remonstrated, "Tut, tut, tut, tut!" The house finches and sparrows cheeped and chattered up and down the ledge; and from the porch railing, the elderberry bushes and the lemon tree, the grosbeaks called softly and plaintively, "Hey you! Hey you!"

These were the sounds of summer as the younger generation grew up and Ken and I grew older.

Johnny and the Night Visitors

My life list of birds was grow-
ing rapidly, too rapidly. While my greed was assuaged, my common
sense warned me of lean pickings ahead since there were only a
limited number of birds in our area and a new species seen in the
present meant one less in the future. A bird watcher's Utopia would
have to include a system of rationing that would allow you a new
bird on your birthday, for instance, another at Christmas, and perhaps a third on the Fourth.

This suggestion was prompted by the appearance on our ledge
one Christmas morning of a white-winged dove, a species rare in
these parts and new to us. I mentioned to a friend that it was the
best present we ever received, and the following Christmas he
brought over a three-foot manzanita tree with winter pears wired
to its branches and a partridge leashed at its tip with a golden
ribbon. The partridge would also have been a new bird for us if it
hadn't been made of clay. A year and a half was to elapse before

Kay Ball found us a real partridge on the campus of the University of Alberta at Edmonton.

Our list of Home Visitors, that is, birds seen at or from our feeding station, was also growing rapidly, and not always according to pattern. Some birds which we had good reason to expect since they were frequently seen in the vicinity never showed up, such as the western kingbird, Say's phoebe, rough-winged swallow, cañon wren, loggerhead shrike, western bluebird, lark sparrow. Others arrived which we had no reason to expect—Scott's oriole, rose-breasted grosbeak, catbird, Grace's and Tennessee warblers, summer tanager—and one of these, Home Visitor No. 103, was a bird we didn't even know existed.

I was in the kitchen preparing the dogs' breakfast one morning when a piercing whistle suddenly split the air. It was as loud as a flicker's, with a clearer and sweeter tone. When I heard it again I knew it was no bird I knew, perhaps no bird at all, but a boy whistling a signal to a friend. I dropped everything and rushed into the living room for my binoculars. As it turned out, I didn't need them.

The whistler was perched in the Australian tea tree at the east end of the ledge, eating one of the doughnuts I'd just put out. His brilliant yellow-and-black plumage and long, sharp, cone-shaped bill marked him as an oriole, but he was bigger than any oriole of my acquaintance, including the rare Lichtenstein's oriole of the Rio Grande delta region of Texas. Our new visitor was about the same length as a scrub jay, though he seemed considerably larger because more of his length was body and less was tail. But the most peculiar thing about him was revealed in a closer study through binoculars: at the outer corner of each yellow eye he had a triangular patch of bare skin, sky-blue in color.

The sky-blue patches simplified the task of identifying the bird. He was a species of South American oriole called a troupial. I found a picture in the Austin-Singer *Birds of the World* which clearly showed the eye patch, the black hood and tail, the bright underparts and full color. There was one puzzling difference, though—the troupial in the picture was a deep orange, and our visitor was yellow.

I called Waldo Abbott at the Museum of Natural History. He

said a bird of similar description had been reported to him by a Mrs. Frank Kennedy who had a feeding station in the center of the city, a block from the courthouse. He'd gone down to see the bird and identified it positively as a troupial. There seemed little doubt that the troupial in Mrs. Kennedy's fig tree and the one in our tea tree were the same bird, since the two feeding stations were less than three miles apart, as the crow flies. But I had to be sure so I drove over right away.

Mrs. Kennedy didn't know exactly how long the troupial had been with her. She first became aware that something had been added to her garden by observing that something was being subtracted from it. The succulents planted in redwood tubs and hanging baskets around the patio were disappearing. Apparently healthy plants were reduced to mere stalks within a day or so, and sometimes flowerpots were found overturned. Mrs. Kennedy blamed everything on rodents, which she assumed had been attracted to her yard by the grain she put out for the birds. She set traps, but they remained unsprung while the succulents continued to disappear.

Early one morning in May when she went out to fill the bird bath she found the culprit perched on a redwood tub, stripping off the fleshy new leaves of the sedum it contained. The troupial stared at her with his bright yellow eyes, then whistled. Mrs. Kennedy whistled back, and a pact of friendship was thus simply and immediately formed.

The birds that flocked to Mrs. Kennedy's feeding station were mainly the common city birds, mourning doves and domestic pigeons, Brewer's blackbirds and house sparrows. It was natural enough that when the exotic stranger showed up, with his brilliant plumage and bold whistle, he was given a great deal of food and attention. He loved fruit—especially bananas—doughnuts, cake, bread softened with milk or water, and of course, the leaves of succulents. He had his own feeding tray in the fig tree, apart from the other birds, and defended it vigorously. During the twenty-four hours he spent at our house he had no trouble driving off the scrub jays; perhaps they were too flabbergasted by the sight of the oversized oriole to fight back.

Where had the troupial come from? Although some orioles are long-range migrants, the Baltimore and orchard going as far as

South America to winter, and the Bullock to Costa Rica, all the reference books I could find indicated that troupials, like most birds of tropical regions, were non-migratory and stayed pretty close to their part of South America. It seemed reasonable, then, to assume that Trouper had not come to California of his own choice or under his own steam. He was not wearing a leg band, as birds purchased in pet shops usually are, though it was possible that one had been attached and had subsequently worn off with the help of time and the weather and Trouper himself.

I contacted Paul Vercammen, whose private aviary has been described in another chapter. He knew what a troupial was, of course, but he'd never purchased any and they weren't the kind of birds normally stocked by the local pet stores. Someone wanting a troupial might have to go where the troupials were, Colombia or Venezuela.

The word Venezuela jogged my memory. Maracaibo was the place where Pete and Adu Batten had acquired the first inmate of what was to become their zoo, or to put it more accurately, their collection of pet birds, reptiles and mammals. I called Adu on the phone. She told me that she and Pete had picked up a couple of troupials in Maracaibo some time ago, but they had escaped the previous fall while being transferred from one cage to another. All attempts to find them had failed and they were presumed dead. Both birds had been adult males, bright orange in color.

I told Adu about Trouper and his golden-yellow feathers, and asked if she was positive about the color. She said the birds were orange when they escaped, but they would have had a moult since then and the color of their feathers might be influenced by diet. She used to feed them oranges every day, just as the flamingos were fed a certain kind of shrimp paste to keep their plumage pink. I thought of the sea otters we frequently saw in the kelp beds off the coast of Monterey and the Big Sur. Their very bones are dyed purple by the pigment in the sea urchins that form a large part of their diet.

Adu was pleasantly surprised that a troupial—possibly two— had managed to survive for six months on its own. Or to a considerable extent on its own. Mrs. Kennedy did provide handouts, certainly, but it was Trouper himself who'd discovered the food value of succulents. Or was it the food aspect that had attracted him in the first place? Perhaps, in his native environment, he used succulents as a source of water the way many inhabitants of our California desert do. My private picture of Venezuela had always been that of a vast and lush rain forest. Adu made some corrections in the picture. Though all of Venezuela was very humid, actual rainfall occurred heavily only in the mountain and foothill regions. Maracaibo itself, at sea level, received barely enough rain to support scrub vegetation.

Three of the mysteries about Trouper had been tentatively solved: his place of origin, his fondness for succulents and the color of his plumage.

During the next year Trouper became well known in the neighborhood. Mrs. Kennedy had learned to imitate his whistle—or, more likely, he'd learned to recognize hers, since the bird's whistle and Mrs. Kennedy's sounded completely different to me. Anyway they understood each other, and when our Audubon members went to visit him, Mrs. Kennedy was usually able to call him down from the date palm where he took his siestas.

When the spirit moved him Trouper would leave the Kennedys' place for a few hours—or a few days—and catch up on what was happening in the outside world. He returned from one of these excursions sadder, wiser and without a tail. The life of a *bon vivant* had made him a bit too casual in his relationship with cats.

We have had many tailless birds at our feeding station during the past five years. Like Trouper, they could all fly fairly well for short distances. None of them stayed long, however. Some, lacking the quick maneuverability made possible by a tail, met an early death; others grew new tails and became once again indistinguishable from their friends and relatives. The longest stay was on the part of a scrub jay who'd been born without the slightest stump of a tail and remained that way. His appearance was apt to mystify visiting bird watchers who, seeing him in the distance in a bad light, identified him as everything from a quail to a flicker.

To the layman, accustomed to the slow growth rate of such things as human hair and fingernails, it is amazing how quickly a bird can replace pulled-out feathers. The stub of Trouper's new tail was visible within three days, within three weeks the tail was fully grown again. He was in no hurry for further adventures though. For some time he stuck pretty close to his feeding tray in the fig tree and the fresh batch of succulents Mrs. Kennedy had put around the patio. Then he started out on another series of excursions. He appeared once more at our house and three times at our neighbors', who had a mission fig tree like the one Trouper was accustomed to. The Museum of Natural History received reports from various parts of town about a strange, large, black and orange-yellow bird with a loud, shrill whistle. It was suggested by one of our Audubon members that we keep track of Trouper's whereabouts the way a general keeps track of his men in battle, with colored pins and a wall map. I didn't purchase such elaborate equipment, but I did plot Trouper's course on an ordinary street map of the city. He kept within a radius of about two and a half miles from home, i.e., Mrs. Kennedy's, and his most frequent appearances were near East Beach, within a couple of hundred yards of his point of escape.

It was a peculiar winter. Starting out with a good five-inch rain in November, it was almost completely dry in January and February. In March the rain began again with two and a half inches, and April turned up as the wettest on record with nearly seven inches according to the Santa Barbara weather charts, eight and three-quarters inches according to our rain gauge—all of it in the first nine days of the month.

Rain or no rain, Trouper suffered a sudden attack of spring fever and off he went. Eight days passed—his longest period of absence so far—and Mrs. Kennedy called and asked me if I'd seen him. I hadn't. Nor were any reports of him phoned in to the Museum of Natural History. News of his absence and a complete description of him were passed along the Rare Bird Alert and also published in our local Audubon monthly, *El Tecolote.* Every birder in town was on the lookout for him, but he was never seen again.

Perhaps he went back for a return engagement with the same cat and this time, weighted down by rain-soaked feathers, he'd lost more than a tail. I would like to think, instead, that the spring fever spread throughout his bloodstream and he had begun the long flight home to Maracaibo, following his heart.

Nearly every feeding station in southern California has had its share of escaped parakeets. At our place they usually flew in with a flock of other birds such as house finches, blackbirds, English sparrows or mourning doves. Some stayed only a few minutes, others were in the neighborhood for two or three days before disappearing. In July, 1962, a turquoise and white male remained for nine days, always arriving and departing with what seemed to be the same group of Brewer's blackbirds. Escaped birds like parakeets usually manage fine during the daytime. It is the darkness that brings danger because they haven't learned the necessity for adequate cover at night, and they become easy prey for owls.

The record stay at our feeding station was set by a blue parakeet with a chartreuse head who first appeared on the ledge in March of 1964. The flesh color of the cere, the horny area between bill and forehead, marked her as a female.

Her difference from our previous parakeets was noticeable immediately: she didn't join up with other birds for companionship or security. She arrived on the ledge alone, scurrying back and forth and round and round on her short, stubby legs like a mechanical toy that had wound itself up. When she finished eating—she ate only seed, I never saw her even taste any of the cake crumbs or doughnuts or similar food available—she retired to the tea tree to clean and hone her beak on the rough bark. It would be fanciful to think she chose this particular spot because both the tree, *Leptospermum laevigatum,* and she herself, *Melopsittacus undulatus,* had their origin in Australia. Most likely she chose it because it offered a safe and convenient perch.

During the month that followed she appeared half a dozen times a day on the ledge and in the tea tree and we also saw her at various other places in the neighborhood. As it became obvious that she felt at home in our area and intended to stay, we gave her a name, Blue Betty, bought some special delicacies parakeets were supposed to like and put them in the tea tree. Egg cakes and salt licks and sprays of wild millet were attached with pipe cleaners, and from B.B.'s favorite perch we hung three compressed-seed balls with a wooden perch at each ball. These additions to the doughnuts, bunches of grapes and suet-filled pine cones aleady there made *Leptospermum laevigatum* look like a Christmas tree decorated in pop art style.

B.B. gave no sign of even noticing the delicacies purchased especially for her. The house finches went crazy over the millet sprays, and by day the pigeons and by night the opossums consumed the salt lick. The scrub jays hammered away at the egg cakes, which were considerably harder than their name suggested, and every evening the rats gave us an exhibition of wild and wonderful acrobatics as they maneuvered up and down the string that connected the seed balls.

Quite a few parakeets came and went that year, including an exquisite white male with a cornflower-blue rump and a hint of blue wash across his chest. (A parakeet expert I know tells me that birds bred for albinism, as this one probably was, are less robust and long lived than ordinary birds, and that unpigmented feathers are more susceptible to wear and tear.) In each case I tried to contact the bird's owner, by phoning the Humane Society, the Animal Shelter and the Museum of Natural History, and by checking the lost and found ads in the local newspaper. After we'd made all possible attempts we would sit back and watch the ex-prisoners enjoying their freedom, careening down the canyon like huge mad butterflies or bustling around the ledge like sanderlings around an ebbing wave. Sometimes, in the company of drab little house sparrows, they looked like jungle flowers blown by the wind. For a bird any cage is too small, and freedom is not an abstract word; it is Blue Betty and her transient kin moving across an open sky.

March rolled around once more and the wild birds began their songs of claiming and proclaiming, their nest building and incubating, and finally bringing their babies to the ledge and the porch railing. All this family activity made B.B.'s aloneness more apparent, and to me, more pathetic. Parakeets seem to form a stronger pair bond than most birds and I'd had in mind for some time a scene where a hearty young male would land on the ledge, take one look at B.B., and it would be instant love.

During that spring three parakeets came and went, all females. The season was nearly over when, on June 15, a green parakeet appeared whose larger size and bluish-gray cere marked him as a male. We named him Green Gus. Though Gus and B.B. both fed off the ledge several times a day, it was two weeks before their paths crossed, in the late afternoon of June 29. The scene began to unfold just as I'd imagined it—Gus took one look at B.B., and sure enough, it was instant love. He started chasing her madly around the ledge, dodging sparrows and blackbirds and hopping over bandtails.

Perhaps Gus's approach was too importunate, or his timing was wrong—it was, after all, the supper hour and B.B. was undoubtedly hungry—or perhaps B.B. had been alone so long that she'd grown to prefer her own company. From ledge to tea tree, cotoneaster to eucalyptus, pine to porch railing, B.B. fled her suitor. When she had the chance she stopped to pick up a few seeds and swallow them with nervous haste before Gus caught up with her again. She could fly better than he could, probably because she'd spent more time in freedom, and by sunset he looked pretty tired and discouraged.

B.B. had given every indication that she considered the whole business extremely annoying, so I was taken by surprise the following morning when the two of them arrived for breakfast together. A couple of times during the meal Gus remembered his passion, but both his advances and B.B.'s retreats looked rather perfunctory. Anyway, some kind of amicable understanding seemed to have been reached.

It lasted three days. On the fourth B.B. began to show signs of restiveness. She had, after all, been the number-one parakeet in the neighborhood for well over a year and it must have been difficult for her to share the billing—and the cooing. Her irritability increased daily. Twice I saw her peck Gus viciously on the back of the neck and send him plunging for cover into the thick foliage of the pittosporum.

On July 6, exactly a week after the two parakeets first met, B.B. appeared for breakfast alone. She ate in a more leisurely manner than she had for some time, and after breakfast she retired to the tea tree to preen her feathers and hone her beak, and now and then doze off. There was an air of complacency about her, as if she was perfectly sure her grooming wouldn't be interrupted or her sleep disturbed.

She was right, of course. It's possible that Mr. Rett's theory about the danger to parakeets from owls applied in Gus's case. More likely, though, B.B. decided that rather than lose her pleasant, peaceful life as a spinster, she preferred to lose Gus. Whatever her methods—and those two vicious pecks I'd seen her give him surely offer a clue—we never saw Gus again.

The three dogs, Johnny, the Scottish terrier, Rolls Royce, the red cocker, and Brandy, the German shepherd, paid little attention to our exotic bird visitors. To them a troupial was no better or worse than a robin. But the unfeathered four-footed wildlife kept them in a state of excitement, especially at night.

Johnny had a regular raccoon watch. As soon as the sun set, he took up his position at one of the two small louvered windows that had been put in below the main picture window for ventilation. Typically, the louvers never quite closed tightly and John would sit with his nose pressed against the slits, sniffing the evening air, his beady little eyes peering into the darkness. He ignored the rats, who were too common to bother about, and the possums, who were too slow and dull to arouse his interest, and he concentrated on the raccoons. Probably the basic reason for this is that his sight and hearing were failing with old age and the raccoons were the easiest of all our night visitors to hear coming and to keep track of once they'd arrived.

Even if the house was full of people and the hi-fi was fying its highest, the approach of the raccoons could hardly go unnoticed. It was announced by a series of loud, high-pitched shrieks. After this would come the snapping of twigs and crackle of oak leaves and eucalyptus; then, when they reached the silverleaf cotoneaster which was their staircase to the porch, there would be another series of shrieks. As far as I could tell, the raccoons' fights, which were not confined to mere vocalizing, had to do with the order of ascent, first up the path from the creek, then up the tree to the porch railing. During the mating season, which seemed to last a good part of the year, these noisy sessions were more prolonged and even noisier and were mistaken by most of the neighbors for tomcats fighting.

If I happened to be working late in my office I would see the cotoneaster begin to shake violently—although this kind of coton-easter (*pannosa*) is usually referred to as a tree, it is, in fact, a shrub, and not meant to support the weight of twenty-five- to fifty-pound mammals. I'd hear the rustle of leaves and the *thump, thump, thump, thump,* as one after another of the raccoons jumped from the porch railing onto the ledge.

This was the moment Johnny had been waiting for since sunset. His tail would shoot straight up into a black furry exclamation point, stay there for a minute or two as if paralyzed with astonishment, and then it would start to wag. Guests seeing this performance for the first time invariably thought it meant that Johnny wanted to get out on the ledge to play with his new friends. Certainly he wanted to get out, but the purpose wasn't play and the tail wagging was simply a nervous habit. I have seen him do the same thing just before he leapt for the throat of a hundred-pound malamute. Years of experience—and veterinarians' bills—have taught me that most male Scotties are inveterate fighters, long of tooth and short of tact.

Johnny's raccoon watch was watched on the other side of the window by the raccoons' dog watch. There were three raccoons to begin with, two males we called Rascal and Pascal, and a blithe and bonny female named for our fellow zoophile, Mary Hascall. A plentiful supply of one of their main dietary staples, acorns, supplemented by the hard-boiled eggs and peanut butter sandwiches we provided, had given them thick glossy coats, and moist black noses that shone like patent leather.

Moving in single file along the ledge, the three of them would pass the louvered window beside my chair with barely a glance. But when they reached the window where Johnny was lying in wait, they rose up on their hind legs like little dancing bears and began going through all kinds of dodging and ducking and swaying movements, as if in time to Johnny's soft, ominous growls.

They also jabbed the air with their front paws in a manner that reminded me of the workouts of a punch-drunk fighter I used to see on the beach. Almost every day he came down to shadowbox on the wet sand. He chose early morning or late afternoon when the sun's rays were oblique and lengthened his shadow into a formidable opponent. Watching his shadow intensely, almost as if he expected it to make the first move, he would jab and feint, lunge and retreat, weave and bob, twist and twirl. Such a performance invariably attracted an audience, especially kids, many of them Mexican-Americans who stood and watched, half-envious, half-contemptuous. They called him Gavilan and I am not sure to this day whether the reference was to Kid Gavilan or to the numerous gavilans (sparrow hawks) that frequented the playing fields nearby. They called him other things too, but he didn't seem to mind. There wasn't a shadow on the beach he couldn't lick, just as there wasn't a Scottie on the other side of the window that our raccoons couldn't stand up to.

Another raccoon joined us that spring, and in early August the first babies were brought to the ledge, the most irresistible trio I've ever had as guests. They were then about two months old, weighing as many pounds and looking like exact miniatures of their parents. At this stage the mother was extremely protective and did her best to shield them with her body when they had to pass Johnny's window. This wasn't easy when they got older and more venturesome and so she had to teach them the art of self-defense. These early lessons included, of course, the shadowboxing routine meant to outwit and confound Johnny.

Perhaps the sight of seven raccoons going through such ridiculous motions proved too much for Johnny, or perhaps it was simply that old age began creeping up on him. Each night his raccoon watches started later and ended earlier, and finally, as winter approached, they ceased altogether. The raccoons didn't notice his absence immediately. They took it for granted that he was on his side of the window just as surely as they were on theirs. Eventually one of the younger members of the group became curious, put his front paws up on the window sill and peered inside. Seeing no sign of Johnny he got bolder and pressed his forepaws and his nose against the glass.

To animals which are mainly nocturnal, like raccoons, the sense of touch is often more important than vision and becomes highly developed in a number of organs. Our raccoons loved to explore things, both with their slim, dainty forepaws and their restless little noses that seemed constantly in motion, sniffing, probing, twitching. I've frequently watched a raccoon as he took stock of an item of food I'd never put out previously. He would see it and smell it first, of course, but the main investigation was done by touch. He stroked it slowly and carefully with his front paws, then felt all around it with his nose. If the item of food didn't pass the test I would find it on the porch or ledge the next morning untasted, without so much as a tooth mark on it. Raccoons are supposed to be omnivorous; ours were not.

If the raccoon decided the new food was worth a try, he would pick it up in his front paws, put it in his mouth and carry it to the large ceramic saucer that served as a bird bath at one end of the ledge. Here he would wash it vigorously, so vigorously that the food frequently disintegrated like a piece of cake tossed in with the family laundry. Eventually the raccoons stopped this practice of washing their food, and just about in time too—I was getting thoroughly sick of cleaning up the mess in the bird bath every morning.

Once Johnny's absence was discovered by the young raccoon, all the others came to the window and took turns looking in to see what had happened. It became a nightly routine: *Oh dear, what can the matter be? Johnny's so long at the fair.*

Sometimes, perhaps by accident, perhaps by design, they would tap the glass with their claws. The noise didn't wake up Johnny but the other two dogs would charge over to the window, barking at the top of their lungs. The raccoons merely stared, as though in disapproval, at such a lack of gamesmanship. It was funny the way they paid less attention to the noise of the big German shepherd and the hysterical spaniel than they did to the almost inaudible growls of the little Scottie. That they showed good judgment can be attested to by a tree surgeon, now nameless but not forgotten, who has the dubious distinction of being the only person ever bitten by one of our dogs. After trimming the trees on the adjacent property he climbed over the concrete wall into our patio to pick up a fallen limb. "I was keeping my eye on the two bigger dogs," he said, several stitches later. "I never thought of watching the runt."

The raccoons were smarter. They watched the runt.

Our possums were as tame as the raccoons, but it was a different kind of tameness. The raccoons had sized us up carefully and decided we were O.K., the possums simply seemed oblivious to our presence and carried on their affairs as if we weren't there.

One of these affairs was a knock-down-drag-out fight that started low in the tea tree and got higher and higher until the battle between the two twelve-pound beasts was being waged on the uppermost branch which was hardly more than a twig. Underneath the twig, a long, long way down, was solid concrete. The possums might have survived such a fall but they couldn't have escaped injury of some kind, so I tried to stop the fight by pounding on the window and shouting at them. The only effect this had was to draw the dogs into the action, which in turn drew Ken out of his study.

Ken took the situation in at a glance—not too surprising since it involved a couple of fighting possums, three furiously barking dogs and a large over-excited woman—and decided to try a different approach. He would coax the pugilists down from the tea tree with food. Grabbing a box of cookies out of the cupboard he went down to the patio, turned on the floodlights and began placing cookies underneath the tea tree where the possums couldn't help seeing them. That is, the possums couldn't help seeing them if they looked down. Only they didn't look down. They looked at each other, and the battle continued. To attract their attention Ken threw a cookie at them. It missed. He threw a couple more and they also missed, but as his temper got worse his aim got better. The fourth cookie clipped one of the possums on the nose and the fifth hit his opponent square in the eye. Both animals loosened their grips and peered down as Ken let go with another round of ammunition.

Possums are not very bright but I think even they recognized that there was something unusual about being attacked by Nabisco Vanilla Cremes.

When the young raccoons were about two-thirds grown, the parents began treating them not as their own offspring any more but as unrelated adults in competition for the food supply. Fights were shrill and frequent, on the porch and ledge, in the cotoneaster tree, on the patio and on the lower terrace beside the concrete bird bath which was knocked over nearly every night. During the winter one pair of raccoons deserted us, presumably to seek more peaceful surroundings. For the others a system was eventually worked out, much like the pecking order among birds.

The large male arrived first. He climbed up the cotoneaster alone, inspected the food in the wooden dish and on the deck of the porch and ate what he fancied. The same procedure was repeated on the ledge, and it was all done in a very leisurely manner, as if he couldn't have cared less about the four hungry creatures who were waiting. The next diner was the female, and after her, the three young ones.

By the time their turn came, there was usually nothing left but bread crusts and orange rinds and half-eaten grapes, so I decided to even things up a bit. As soon as the two adults had eaten and gone on their way, I would sneak extra food out to the youngsters, hard-boiled eggs, bananas, cheese, doughnuts, bread and honey. They caught on to this arrangement very quickly and I would find them waiting for me just outside my office door. When I opened the door they would put on a show of scampering away in terror, but it wasn't very convincing. The young members of any species are bolder than their elders—or perhaps more trusting.

With a house to run I couldn't devote all my time to raccoons and I was sometimes late putting out the food. When this happened they jogged my memory by rearing up on their hind legs and tapping on the windows. Every section of glass accessible from the porch or ledge bore the tracings of their delicate forepaws and the smudge marks of their wet little noses. In the beginning the dogs made a terrible racket when they saw the three black-masked faces peering in at them. Eventually a truce was reached and it became a nightly routine for the three dogs on the inside of the window, and the three raccoons on the outside, to stand and quietly size each other up.

It seems a fairly safe assumption that neither group arrived at a very favorable opinion of the other. It must remain an assumption, however, since the two groups never met in the open as far as I know. When the dogs were let out in the evening they stayed on the front part of the property and the public road, as if they realized that after dark the canyon belonged to the night visitors.

Rainbirds on the Roof

It was the first day of autumn, 1964. Those Santa Barbara residents who lived within a block or two of the sea woke up to a dense fog and the ominous warnings of the foghorn at the end of the breakwater. The rest of the city was awakened by the brilliant rays of a September sun and realized it was going to be a hot day. How hot none of us could ever have guessed

The summer that was ending had been one of drought, as usual. The last rain measurable on our gauge was a tenth of an inch in May. September occasionally brings some moisture—the hundred-year average is about a quarter of an inch—but it is better known for bringing our hottest and driest days. For us this is the month of santanas, the scorching winds that blow in over the mountains from the Mojave Desert, a vast area covering some 14,000 square miles.

We are accustomed to sea winds and their ravages: tons of kelp strewn along the beaches, alive with tiny octopi and starfish and skate eggs that look like black plastic comb cases; boats escaped from their moorings, loose anchors and racing buoys, dead fish and sea lions and leopard sharks; battered sea birds, surf scoters and whitewings, all kinds of gulls and terns and cormorants, western grebes and horned grebes, arctic loons and red-throated loons; and once—and only once, thank Heaven—the newly severed head of an enormous wild boar, brought to my reluctant attention by our German shepherd, Brandy.

Sea winds may be violent and cruel, but in a coastal town they are a natural part of life. Santanas are strangers, intruders from the other side of the mountains. They are not polite or kindly strangers. We give them no welcome and they in turn come bearing no good will. One of them almost cost our city its life.

A santana ordinarily arrives on a calm, quiet night. Some people claim it gives no warning, others sense its approach or "feel it in their bones." Nothing psychic is involved, and no bones either, merely skin and mucous membranes reacting to a rapid lowering of humidity and rise in temperature. In southern California the temperature always goes down with the sun, and this rule is broken only by the arrival of a santana.

On one of these calm, quiet nights in September, a person may become suddenly aware that changes are taking place. There is a rustle of leaves, the squawk of a gate swinging, the bang of a screen door. A gust of wind roars down the canyon, and the eucalyptus trees begin to writhe. Leaves begin rushing past the windows like refugees fleeing the forest, and the hard little seed pods of the tea tree tap the glass like animals' claws. If, at this stage of the game, all doors and windows are locked, drapes pulled, and the drafts of fireplaces closed tight, it won't do much good. The dust seems to penetrate the very walls, and every flat surface in the house is soon covered with it. Skin is taut, throats parched, eyes gritty, tempers short. In a santana the milk of human kindness dries up like everything else.

In general, sea winds are fairly strong and steady, and desert winds come in gusts. Sometimes both are blowing simultaneously and between gusts of the desert wind the sea wind rushes in. Then there begins a tug of war between them with the city caught in the middle, a nervous referee for a battle of giants who haven't read the rule book. Temperatures go up and down so rapidly thermometers haven't time to register them accurately—and the range is wide, fifty or sixty degrees.

By sunrise the battle is over, the friendly wind is resting, the stranger has fled, the cleanup begins. Branches and leaves, and the litter blown out of overturned trash cans must be picked up; trees and shrubs and flowers must be hosed down to remove the dust that clogs their breathing pores; damaged bird feeders must be fixed and rehung, and the dirt and debris cleaned out of the bird baths. If we're lucky, the stranger won't come back the next night. . . .

The morning of September 22 was windless. The heavy fog that had blanketed the coastal area at dawn was burned off by the sun before nine o'clock and the mercury in the official temperature gauge, which is located at the shore, began to rise rapidly, up through the seventies into the eighties. Our area, at an elevation of about 550 feet, was a good deal hotter, a situation that was reversed only on very rare occasions.

I had watered heavily the previous afternoon, using the rainbirds on the roof in spite of the outraged protests of the scrub jays. We had had these roof sprinklers installed several years before by an off-duty fireman after the Montecito fire chief had urged all hill and canyon dwellers to be prepared for an emergency as the layers of brushwood grew higher and thicker and more dangerous. The emergency hadn't occurred, but we used the rainbirds to cool the house and to water a considerable part of our property.

Few people had taken the fire chief's advice. Rainbirds on a roof were so uncommon that at first when we used ours, passing motorists would stop and stare, and one even inquired if we'd broken a water main. If the effect was peculiar from the outside, it was doubly peculiar to sit inside and listen to rain pounding on the shingles, to see it pelting the windows and gushing out of the eaves troughs, while just beyond the walls of water a brilliant sun shone from an unclouded sky. Ordering up a private rainstorm in the midst of a California summer is as close to playing God as I care to come.

But the three rainbirds, even twirling full tilt, were no match for the September heat and drought. All traces of moisture had disappeared by midmorning the next day, and the temperature was in the nineties and still rising. The birds coped with the heat in several ways. The yellowthroats napped in a sheltered spot down by the creek. Some of the English sparrows and blackbirds cooled themselves by breathing rapidly through open beaks. The hooded orioles and Anna's hummingbirds drank nectar from the golden hearts of the trumpet flowers and the mockers crushed the ripening elderberries and eugenias. The wrentits kept in the shade, foraging in the dense poison oak that was reddening the canyon slopes. All half dozen bird baths were in continual use, the champion bathers being the house finches, who looked like miniature rainbirds as they hurled water madly in every direction at once.

None of our winter birds had arrived yet, though several species were due any minute—white-crowned sparrows, Lincoln and fox sparrows, pine siskins and Audubon warblers. Many of the summer visitors had already departed—all the swallows, the warbling vireos, Bullock orioles, Wilson warblers, western tanagers and black-headed grosbeaks. (The two latter species were to return mysteriously at the beginning of December, stay a month, and vanish again.) Summer birds still present included Vaux' swifts, hooded orioles and the lone yellow-breasted chat who spent a month with us every year. We also had two interesting and unusual guests, a white-winged dove, normally a desert dweller, and a ringed turtle dove, seldom seen here in the wild but familiar to people who frequent certain parks in Los Angeles where the species has become well established. The white-winged dove had recently arrived, on September 3, the turtle dove had been with us since July.

This, then, was the population of our feeding station on the morning of September 22, 1964. Elsewhere in the country the Warren Commission was still weighing the evidence against Lee Oswald; L.B.J. predicted tax cuts to the Steelworkers' Union; Goldwater hit the campaign trail in Oklahoma; the Phils were 5½ games up on the Cincinnati Reds; and Napa County in northern California had been declared a disaster area by Governor Brown after a forest fire had burned ninety square miles and was still raging out of control. One section of it was traveling at a rate of more than a mile an hour.

For some time Ken and I had been planning to buy an acre or two and eventually build a house. Every now and then when a new parcel of land came on the market we would make arrangements through a real estate agent to inspect it. That morning at eleven a young man took us out to see three acres in the foothills at the opposite end of Montecito. The owner, John Van Bergen, an architect, lived with his wife on the adjoining property in a house he'd recently designed and built himself.

We admired the Van Bergen house and its magnificent panorama of miles and miles of coastline. The region was somewhat higher than where we were living—which meant that it was more than somewhat hotter and dryer—and the terrain was steep. But my main objection to the place was the fact that it would not support an abundance of bird life. There was no source of water nearby, and the vegetation was limited to those native plants which could tolerate prolonged periods of drought, various types of shrubs which are usually grouped together under the name chaparral, and a few small live oak trees.

I had another objection. The climate, in conjunction with many years' accumulation of underbrush, made the place an even greater fire hazard than a wooded canyon like ours. If the Van Bergens, newcomers from Chicago, realized this they didn't show it. Neither did the insurance companies. In response to my question Mr. Van Bergen said they paid the same insurance premiums as anyone else, though certain precautions against fire had been built into the house, such as a flat roof which held a three-inch layer of water.

It was one o'clock when we left the Van Bergens. We drove down to the beach club, had a cold lunch and headed for the surf. On the ramp to the beach I was detained by a friend who wanted to ask me a bird question, and it was here that one of the lifeguards from the pool caught up with me. A message had just been received in the office from Richmond Miller, the young, newly elected president of the Santa Barbara Audubon Society. Rich, failing to reach us at home, had called the beach club to leave word that a fire had been reported on Coyote Road below Mountain Drive. He didn't know how big a fire it was, but in that area, in that weather, even a glowworm was dangerous.

I thought of the fire raging through Napa County, traveling more than a mile an hour; the intersection of Coyote Road and Mountain Drive was half a mile crows' flight from our house. From where I was standing I could see the smoke rising in the air, black and brown and gray, changing color with the fire's fuel. I asked the lifeguard to call Ken in from the sea and tell him we had to go home.

At 2:02 P.M. smoke had been reported in the Coyote Road–Mountain Drive region by an unidentified woman. A minute later an off-duty fireman living in the area confirmed the report and the Coyote fire, as it came to be known, officially began its long and dreadful journey.

Its initial direction was up. At 2:23 it jumped Mountain Drive and the first houses in its path began burning. By 2:30 two planes were dropping fire-retardant chemicals. On the way home we could see the stuff falling like puffs of pink clouds out of a technicolor dream. Fire Retardant Pink was to become, in certain parts of Santa Barbara, the fashionable shade worn by many of the luckier houses, garages, cars, boats, corrals, horses, burros, dogs, cats, people, and at least one highly indignant peacock. The reddish color, by the way, was deliberately added to the formula to make hits and misses more apparent.

When Ken and I pulled into our driveway we met Bertha Blomstrand, the widow who lived across the road from us. She'd come over to check the whereabouts of our dogs in case they might have to be released, and to turn on the rainbirds. Bertha's action was the kind that typified people's attitude toward the fire right from the beginning: it was going to be a bad one and we were all in it together. The three of us stood watching the blaze and the smoke half a mile away, and listening to the shriek of sirens, the rhythmic clatter of the rainbirds and the roar of the borate bombers as they followed the sporty little yellow lead plane that showed them where to drop their loads. It was to be some time before the ordinary quiet sounds of an ordinary day were heard on our street again.

From our living room we saw houses on Mountain Drive burning unchecked. Wind-driven sparks landed in a large grove of eucalyptus and the oil-rich trees virtually exploded into flames. One of the houses in the direct path of the fire had been built by a local writer, Bill Richardson, for his family. It seemed certain to be destroyed, but at the last crucial moment a borate bomber scored a miraculously lucky hit and the place was saved along with a pet burro, four dogs and all of Bill's manuscripts.

It was three o'clock.

During the next hour men who'd served in World War II were surprised by the sudden appearance of an old army buddy, a B-17 Flying Fortress which had been sent down from Chino in northern California carrying 2000 gallons of fire-retardant fluid. By this time half a dozen other planes had arrived from Los Angeles as well as some helicopters, each capable of carrying 50 gallons of the fluid. A combination heliport and firecamp was set up on the athletic field of Westmont College, a private coeducational institution whose property line was two hundred yards from our own.

Late afternoon also brought the first carloads of sightseers, the first wave of telephone calls and the first outbreak of contradictory rumors:

A storm front was heading our way from Oregon and rain would start any minute. No rain was in sight for a week.

Firefighters were coming from every part of the southwest, including the famed Zuñi Indian crews from New Mexico, and the fire would be under control within a few hours. No firefighters could be spared because so many other areas were highly flammable, and the entire city of Santa Barbara was doomed.

Every householder was to soak his roof, walls, shrubbery and trees. Water was to be conserved to keep the pressure from dropping.

We were spared a great many rumors because our only radio wasn't in working condition. This lack of communication proved to be a blessing in disguise. There was an advantage in not knowing exactly how bad things were until after they were over.

As for the phone calls, it was gratifying to receive so many offers of sanctuary, some from people we hadn't been in contact with for years. Yet, as the hours passed and the phone kept ringing, we began to look on it as an insatiable monster demanding our continuous attention. The news it gave us in return was mostly bad—the fire was still going up the mountain, but it was also moving rapidly southward, in our direction, and two hundred acres were burned, including the houses of several people we knew. The only piece of good news was the information about the borate bomber saving Bill Richardson's place with a direct hit of fire retardant.

As soon as the roof and the plantings around our house were thoroughly soaked, I turned off the rainbirds. The scrub jay, who'd been squawking ever since they were turned on, left his griping post in the pine tree and came down to the ledge to remind me that all the food had been washed away. I put out more and the other regular customers began drifting in, the mourning doves with their two uncommon cousins, the turtle dove and the whitewing, band-tailed pigeons, cowbirds, blackbirds, the hooded orioles and the lone yellow-breasted chat, towhees, house finches, song and English sparrows. The birds were perhaps fewer in number than usual, and one oriole and some of the English sparrows showed heat reaction, increased respiration through open beaks.

As the afternoon wore on and workers began leaving their jobs for the day, the stream of cars on our narrow little road increased. What kind of people were in these cars? I will quote one of them and let the reader judge for himself. A young man pulled into our driveway and shouted at Ken who was on the roof readjusting a rainbird:

"Hey, how do we get to the houses that are already burning?"

Darkness fell. At least it should have been darkness, but on the mountains a strange, misplaced and molten sun was rising and expanding, changing the landscape into a firescape. Instead of the normal quiet sounds of night there was the constant deafening roar of helicopters landing and taking off from the camp on the Westmont College athletic field. The borate bombers had stopped at dusk because they couldn't operate over the difficult terrain in the dark, and without chemicals to impede its progress the fire was spreading in all directions at once.

I took the raccoon food out to the ledge as usual. The cotoneaster tree remained still and silent, and no moist black noses pressed against the window beside my chair, no dainty little paws tapped the glass. The raccoons' absence emphasized the eeriness of the night. It was the first time in many months that they had missed us and we didn't know whether they'd fled the fire or were simply lying low because of the noise and confusion. Raccoons are not particularly shy but they're sensible enough to want to avoid trouble. Every year on the last night of October, for instance, they stayed out of sight until every witch and ghost and skeleton and every pirate, clown and batman had gone home to count his loot, and all the neighborhood dogs had finished their Halloween barking binge. For the raccoons, was this a flight for survival, or just another Halloween?

During the early part of the evening the hundreds fighting the fire and the thousands watching it never really doubted that it could and would be brought under control. Then at nine o'clock, the eventuality which some of us had been secretly dreading suddenly came. The first gust of a santana rushed down from the crest of the mountain, driving the flames before it like teams of dragons. It soon became obvious that the fire was going beyond the control of men and machines. If it was to be stopped it would have to be stopped by nature herself. Not only was it spreading at a fantastic speed, it was being forced by the santana to backtrack, destroying whatever had been missed or only half burned the first time.

That night Bill Richardson's house, miraculously saved by a borate bomber in midafternoon, burned to the ground.

The stream of sightseers continued. Our street, Chelham Way, is a circle, it goes nowhere, so only a very small percentage of the cars passing were on legitimate business. One of these stopped at the entrance to our driveway and the man behind the wheel asked us how to get to a house in the neighborhood where an elderly woman lived alone and might need help. He added, "Aren't you Mrs. Millar?"

I said I was.

"We met this morning. You were at our house looking at the acreage we have for sale."

It was John Van Bergen and his wife. Less than twelve hours previously, we'd been talking to them about fire insurance rates and I'd been surprised to learn that they didn't have to pay higher premiums than we did.

There was no time to discuss the ironies of fate. We gave the Van Bergens the information they wanted and they drove on. Later that night they telephoned and offered us refuge from the fire, but by that time we'd decided that if we were forced to evacuate we would go to Ping and Jo Ferry's. We had a number of good reasons for our choice, perhaps the chief one being that when Jo Ferry called she had particularly invited our three dogs to come too. Many people had indicated willingness to take us into their homes, but they didn't especially want to entertain a dour and elderly Scottie, a nervous spaniel and a German shepherd the size of a pony.

Quite a few of the houses on Chelham Way and other streets in the vicinity had already been evacuated. At eleven forty-five the official order came from sound trucks going slowly up and down blaring out the message: *"This area must be evacuated. You have ten minutes to get out of this area. This area must be evacuated in ten minutes. You have ten minutes. . . ."*

It was enough. I grabbed a coat and three leashes. Ken put Brandy and Johnny in the back seat of the car and Rolls Royce in the front. Then he leaned down and kissed me and handed me the car keys. "Drive carefully."

"I thought you were coming with me."

"Drive carefully," he repeated. "And don't try to get in touch with me by phone. I'll be out on the ledge with a hose."

The sound truck went by again: *"This area must be evacuated immediately. You must leave now. This is your final warning."*

As I backed out of the driveway I saw Bertha Blomstrand climbing a ladder up to her roof. I called to her. She looked down at me and shook her head grimly. Her meaning was clear: everything she had worked for all her life was in that house and she wasn't going to abandon it.

She looked frail and impotent in the light of the fire that was now surrounding us on three sides, and the odds against her were formidable. Yet I know of dozens of houses that were saved in this manner—by one determined person with a garden hose—after the situation became so bad that firefighters and equipment couldn't be spared merely to save buildings, but had to be used for the much more important job of keeping the fire from spreading.

"This is your final warning."
I joined the sad little procession of vehicles evacuating our street. Some had obviously been packed earlier in the evening. There was a pickup truck loaded with furniture and bedding held in place by two frightened children, a station wagon carrying suitcases and camping equipment, a tiny sports car jammed with Westmont College girls and their collections of photographs and folk-song albums and books.
All I had was a coat and three leashes.

The Ferrys lived then as they do now on a knoll overlooking the Bird Refuge and the sea beyond. Ping was away on a business trip but Jo was waiting for me with her youngest daughter, Robin, a professional rider who'd driven up from the stables in Somis as soon as she heard about the fire. They both seemed calm, even cheerful, as though the glow in the sky and the pervasive smell of smoke were caused by nothing more than a Boy Scout marshmallow roast or a backyard barbecue. Zorba, the spaniel, represented the facts more accurately—he took one look at my dogs, barked nervously and fled to the rear of the house. Mine set off in pursuit and the game began that was to last, quite literally, all through the night.
Instead of making good use of the time by getting some rest, Jo and Robin and I sat in the library for a while and talked. Robin especially was to regret this since she was drafted to spend the next two nights helping look after some reluctant and difficult refugees at the polo field—150 show horses, mainly hunters and jumpers.
Eventually Jo showed me upstairs to my room, gave me a sleeping pill and said goodnight. There was a small radio beside the bed, and while I knew it would bring only bad news at this point, I couldn't resist turning it on. A man was announcing in a voice hoarse with fatigue that fifteen houses had been destroyed and a thousand men were battling the fire on a ten-mile front. There was no hope of containment as long as the santana kept blowing. Flames were fifty to seventy feet high and had already reached Cold Spring Canyon on the northeast, Gibraltar Road on the northwest, and Sycamore and Rattlesnake canyons on the west.
I turned off the radio and sat on the edge of the bed, the report-

er's words echoing in my ears. I knew those canyons well and had spent many good hours birding in them, especially Rattlesnake Canyon. It was the topography, not the rattlesnakes, that had given the place its name, and the wildlife I encountered, except for deer and rabbits and the occasional red fox and coyote, consisted mainly of birds.

At the old stone bridge that marked the canyon's mouth, hundreds of wintering robins and cedar waxwings fed voraciously on toyon and coffeeberries and the miniature apples of the manzanita. Oregon juncos and hermit thrushes bathed in the shallow pools, Bewick wrens picked their way fastidiously through the underbrush, pausing to catch a bug or denounce an intruder, and redbreasted sapsuckers played hide and seek with us around the trunks of the live oak trees. Wide-eyed kinglets rattled from leaf to leaf, every fidgety-twitchy movement distinguishing them from their look-alike but more phlegmatic cousins, the Hutton vireos, which were found in the same area though less frequently. The difference between the two species became unmistakable when two male kinglets met and the top of each tiny head burst into a crimson rage.

When spring came to the canyon, shooting stars, owl's clover, blue-eyed grass and milk maids bloomed in the sun, and in the shadier places, fiesta flowers and Indian pinks, woodmint and the little green replicas of artists' palettes that are called miner's lettuce because the forty-niners used them for salads. It was then that the phainopeplas arrived to nest in the mistletoe, the lazuli buntings in the silver-lined mugwort along the stream, the Wilson warblers under the blackberry vines, the black-chinned hummingbirds in the sycamores, the cliff swallows under the stone bridge already occupied by a pair of black phoebes, the olive-sided flycatchers in the pines, and Hutton vireos in the oaks, the western wood pewees and Bullock orioles in almost any tree or bush.

No summer rains fed the creek and by September some parts of it had turned to mud and some to dust, and the slow trickle of water was only a reminder of the past winter and a promise of the one to come. Along the banks the leaves of the poison oak turned orange and red, and its smooth white berries were eaten by wrentits and California thrashers. Audubon warblers were everywhere, from the tops of the tallest trees where they flew out after insects like flycatchers, to the ground where they foraged like buntings. From ceanothus and chamise came the golden-crowned sparrows' sweet pleading, "Hear me! Dear, hear me!" Pine siskins and American goldfinches gorged on the ripening seeds of the sycamores and alders, and high in the sky, white-throated swifts tumbled and turned and twisted with such speed that no single bird could be followed with the binoculars. (W. L. Dawson, in *Birds of California,* estimated that a white-throated swift which lives for eight years covers a distance equal to ten round trips to the moon.) Among the fallen leaves brown towhees foraged, both feet at a time, sounding like a whole battalion of birds, while tiny gray gnatcatchers searched the limbs of the pepper trees for grubs, and bushtits bickered through the oaks, followed by other little birds attracted by their antics and gay gossip—Townsend and Audubon and orange-crowned warblers, plain titmice and Hutton vireos, and in some years, mountain chickadees and red-breasted nuthatches.

This was Rattlesnake Canyon. I thought of all the small confiding creatures who lived in it and I wept.

The sleeping pill Jo Ferry had given me hit me very suddenly. I don't know what it contained but I can vouch for its effectiveness: I slept through the arrival and bedding down of my fellow refugees, a family of eleven with all their household pets, including a snake and a parakeet.

I woke up at dawn and became immediately aware of a change in the atmosphere. I was cold. The air coming in through the window was gray not with smoke but with fog, and it smelled of the sea, of kelp and tar and wet pilings. The santana had stopped.

I put on my coat, picked up the three leashes and made my way through the quiet house out to the driveway. Zorba, the Ferrys' spaniel, was stretched out, dead to the world, under an olive tree. My three dogs were arranged around the car, panting even in their sleep, as though this was merely a short recess in a long game. At the sound of my step they were instantly alert and eager to go home. They hadn't the slightest doubt that there was still a home for them to go to. Their only anxiety seemed to be that they might have to be separated from me, so they all insisted on riding in the front seat. It was a cosy trip.

At the top of Barker Pass there was an abrupt change in the weather. The fog dropped away like a curtain and the air was hot and dry and windless and ashes were falling everywhere, some particles as fine as dust, some large as saucers. On Sycamore Canyon Road I came across a roadblock, but after a brief exchange of words I was allowed through. The men in charge looked too tired to argue. They had been up all night like hundreds of other volunteer workers—students from the university and from City and Westmont colleges, Red Cross and Salvation Army workers, civil defense and National Guard units, radio hams, firemen's wives manning the stations while their husbands fought on the front lines, nurses and nurses' aides, teachers, city and county employees, and such a varied assortment as the members of a teen-age hotrod club, a folk-dancing group, and a contingent of deep-sea divers from one of the offshore oil rigs.

I turned into Chelham Way.

 **16**

Fire on the Mountains

It was like the fringe of a bombed area. The houses were still standing but deserted. In one driveway a late-model sedan was parked with a small U-haul trailer attached to the rear bumper. The trailer, heaped with clothes and bedding, had been left unprotected and the top layer of stuff was black with ashes. The sedan, however, was carefully covered with a tarpaulin. Perhaps its owner was a veteran of the disastrous 1955 Refugio fire, when a great many of us learned that ashes falling through atmospheric moisture made a lime mixture which ruined even the toughest paint.

Halfway around Chelham Way was a narrow black-top road leading to Westmont College. A locked gate kept the road unused except in emergencies. Beyond the gate, which had been opened, I could see a large section of the athletic field where the main fire-camp had been set up the previous day. Here, where Ken and I used to walk our dogs, where we watched robins in winter and track meets in spring, this place meant for nothing more than games was now headquarters for hundreds of men, a kind of instant village. Here they ate at canteen tents, slept on the ground, received first aid for burns and cuts, were sent off in helicopters, fire trucks, buses, pickups, jeeps, and brought back to begin the cycle all over again.

The noise was deafening, most of it caused by the arrival and departure of helicopters and the shriek of sirens and blare of loudspeakers. The "helitack" units of the Forest Service consisted of the pilots themselves, the fire jumpers wearing heavy canvas suits to protect them when they leaped into the brush, and ground crews, in orange shirts and helmets, whose job was to prime and space the copters and keep them out of each other's downdraft.

The scene, with its backdrop of blazing mountains, was unreal to me. Even the wounded men being brought in by helicopter looked like extras from the Warner Brothers back lot and the sirens of the ambulances as they left the field seemed like part of a sound track. The dogs knew better. They began to whine, so I let them out of the car and told them to go and find Ken. They didn't hesitate. It was a good place to get away from.

Beyond the road leading into the firecamp was the top of our canyon. This part, which belonged to Westmont College and had no structures on it, had been completely burned. The ancient oak trees were black skeletons rising from gray ashes, and many eucalyptus, cypresses and Monterey pines had been reduced to stumps, some still smoldering. But where the row of houses began, along each side of the canyon, the burning had terminated. There was no evidence that the area had been wetted down nor any reddish stains indicating the use of fire retardant; no firebreak had been bulldozed and no hose laid. Yet at that one particular point the fire had stopped.

I learned later what had happened. At two-thirty in the morning, just when all hope of saving our canyon had been abandoned, the santana ceased as abruptly as it began and the wind pressed in from the sea, cool and moist. Temperatures dropped, humidity rose, and the flames were pushed back toward the mountains. It was during this lull that the Los Angeles *Herald Examiner* went to press with the front-page headlines "SANTA BARBARA SAFE. FIRE SHIFTS: 18 HOMES LOST." By the time I got to read those headlines Santa Barbara was surrounded on three sides by an inferno and a hundred more houses had been lost.

I stopped the car. Through the binoculars I kept in the glove compartment I examined hollows where smoke was still rising and stumps still smoldering unattended. At any moment they could burst into flames again and the santana could return. It had taken a miracle to save our canyon and there was probably only one to a customer. I rushed home to call the fire department.

Ken was asleep on the living-room davenport, a scribbled note on the coffee table beside him instructing me to wake him up when necessary. He didn't stir even under the barrage of dog greetings.

Most of the telephones in the region were out of commission by this time. Ours was still working, though it failed to solve much. The fire department, I was told, had no trucks and no men available; people spotting areas which were still smoking were urged to cover them with dirt and/or douse them with water. I grabbed a shovel and a length of garden hose and headed back up the road.

During the windless morning the fire went through a semiquiescent phase. There was unofficial talk of "early containment," and a few evacuees began returning. Though the area where I was working still smoldered in places, other people had arrived to assist and the general picture looked good. By noon I felt secure enough to go home for some lunch. The only wildlife I'd seen all morning was an indignant family of acorn woodpeckers living in a nearby telephone pole, and a badly frightened and half-singed fox who came scurrying up from the bottom of the canyon.

Over tea and sandwiches Ken told me how he'd spent the night dousing sparks and embers that fell on the roof and in the underbrush. He had done his job well. Too well. The tea tree's natural tendency to lean had been encouraged by the excessive water and it now lay on its side on the ground. Many trees were lost to fire during that week; our tea tree was probably the only one lost to flood.

We were finishing lunch when my sister called to tell us the fire had started on another rampage. By midafternoon the "early containment" theory had been blown sky high—and sky high turned out to be the precise description. The flames jumped El Camino Cielo, the sky road, and were racing down the other side of the ridge, with nothing whatever to stop them. Ten borate bombers were in operation, but dense smoke and wind conditions had grounded all of them and the fire roared unchecked into the back country, Santa Barbara's vulnerable watershed.

El Camino Cielo was the road along the top of the first main ridge, starting at the east end of Montecito and continuing west past the city of Santa Barbara, San Marcos Pass, Santa Ynez Peak, its highest point at 4292 feet, and ending at Refugio Pass. Along this sky road, winter bird watchers were apt to see mountain species which seldom appeared in the city itself—a Clark nutcracker noisily prying open the scales of a pine cone; a varied thrush standing in regal silence underneath a live oak, ignoring the raucous challenges of Steller jays; golden-crowned kinglets and brown creepers, mountain chickadees and red-breasted nuthatches, and sometimes a large garrulous flock of those erratic wanderers, the piñon jays.

The previous December, Jewell Kriger and I had done some advance scouting along Camino Cielo preparing for the Audubon Christmas bird count and we had come across a Townsend solitaire flycatching in the chamise and scrub oak along the sides of the road. A quarter of a mile beyond we found another solitaire. These birds are rarely found on a coastal bird count and we wanted to make sure that at least one of the solitaires would be located when the proper time arrived. Camino Cielo was not part of our regular territory—we were scouting it for Dr. Mary Erickson, ornithologist at the University of California at Santa Barbara. Mary was to head the group covering the area on actual count day, but she was too busy to do any preliminary looking.

The usual procedure in a situation like this was to note the mileage, and if the find was especially important, like the pygmy owls' nest earlier in the year, to mark the spot with something that would attract attention without rousing the wrath of anti-litterbuggers. And others. (I mention "others" because on one occasion, to mark the whereabouts of a pair of black-chinned sparrows, I had carefully built a small mound out of stones, the best material on hand. Half our Audubon Society fell over the stones, and by the time the excitement subsided, the black-chinned sparrows were far away and glad of it.)

Near the pygmy owls' nest we'd been lucky enough to pick up a good-sized piece of board painted red. We couldn't expect such luck to be repeated, and it wasn't. We found no marker in the area that would be readily visible from a moving car. Two more factors were against the Townsend solitaires appearing on our Christmas count. The speedometer on Jewell's car was out of order and the previous weekend Russ Kriger had done one of his enthusiastic cleanup jobs on the car's interior. A search through the glove compartment and the trunk, and even behind the seats, revealed nothing useable as a marker—no polishing cloth or chamois, no piece of rope or empty bottle, no last summer's beach hat or last winter's scarf. I looked at Jewell. She was wearing a white shirt and capris and a yellow sweater the exact shade of the band across the tip of a waxwing's tail.

"Have you ever noticed," I said, "how easy it is to identify a flock of cedar waxwings from a distance? The yellow tailbands show up very conspicuously."

"So?"

"Experiments have shown that yellow is the color most easily seen from the greatest distance."

"Well, you can forget the experiments," Jewell said. "This sweater happens to have been a gift from one of my favorite relatives. It's practically a keepsake."

"You bought it yourself last year. I was with you, I even remember what it cost."

"All right, all *right*. But I want it back."

I assured her that she'd get it back, providing that during the next three days it wasn't eaten by some animal, ruined by rain or blown away by the wind.

I tied the sweater to the top of a small ceanothus bush to mark the spot where we'd seen the first Townsend solitaire. To indicate the location of the second bird I was forced to sacrifice the lace hem of my slip, which I ripped off and impaled on a dead oak twig. The lace could easily be spotted by someone who was looking for it, and the sweater was conspicuous enough to prove that the experiments were right: if you want to be seen, wear yellow.

The following Sunday was count day. As usual there was a last-minute mixup and El Camino Cielo, which was to be Mary Erickson's territory, was assigned to someone else. I didn't know about this until the following Tuesday afternoon when the group captains and other interested people met in the junior library of the Museum of Natural History to make their official reports and add up the number of species and the number of birds seen between dawn and midnight on the Big Day. No one had remembered to have the heat turned on in the library ahead of time and we all sat around a table, huddled in coats.

The total number of species that year was 166, good enough to place us fifth in the nation, just one up on Freeport, Texas, and Oakland, California, tied at 165.

I greeted Mary Erickson, who was sitting across the table from me, and asked her what mountain species she'd found up on the ridge. She told me she'd been assigned to a beach and slough area instead.

A woman I'd never seen before volunteered the information that she had helped cover Camino Cielo, and except for a Steller's jay and a varied thrush the place had been very disappointing, bird-wise. She'd obviously missed the Townsend solitaire, so I didn't mention it.

The library was much warmer by this time and people were starting to take off their coats. The newcomer made a ceremony of removing hers, as though she wanted to make sure everyone noticed the costume she had on underneath. Everyone noticed all right. Especially me. Over a plaid wool skirt she wore a yellow sweater the exact shade of the band across the tip of a waxwing's tail.

She saw me staring at the sweater. "Like it?"

I nodded.

"You'll never believe where I got it."

It was at that point, I suppose, when I should have taken her aside and explained the situation, but I didn't. Instead, I listened in a kind of numb silence while she described to us how she'd seen the sweater, flapping in the wind, stopped the car and went over to investigate.

". . . And there, tied to a bush, was this perfectly good sweater which turned out to be exactly my size. I couldn't leave it out there in the weather to be ruined, so I brought it home and laundered it. And lo and behold, here it is and I am. It makes you wonder though, doesn't it? What kind of a nut would leave a perfectly good sweater tied to a bush in the middle of nowhere?"

The answer seems inescapable: my kind.

The second night of the fire came on. At seven-thirty the heavy winds which had been blowing all afternoon at the upper elevations reached the foothills, and many of us found out for the first time what the term "wildfire" really meant. The whole mountain range seemed to explode, and flames were suddenly roaring down toward the city itself, through San Roque Canyon, Laurel Canyon, Mission Canyon, where the Botanic Garden was situated, all the way to Romero Canyon at the northeast end of Montecito. Because of the winds and approaching darkness the borate bombers stopped operating, and by this time too, there was a drastic drop in water pressure.

Mass evacuations began, with some motels and hotels offering free rooms, and moving companies volunteering trucks and vans. Many people were double evacuees who'd fled Sycamore and Cold Springs canyons the first night and were now forced to flee their places of refuge; and before the fire was over, there was even a small band of very tired and jittery triple evacuees.

Our Chelham Way situation, which had been fairly good all day, was suddenly ominous again as the fire turned back in our direction. I thought of the house on Mountain Drive that had been saved in the afternoon only to be burned to the ground at midnight, and I wondered what similar ironies fate might be preparing for us.

Blessing counters and silver lining searchers found a plus in a negative: there were no sightseers. The noise from the firecamp, however, was incredible, a continuous roar of helicopters arriving and departing, the blaring of air to ground loudspeakers, the shrieking of ambulance and fire truck sirens. It was decibels rather than danger which strained my nerves to the breaking point and convinced Ken I'd be better off elsewhere.

Jo Ferry called to repeat her invitation of the previous night, but Ken decided that this time more constructive action was necessary than simply sending me off with the three dogs. He made arrangements with my brother-in-law, Clarence Schlagel, to bring his pickup truck over. After a series of delays caused by roadblocks Clarence arrived with the truck and we loaded it with our main valuables, manuscripts and books. We owned no art originals, no fine china or silver, no furs, and I wore my two pieces of jewelry, my wedding ring and my "lucky" bracelet which had been a present from our daughter, Linda, many years before. (Some people we knew, trapped in the fire by a sudden, violent change of wind, used their swimming pool as a depository for their silver, jewelry and furs, including a beaver jacket whose original owner wouldn't have minded at all.)

It was agreed that I would go to the Schlagels' house with the two smaller dogs, leaving Brandy with Ken. That way Ken could rest at intervals during the night knowing that Brandy would wake him up if anything unusual happened. German shepherds have a highly developed sense of propriety and when things go wrong they indicate their disapproval readily and unmistakably. Having Brandy in the room was like having an alarm clock set to go off in any emergency.

I rode in the truck with Johnny sitting quietly beside me and Rolls on my lap, trembling and whining all the way, partly out of fear and partly anticipation of spending another night chasing around the Ferrys' house with Zorba. He was in for a disappointment: no chasing was allowed at the Schlagels' place because there were too many chasers and chasees, and to avoid a complete shambles the animals had to be kept separated as much as possible. I counted four cats—a fat, ill-tempered orange tiger bought for Jane when she was a baby, an alley cat who realized he'd struck it rich and seldom left the davenport except to eat, and a pair of tabbies abandoned by a neighbor who'd moved away; Jane's pygmy poodle with the giant name of Cha Cha José Morning Glory, my sister's burro, Bobo, who had a loud, nervous hyena-type laugh he seemed to reserve especially for me, and Clarence's four Shetland ponies. Sibling rivalry was rather intense on occasion, and the arrival of Johnny who loathed cats, and Rolls who hated horses and rapidly learned to hate burros, didn't improve matters. There were many times during the night when I would have welcomed the sound of helicopters and fire sirens to drown out some of the yelping, yowling, whinnying, barking, and above all, Bobo's wild bursts of laughter.

I woke up at dawn, leashed my two dogs and took them for a walk down the road toward the sea. When I faced that direction everything seemed quite normal. The light breeze smelled of salt and moist kelp. Mourning doves and brown towhees foraged along the sides of the road and bandtails gathered in the eucalyptus trees, getting ready to come down to feed. Brewer's blackbirds and brown-headed cowbirds were already heading for the Schlagels' corral, Anna's hummingbirds hurled themselves in and out of fuchsia blossoms and the bright red bushes of callistemon and torches of aloe, while half a dozen dogs vehemently denounced me and the company I kept.

When I turned to go back, the whole picture changed abruptly. I remember thinking, with terrible surprise as if I hadn't been aware of it before, *Our mountains are on fire, our forest is burning.*

Returning to the house, I found my sister and brother-in-law in the kitchen making breakfast and listening to the radio. It had been a disastrous night. With winds in forty-five mile an hour gusts and flames towering as high as two hundred feet, the firefighters didn't have a chance. Twenty-three thousand acres and over a hundred buildings were now destroyed and still the fire roared on, unchecked.

Fire, like war, is no respecter of age. Lost hysterical children wandered helplessly around Montecito village, and Wood Glen Hall, a home for the elderly at the opposite end of the fire area, was evacuated when the building filled with smoke.

Fire operates without any rules of fair play. Carol Davis of the University of California at Santa Barbara was helping the residents of Wood Glen Hall carry out their possessions when she learned that her own house had been destroyed and the only things saved were four books and a few pieces of clothing.

Fire makes no religious distinctions. The Catholic Sisters of Charity were burned out, the Episcopalian retreat on Mount Calvary lost a building, and a residence hall was destroyed at the Baptist Westmont College.

Fire has no regard for history or politics. Several buildings were burned to the ground at San Ysidro Ranch, the site of one of the old adobes constructed when Santa Barbara was under Mexican rule, and the place where, in 1953, a young Massachusetts senator named Kennedy brought his new bride, Jacqueline Lee Bouvier, on their honeymoon.

Fire does not defer to beauty, either natural or man-made. A multimillion-dollar art collection belonging to Avery Brundage was destroyed, and some parts of the Botanic Garden were ravaged, including the majestic grove of sequoias, the largest of trees, where in the winter we could always find the tiniest of warblers, Townsend's, and in the spring the almost as tiny Oregon juncos nested under the fragrant heart-shaped leaves of wild ginger.

Even the firecamp itself wasn't spared. Flying embers started a blaze right in the middle of it and burned an area the size of a city lot before it was extinguished.

Around Santa Barbara that morning few people had a good word to say for Prometheus.

Ken phoned while I was feeding the dogs to tell us that he and Brandy and the house had come through the night in fair shape. Once again the flames had reached the head of our canyon and turned back as the winds shifted and though live coals had left holes in some roofs and all exterior areas were a mess, not a house on Chelham Way had been lost.

Other people weren't so lucky. Of my fellow refugees at the Ferrys' house, two were completely burned out: Robert M. Hutchins who lived in Romero Canyon in Montecito, and Hallock Hoffman who lived miles in the opposite direction above the Botanic Garden.

Every disaster has its share of ironies. Perhaps the Coyote fire seemed to have more simply because they happened to people we knew. One of them involved an old wooden shed which was on the Romero Canyon property where the Hutchins had built their house several years before. The shed was being used to store the antiques Mrs. Hutchins had been gathering from various parts of the world for her art shop. When it became inevitable that fire was going to overrun the area, the antiques were removed by truck and taken to—where else?—the Ferrys' house. No collector of ironies will be surprised to learn that the old shed, highly inflammable and containing nothing whatever of value, was the only building in the area untouched by flames.

One of the most eloquent of all the pictures taken during and after the Coyote fire was a shot of the formal gardens of the Brundage estate. It showed a marble Athena looking coolly and imperturbably through the bare black bones of trees toward the ruined mountains. No caption was needed; *Ars longa, vita brevis.*

During that early Thursday phone call, Ken also told me what I'd already guessed: during the night the Van Bergens' house, which had been offered to us as a sanctuary from the fire, was completely destroyed. Afterwards I learned some of the details from the Van Bergens themselves and from people who'd been watching from below.

The house, situated on a knoll at an altitude of about seven hundred feet and constructed of glass and stucco in a distinctive, semicircular design, was easily identifiable for miles around. Dozens of observers saw the flames advancing on it and they were all unanimous on one point: the place did not burn, it was consumed—and with such rapidity that there was hardly a trace of smoke. Less than twenty minutes elapsed between the beginning of the fire and the end of the house. Evidence of the fantastic heat generated during that time was discovered later in the week when the Van Bergens started sifting through the ruins. The glass and the aluminum framing of the windows had oozed together in an incredible mess and the porcelain on the kitchen sink had completely melted. Since this stuff is applied at a temperature of 3000° F., firemen estimated the fire at that point to be between 3000° and 4000° F.

After breakfast, Johnny and Rolls and I said goodbye to the poodle, Cha Cha José Morning Glory, to Bobo, who let out one last triumphant guffaw, and to the cats Goldie, Neighbor, Neighbor Junior and Sneaky, and the ponies Heidi, Slipper, Tammy and Shasta. None of them showed the slightest regret at our departure.

It was still very early in the morning when I arrived home. For us the fire which had threatened on three sides was over. For others it was just starting. By noon 23,000 acres had burned, more than 2000 men were on the front and preparations were being made to start the backfire that was really to backfire and cause the first death.

Our house and yard, in spite of a covering of gray ash, looked beautiful to me because they were still there. Something was missing though. I noticed as soon as I walked in the front door that the ledge was vacant and the food I'd put out the previous night was untouched. The mourning doves and band-tailed pigeons, normally seen at any hour of any day, were missing. So were our unusual visitors, the ringed turtle dove and the white-winged dove. The only bird life in evidence was a small flock of green-backed goldfinches in the bath on the lower terrace. They were bathing merrily in the gray ash-coated water as if it were the clearest, freshest mountain brook.

The most obvious absence, however, and the most mysterious, was that of the scrub jays. I took some peanuts out to the wooden dish on the porch railing, a maneuver that under ordinary conditions would have set the canyon echoing with their harsh cries of "Hurry up, hurry up, hurry up!" and brought jays down from every tree and rooftop. Nothing happened. The acorn woodpeckers didn't respond either, but I didn't expect them to; it was now the final week of September, the month when the acorns were beginning to ripen and there was work to be done. The only bird who appeared for the peanuts was Houdunit, the brown towhee. This was predictable since he seldom ventured more than fifty feet from the house and knew all the things that took place in and around it almost before they had a chance to happen.

We were feeding about a dozen scrub jays at this time, most of whom had been raised on the ledge and were very tame. The word tame might give the impression of birds trained to sit on shoulders and do tricks and the like. That impression would be wrong. Our jays were tame in the sense that they were part of the landscape, like the eucalyptus trees and the cotoneasters; their voices were as familiar to us as Brandy's basso-profundo bark or Johnny's howling at sirens; our lives and their lives were entwined, so that you might say we were all part of the same biota.

In the course of the morning a number of the usual birds came to the ledge to feed—house finches, a pair of young song sparrows, cowbirds and blackbirds, a lone flicker and a mockingbird. The scrub jays remained absent, as did the band-tailed pigeons, the three species of dove and two house wrens who'd been with us since spring. We never saw any of them again.

When a major disaster is over, there are immediate estimates of losses in terms of dollars and cents. The Coyote fire, which continued for more than a week, is said to have been started by a woman burning rubbish to avoid the admission fee to the county dump. She saved fifty cents. It cost the rest of us $20,000,000.

The cost in wildlife was much more difficult to assess. The creatures given sanctuary by the Humane Society ranged from African goats to ducks and peacocks, but these were pets. Reports of actual wildlife, especially of birds, were few and vague. An account of birds flying up out of the burning trees and falling back into the flames, I was unable to verify—let alone check what kinds of birds and whether they were all the same and how many there were, and so on. The number of injured birds brought to the Museum of Natural History was no higher during and after the fire than before it.

Bill Botwright of the Santa Barbara *News-Press,* describing his patrol of the fire area during the first night's lull when the santana stopped, told of seeing "two large birds blundering blindly in the red glare." He thought they were crows, but they could have been band-tailed pigeons which are only slightly smaller, fourteen to sixteen inches as compared with the crows' seventeen to twenty-one inches. Dick Smith, of the same newspaper, who covered the rugged back-country regions in his triple roles of artist, topographer and naturalist, told us that the only birds he saw actually fleeing the fire were quail running out of the underbrush, and that on dozens of trips into the area after the fire he didn't come across a single carcass or skeleton of a bird. This doesn't mean that no birds were destroyed, only that evidence of such destruction was reduced to ash. Bird bones are light and hollow; they can be, and often by accident have been, cremated in a backyard barbecue pit.

In the absence of eyewitness accounts and even one corpus

delicti, we had to depend on circumstantial evidence as well as facts. The main fact was that before the fire we had feeding on our ledge every day a flock of approximately a hundred band-tailed pigeons, half that many mourning doves, one white-winged and one turtle dove, ten or twelve scrub jays; and feeding in and under the shrubbery around the house, a pair of house wrens. None of these birds reappeared after the fire. (Our last sight of the Vaux' swift on the first night of the fire has been described in an earlier chapter.)

A number of people have suggested that the disappearing birds sensed danger and flew away to a safer area. There are several reasons why I can't believe this. If the pigeons, doves and jays took flight when danger was imminent, why didn't the house finches, towhees, blackbirds, cowbirds, song sparrows, goldfinches, hummingbirds, thrashers, titmice, flickers and so on?

You would also expect that when the danger had passed, the birds that had fled would begin returning. The feeding station was their home, as far as wild birds can have a home. There they ate their meals and met their neighbors, and sunned in the good weather and took shelter in the bad. Many of them had been brought to the ledge the first day they could fly and they accepted Ken and me and the three dogs, moving around on the other side of the glass or on the patio below, as part of their daily routine. I have previously described the tameness of the jays. As for the doves and pigeons, they had become so unafraid that it took several smart taps of a folded newspaper on the window or the porch railing to chase them away when I wanted to turn on the rainbirds. Even then an occasional juvenile would refuse to budge, and would stand glaring at me through the bogus rain with an expression that clearly meant, who did I think I was—the *owner* of the ledge?

If any of the missing birds had come back I would have recognized them instantly, not as individuals but as former freeloaders who knew their way around the premises. Newcomers arriving at the feeding station were easy to spot.

A very small minority of these were stragglers too hungry, too exhausted or too sick to act in their normally cautious manner. The rose-breasted grosbeak which appeared on October 30,

1963, was a good example. This grosbeak, a bird belonging east of the Rockies, must have been somewhat flabbergasted to find himself not only west of the Rockies, but west of the Sierra Nevada as well; in fact, right at the Pacific coast on our ledge. He ate almost continuously the first day, oblivious to the other birds and to the movements of people on the other side of the window, including a flock of bird watchers who'd responded to the Rare Bird Alert I had put out as soon as the grosbeak arrived. On the second day he was considerably more skittish and his appearances on the ledge were so sporadic that one determined out-of-town birder had to wait two hours for a glimpse of him. By the fourth day, rested, well fed and in good health again, he was completely wild and independent, and that afternoon he was on his way.

The rose-breasted grosbeak had reversed the usual behavior pattern. Normally a new bird arrives shy and wild and gradually becomes tamer. The first Brewer blackbird, for instance, approached the feeding station quietly and by himself. From an unobtrusive perch in the loquat tree he studied the proceedings for more than a week before he flew down with the other birds, at first on the lower terrace, eventually on the ledge.

The most extreme case of wariness was the crow. He spent an entire winter watching the place from the tops of the eucalyptus trees and the Monterey pines. The opening of a door or window, the turning on of a sprinkler, the slightest movement that was unexpected would send him flying off, squawking invectives at us and warnings to his friends. Only when there were babies to be fed did he come down for food. He was so quick and quiet about it that I didn't even suspect he was responsible for the whole doughnuts disappearing as soon as I put them out in the wooden dish outside my office window. Though I had no evidence against the scrub jays I blamed them, on general principles. Then one morning when I went into my office to begin work, a black flash crossed the corner of my vision and the thief was identified. I duly apologized to the jays, who are blamed by nearly everybody for nearly everything.

The crow and the rose-breasted grosbeak provided good examples of the two types of behavior which made newcomers to the feeding station easily recognizable.

The first band-tailed pigeon to arrive after the fire showed no signs of familiarity with the place. He perched, just as our initial bandtail had done years previously, on a eucalyptus limb over the drip bird bath. When I went over to the window and raised my binoculars he flew away. Shadows on windows couldn't be trusted and binoculars were weapons that might be used against him. He was a stranger. So, too, was the first scrub jay after the fire, and the first mourning dove. No white-winged dove, turtle dove or house wren appeared again at the feeding station.

What had happened? We can never be completely sure, but there seems little doubt that the missing birds were destroyed while they were asleep. Once birds are settled for the night they are hard to disturb. Eyes closed, heartbeat slowed, head tucked under wing and claws locked in position, the sleeping bird is practically oblivious to noise, light and movement: airplanes, sirens, searchlights, high winds, cloudbursts, auto horns, band concerts—and fire. The odor of smoke, a cogent warning of danger to so many furred creatures, is lost on the feathered ones. Sense of smell is poorly developed in birds since there is little need for it in their atmospheric environment.

The band-tailed pigeons, I had learned, used an old Monterey cypress at the head of the canyon as their favorite roost. It seems likely that when the sun set the first evening of the fire, some of the doves and pigeons were roosting in the same cypress, or in the oaks and pines nearby. At nine o'clock the santana began, and in the course of the night the entire area was overrun by flames. The oak leaves burned like paper, the cypress and pine needles like oil-soaked toothpicks.

There were no reports of scorched doves or pigeons, or of smoke-blackened jays. I would like to believe that the birds were lost only to us, that they fled the fire in safety and found food and water and shelter in someone else's yard. Perhaps they did.

It is difficult to tell what events were the direct result of the fire and what might have happened anyway. In the case of the house wrens, for instance, many of these birds desert the inhabited areas in early fall and spend the next six months in the brush-covered hills preferred by the Bewick wrens and wrentits. Their disappearance on the day the fire started, September 22, may simply have been a coincidence. Perhaps the palm warbler which came on September 25 would have come, fire or no fire; it provided us, however, with the first record of this species in Santa Barbara.

Members of the Audubon Society were asked to be on the lookout for unusual birds, and for noticeable increases or decreases in the number of the ordinary birds. Those who expected disastrous changes were pleasantly surprised by the normal pattern of the migrations:

The white-crowned sparrows arrived for the winter on schedule, on September 24, while the fire was still raging.

The Audubon warblers appeared the next day.

On the 28th, the hooded orioles left for Mexico, the Nashville warblers passed through on their way south and the last of the yellow warblers of the season were observed. On that day too the Oregon junco returned.

On October 3 our pair of Lincoln sparrows came back at the same time as the first dozen golden-crowned sparrows, always a week or two later than the white-crowns.

On October 8 the yellow-breasted chat concluded his yearly late-summer stay with us. I don't know where he went but I'm willing to wager it was a banana-growing region. He was the only wild bird at the feeding station who always showed a distinct preference for bananas.

October 24 marked the return of two myrtle warblers a month later, as usual, than their look-alike cousins, the Audubons.

On November 17 a slaty fox sparrow arrived, followed three days later by one of the rusty subspecies. This was exactly on schedule as far as the feeding station was concerned. Fox sparrows are reported to reach southern California in mid-September and have been seen in Santa Barbara as early as September the 1st, but my records show only one arrival even close to that, on September 28, in 1961; the others have all been in November.

November also brought a burrowing owl, the first of this species to visit us, and he was duly recorded as home visitor No. 106. It's possible that his appearance was indirectly caused by the fire since this species is not normally seen in canyon areas like ours. However, these birds aren't always predictable. According to a report in *Audubon Field Notes* (Volume 19, No. I), a burrowing owl had, during the previous month, come aboard a ship about sixty miles south of San Clemente Island.

What, then, were some actual results of the fire and what birds were affected?

As might be expected the birds suffering most heavily were terrestrial species poorly equipped to escape by flight. The number of quail found on the Christmas count three months after the fire was 170, compared to 604 found the previous year, and the number of California thrashers was 19, compared to 41. Fringe areas of the fire, such as certain sections of the Botanic Garden, demonstrated an apparent increase in wrentits. These retiring little birds were not only more numerous, they acted bolder than normal and were consequently easy to observe. The overall picture turned out different, however. The 85 wrentits reported on the Christmas count showed a 50-percent decrease from the previous year. It seems more than likely that these three species, quail, thrashers and wrentits, suffered considerable losses in the fire.

Another ground dweller, the Oregon junco, showed an apparent increase because many flocks took to foraging in the burned-over areas and were easy to see in the absence of vegetative cover. Almost a thousand were reported on the Christmas count, double the previous year's 474. The following year, when the ground vegetation was just about back to normal after a vast reseeding program, the number of juncos also returned to normal, 430; but wrentits remained at a low 84, thrashers at 24, and quail at 330.

Our most personal loss could not be attributed directly to the fire, yet I think it played a part. Johnny, our Scottish terrier, was thirteen at the time and his two wild nights as a refugee did nothing to lighten the load of his years. Up until then he'd been in good health, though his muzzle was long since gray and it had become increasingly apparent that either he was getting lower or the ground was getting higher.

His deterioration after the fire was very rapid. He began losing his hearing and his teeth, and an infection in his nose and eyes proved resistant both to all kinds of antibiotics and to cortisone. He also developed a heart condition which required a digitalis pill twice a day.

The usual technique of administering pills to animals involved a kind of force-feeding most unsuitable to a dog of Johnny's advanced years and enormous dignity, as well as tender jaws. We therefore spent a considerable percentage of our time devising ways and means of concealing the pills in food. They were served buried in hamburger, wrapped in bacon or bologna, smothered in cottage cheese and scrambled eggs, hidden in chunks of cheddar, inserted in cunningly slit pockets in steak or wedged into frankfurters or liver sausage. After the cheese, steak, liver sausage, etcetera was consumed, we'd often find the digitalis pill on the floor. When this happened I thought of Bushman, the massive gorilla who was the star of the Lincoln Park Zoo in Chicago in the days before tranquilizers and tranquilizer guns eased the difficulties of medical attention for larger animals. Bushman died of pneumonia because he couldn't be fooled into swallowing the drugs hidden in his food.

By December, Johnny, blind, arthritic and deaf, had become almost completely dependent. It was a strange fate for this sturdy, self-reliant little creature, this most unlapdog of dogs. He had to be lifted in and out of the red leather chair where he slept, and carried up and down stairs. He could be let out alone in the fenced yard where he knew every plant and weed and blade of grass. Elsewhere, in the field next door, on the path down to the creek, or up the road to the neighboring houses, I went with him, keeping a tactful distance behind so as not to disturb his Scottish pride.

On a foggy evening shortly before Christmas a delivery boy left the fence gate open and Johnny disappeared. We roused the people next door and there began a frantic search by flashlight for a small black dog in a large black night. Eventually he was found on the other side of the circle, sitting calm and composed in a yard once occupied by his girl friend, also a Scottie, named Annie Laurie. She had long since left the neighborhood, and perhaps life itself;

but Johnny was dreaming of happier times, bright days, fast runs, fair ladies.

One morning in mid-February he began hemorrhaging, and at noon he was put to sleep.

The Coyote fire had taken a heavy toll. But for some people who lived far from the fire's perimeter and never gave a thought to its effect on them, the worst was yet to come.

Death and Life in the Forest

The winter weather began on November 9 with an inch of rain, followed after a short pause by another three-quarters of an inch. This made a modest total of less than two inches. Yet it was enough, falling as it did on denuded hills and mountains, to cause severe flooding. Streets near creek beds were buried under four or five feet of mud, and boulders that looked too big to move washed downstream like pebbles. Tons of water-driven debris crushed houses and bridges and retaining walls in its inexorable journey to the sea.

The beaches were strewn with wood, some burned or half burned, some barely scorched, some as big as telephone poles, some small as palm fronds, pine cones and eucalyptus pods. For driftwood collectors it was a paradise, for swimmers, surfers and skin divers, a nightmare. In addition to the serious hazards of floating lumber there was the fact that for several hundred yards beyond the surf the water was as muddy as the lower Colorado River. This brought up another problem: fish can't see any better in muddy water than humans can in a blizzard or dust storm. When Ken swam his usual half mile on the first day of the flood, he had thirteen encounters with fish. Whether he bumped into them or they bumped into him is immaterial. Among our friends in the wet set, not a particularly scientific group, this became recognized as a way of measuring the ocean's visibility—how many ichthyoid contacts Ken made on his daily swim.

Little good comes from a flood. Reservoirs silt up, and topsoil is washed away, carrying with it the seeds necessary to reestablish watershed vegetation.

Fire, on the other hand, is a natural condition of life in the chaparral regions of southern California, and an essential condition if vegetation is to remain young and vigorous. Without an occasional clearing out, the underbrush gets so thick and high that deer and other mammals can't penetrate it and ground-dwelling birds have trouble foraging. When this happens the chaparral, normally rich in wildlife, becomes incapable of supporting its usual share. Fire occurring at twenty- to twenty-five-year intervals is a benefit, a cleaning-out of dead and diseased wood and ground cover. (Before any nature lover sets off into the hills with a pack of matches, it should be noted that more frequent fires result in the destruction of chaparral, and its conversion to a different and less interesting type of vegetation.)

Some forty or more plant species are grouped together under the name chaparral. *Chaparro* is the Spanish word for scrub oak; it also means a short, stocky person, and perhaps this gives, to someone who has never seen it, a better idea of chaparral. Chaparral is short, stocky, tough vegetation, capable of withstanding a yearly drought of six months or more.

Throughout the centuries a number of ways have evolved for chaparral plants to survive burning. Some, like green-bark ceanothus, sprout new leaves directly from the "dead" stumps. Some have woody crowns or burls at ground level, like toyon, or underground, like Eastwood manzanita, which is back to full size in a few years. Others have seeds with a hard coat that must be split open by fire, or else soft-coated seeds which need very high temperatures to trigger their internal chemistry. Among the plants with seeds requiring fire in order to germinate are some of the most dominant and important in the chaparral group of this region—chamise, big berry manzanita, laurel sumac, hoary leaf ceanothus, big pod ceanothus, sugar bush and lemonade bush. All but chamise are frequently used in cultivated gardens.

After the Coyote fire I hiked around the burned areas, observing as a bird watcher, not a botanist. But I couldn't help noticing that greenery started to reappear almost as soon as the earth had cooled. This applied especially to a certain vine, rather similar to a grapevine, which spread along the ground, as lush a green as ever graced a rain forest, and wrapped its tendrils around the blackened stumps of trees and shrubs. This was chilicothe, or wild cucumber. Its appearance had been neither delayed nor hastened by the fire, by the rain that followed, or by any external circumstances at all. When its cycle of growth was ready to begin again, it began: everything necessary for the complete process—leaves, flowers, fruit, seeds—was contained in a giant tuber buried underground.

An example of the chilicothe's self-containment and independence of the outside world was accidentally provided by the local Botanic Garden. To show the public the size of the tubers, one weighing about fifty pounds was dug up and placed in the information center. At Christmas time it started sprouting, and within the next few weeks it went through its entire growth cycle while in a display case. Again the following year, still in the display case, it grew leaves and tendrils, it flowered and fruited and went to seed. It was only during this second cycle that the tuber became noticeably smaller and wrinkled as its water content decreased.

The emergence of the chilicothe was unimportant as far as food or shelter for wildlife was concerned. Yet it appeared to be a signal for the forest to come alive again. After a December rainfall of four and a half inches, oaks that looked ready for the woodpile and seemed to be still standing only because nobody had leaned against them, suddenly burst out with a cluster of leaves here, and a cluster there. No two trees refoliated in quite the same way. These native oaks are accustomed to fires and make strong comebacks, as do the sycamores. Not so the pines, which lack the regenerative powers of the other species. The pines that looked dead were dead. Although a few of them put out new needles at the top, these soon withered and dropped, and nothing further happened.

Such debility on the part of the tree itself must, in order to account for the species' survival through centuries of periodic fires, be compensated for by the durability of the seed or the seed's protective device. Some pines, such as Bishop, knobcone and to a certain extent Monterey, are equipped with closed cones which open and drop their seeds only when exposed to very high temperatures. There is a stand of Bishop pines near Santa Barbara which passers-by assume to be a state or county planting because the trees are all exactly the same size. The actual reason is that the seeds all germinated after the same fire.

During the Coyote fire the eucalyptus trees, especially the most widely planted variety, blue gum, burned very quickly. This was partly because of their natural oil content, which caused a great deal of black smoke, and partly because they were very dry. The deep underground water which carried many large trees through the summer drought was unavailable to the shallow-rooted eucalypts. But their comeback was also quick. In fact, the adaptation of these imports from Australia to a California fire provided one of the oddest sights of the spring and summer. Normally, eucalyptus leaves grow like other leaves, out of branches and twigs. When the branches and twigs, however, were consumed by fire, the leaves grew instead out of the trunk of the tree. They looked like telephone poles which had suddenly started to sprout leaves from top to bottom.

Certain trees took a long time to show signs of regeneration. These included the redwoods in the center of the Botanic Garden and the olive trees on the slopes of a canyon adjoining the Botanic Garden. This grove had been planted for the commercial milling of oil in the 1880s, about the time the first daily newspaper was established in Santa Barbara and the first free library and reading room was opened. The olive oil project was abandoned when cheap Mexican labor became scarce. One of the methods used to keep the workers on the job would be frowned on by present-day union officials: whenever the braceros gave evidence of wanting a siesta, a barrel of wine, carried on a donkey-drawn sled, passed between the rows of trees, and the braceros were bribed with booze on a considerably more generous scale than the British seamen with once-a-day grog.

This olive grove, left untended for years and with a heavy growth of underbrush between the trees, was severely damaged by the fire. The underbrush was the main reason for the destruction, not, as some people believed, the oil content of the wood or leaves. When I walked through the area a week after the fire ended, all the trees looked dead, and continued to do so for a long time. Yet on a visit in mid-January, sixteen months after the fire, I noticed that nearly every blackened stump was showing some greenery at the base.

The heavy rains in November and December had caused the various kinds of grasses to grow thick and tall, and there were birds everywhere: house finches, white-crowned sparrows, golden-crowned sparrows and lesser goldfinches foraged in flocks, with the sparrows providing the dinner music, assisted by two or three invisible wrentits. The brown towhees took part with an occasional *chink,* reminding me of gradeschool monotones who are allowed to accompany their musical classmates by "playing" percussion pie plates or cake tins. Dozens of quail, securely hidden, ticked and talked, discussing the intruder among themselves without bothering to lower their voices. They made it plain that they considered me a *yark* and a *kookquat,* and since I didn't know what a *yark* or a *kookquat* was, I couldn't very well contradict them.

The same visit provided an unexpected bonus, a pair of black-chinned sparrows, male and female, resting on the burned branch of an olive tree. These birds are normally seen only during the late spring and summer in stands of chamise-dominant chaparral in the mountains or foothills. Finding them in January near the city limits was highly irregular. Perhaps the Coyote fire had something to do with their appearance since the species is known to be partial to burn areas where the new vegetation is only half grown.

On my next visit to the olive grove in mid-July, most of the trees gave evidence that they would recover completely in time. Branches growing out of the woody crown were as long as six feet and covered with silver-green leaves.

Even without the braceros and the wine wagon to keep them on the job, there will someday be another crop of olives for the white-crowned sparrows, robins and California thrashers.

The forest was turning green again. For residents of the fire areas the change was gradual. For those who only visited from time to time it was incredibly fast and far, from death to life. At the higher altitudes the white-bark ceanothus had a fresh growth of the tough, wiry stems and sharp spikes which kept predators away from such guests as the green-tailed towhee and the mountain quail. Closer to sea level the green-bark ceanothus was performing a similar function for the lazuli bunting and California quail, the wrentit and lark sparrow.

Soon manzanita apples would again be ripening for the cedar waxwings, toyon berries for the purple finches and mistletoe for the phainopeplas. Oak buds were already appearing for the band-tailed pigeons, and there was promise of a fresh crop of chaparral currants for the hermit thrushes, mountain cherries for the Town-send solitaires, nightshade for the grosbeaks. Through the picture window beside my chair I watched the mountains recover from the fire, each day bringing a new patch of green that turned to violet when the sun set.

As each day of recovery came and went, and each new flight of birds landed on the ledge to feed, I was continually reminded of a letter John Keats sent to a friend in 1817.

The setting Sun will always set me to rights, he wrote, *or if a Sparrow come before my Window I take part in its existence and pick about the Gravel.*

INDEX

ABOUT THE AUTHOR

MARGARET MILLAR is internationally known as a novelist of mystery and suspense. Her books have been widely translated in Europe, Asia and South America. *Beast in View* was given the Edgar Allan Poe award by her fellow Mystery Writers of America in 1956, and the following year she served as president of that organization. In 1965 she received a *Los Angeles Times* Woman of the Year award for "outstanding achievement."

Born in Canada, Mrs. Millar was educated in classics at the University of Toronto. In 1938 she married Kenneth Millar, whose books are published under the name of Ross Macdonald.

In the fall of 1958 the Millars moved into a house in a wooded canyon just outside Santa Barbara. The place was alive with birds, and in the ensuing years of observation and study, Mrs. Millar tabulated 112 species. The present book, her twentieth, tells the story of her adventures with the birds and the other wild things that live in the canyon.

Both the Millars are active conservationists and founding members of the Santa Barbara Audubon Society.